"P's" of successful grantseeking

* pro-active
* plan
* promote your goals
* predetermined goals
* pre-select sources of support
* pre-poposal contact
  (3x incr in chance of success)
  i.e. check # funded in past

* persistent
* politeness

Each of us develops our unique way of viewing the world. Festinger's Theory of Cognitive Dissonance

The Principal's Guide to Grants Success

David G. Bauer

Exclusively distributed by
Classroom Connect™

Internet made easy in the classroom™

1866 Colonial Village Lane
Box 10488
Lancaster, PA 17605-0488

Telephone: (800) 638-1639
Fax: (717) 393-5752
Email: connect@classroom.net

URL: http://www.classroom.net

ISBN 0-590-49217-9

12 11 10 9 8 7 6 5 4 3 2 1 1 2 3 4 5/9

Printed in the U.S.A.

Library of Congress Cataloging-in-Publication Data

Bauer, David G.
The Principal's Guide to Grants Success/David G. Bauer.
p. cm.
Includes bibliographical references.
ISBN 0-590-49217-9
1. Educational fund-raising. I. Title.
LC241.B38 1994 92–39714
370'.79–dc20 CIP

Designed by Joan Gazdik Gillner

Contents

Introduction

This book is intended to assist principals of public and private elementary and middle schools in developing and maintaining a grants system that utilizes grant funds to meet their schools' mission. It is the second book in a three-part series on grantseeking. Book one, *The Grantseeking Primer for Classroom Leaders,* focuses on the teacher's role in grantseeking; book three, *Successful Grants Program Management,* is aimed at the district administrator.

The challenges in seeking and administering alternative sources of funding for public and private elementary and middle or junior high schools require a new and more efficient system to support and monitor the grant-proposal development process. The old system, which was characterized by an assistant district administrator pumping out forms requesting federal entitlement funds and formula grants, is not equipped to deal with the decentralized, site-based management concepts that are dramatically affecting our school/community today. The "new" concepts of local decision making, ownership, and investment provide the principal with opportunities to encourage parents and community to "buy into" the responsibility of educating their children. When parents, teachers, students, and community come together to develop goals, objectives, and curriculum they soon realize the limitations of the educational system's normal resource allocation process. However, with some creativity, they can achieve *their* educational goals by routing their energies toward developing more resources through public and private grants.

The grants marketplace can provide a tremendous resource for your school. In fact, it provides your teachers with billions of dollars' worth of opportunities to change and supplement their curriculum, purchase equipment, and develop new programs. *But they must know how to access the funds.*

The reaction of some school systems to this newly developed parental, teacher, and community interest may be to request that a group's grant or proposal ideas be submitted to a central office, where a hired grant writer looks at the possibility of developing a proposal for outside support. This type of system will not produce the winning grants your school needs. Today's proposals need to include empowered and motivated volunteers who want action, and the principal should provide the crucial link to utilizing this free, inspired source of labor. The principal should:

- Help parents and teachers develop their grant-proposal ideas into a fundable form.

- Play a pivotal role in developing the necessary coordination between the district's central office and the school's grants effort.
- Increase the school's/community's commitment to solving its problems, responsibility for finding solutions, and ownership of its successes.

One advantage in using the grants marketplace to achieve educational improvement is that with a minimum of assistance, volunteers can become involved in preparing proposals. While districts provide varying degrees of support, most grantseekers prepare proposals at their own expense and in their spare time. Forward-thinking administrators should encourage and support this investment of their staffs' and volunteers' time with an efficient proposal development system.

The aim of this book is to describe the basic elements of successful grantseeking. In so doing it summarizes and sometimes repeats information contained in the *Grantseeking Primer for Classroom Leaders.* The material is arranged so that you can evaluate the relevance of and need for each facet of the grants system based on your particular situation. The perfect system does not exist. But the more components of a model grant system that you can adapt and include in your system, the more you can expect from the grants marketplace. As an additional help, each chapter ends with a checklist to help you evaluate and improve your grants system.

Remember, the changes that will be necessary to improve your grants plan may be difficult to achieve. Therefore, use restraint in developing your plan. Read this entire book and then determine what your grants system needs. Discuss with your staff the areas to be improved. Encourage their input and utilize it where appropriate. Discuss with your central administration your school's needs and how administrators can help you address them.

Effective grantseeking is not an accident and has little to do with good luck. From the principal's perspective, the two crucial ingredients for successful grantseeking are good planning and the development of an efficient support system.

Bauer Associates supplies several valuable products and services created to support your school's grantseeking efforts. For a price list of our materials, or to discuss the possibility of having David Bauer conduct a grants-training seminar for your school or district, phone 1-800-836-0732.

CHAPTER ONE

The Principal's Role in Supporting Grantseeking

The possibility of winning a grant gives the principal an exciting opportunity to apply concepts in successful leadership and management. As educational administrators we are challenged to work through those whom we manage to achieve our school's objectives. But it is difficult to develop an environment in which staff members feel sufficiently empowered to willingly invest their time and effort with little regard for up-front payoffs. With the proper introduction, and a support system that responds to legitimate concerns, grantseeking can create this environment. In fact, grantseeking can actually become a vehicle that enables the principal to develop an exciting and cooperative relationship with teachers, support staff, parents, and the school/community.

Encouraging the Grants Process

Agreed, your job is already hard enough with its new and daily- changing responsibilities. You work 70 hours a week, and now you are being asked to get excited about expanding your activities to include *aggressive grantseeking*. But the grantseeking you will be promoting will be based on helping *others* better meet the needs of your students, teachers, and community through *their* active involvement in the preparation of successful proposals. Those who will carry out and support the project will willingly take part in the research and writing if you provide them with a system that *supports their efforts*.

In order to win grants, you must know *where* the grant funds are. Chapter 4 will provide you with in-depth data on the grants marketplace. But the following 1993 estimates will give you an idea:

- Foundations will grant over $8 billion.
- Corporations will grant over $6 billion.
- The federal government will grant over $80 billion.

What percentage of these grants will go to elementary and junior high or middle schools? This is the subject of chapter 4. But the fact is that the percentage going to elementary and middle school education from all three major types of funders has been increasing.

Your school's opportunity to access this 94^+$ billion *grants marketplace* provides you, the school administrator, with a unique motivational tool that can be utilized to develop exciting goals and objectives as well as the projects and programs to achieve educational progress. To top it off, you can do this by using outside resources and without tremendous up-front expenditures.

While some elementary and middle or junior high schools employ grant writers to develop proposals, this is not how grantseeking is conducted by the majority of schools or other nonprofit organizations.

At colleges and universities, the grants office does very little proposal writing. It may perform a search for potential grant resources and provide budgetary, submittal, and sign-off assistance, but seldom does it write the proposal. So who is paid to write a proposal? The answer is no one. The key personnel involved in developing the proposal are paid from the grant once it is approved, and in most cases, the successful project director or principal investigator will receive release time from his or her normal duties to carry out the project. No costs for proposal preparation are reimbursed through grant funds. These are considered costs incurred before the award date, and it is unethical or illegal to claim them.

If individuals cannot receive payment for preparing proposals, why do they do it? One of the motivations to become involved in proposal preparation is simply the opportunity to make a difference, to be involved in developing a solution to a problem. By utilizing techniques that encourage your school's employees and volunteers to become involved and to make a difference, you provide them with the possibility of attracting grant funds that can be used to:

- institute a novel solution to a problem,
- expand a program to new populations,
- provide for increased educational achievement,
- develop the school's resources, such as equipment and facilities.

To begin the process of improving your school through outside grant support, you must know what your school's needs are and where your opportunities lie. One very effective way to find this out is to ask your teachers, parents, staff, and interested community residents to identify the greatest problems and opportunities facing your school. Announce an open forum or special meeting that will focus on setting goals and priorities for your school and on assessing its needs. The meeting may be organized according to area of concern or grade level. But you must inspire a sense of urgency and provide hope that the needed change can take place. The following activity may help you accomplish these goals.

Bring in a stack of play money or several lottery tickets. Let the focus group know that there are billions of dollars in grants available for funding elementary and middle school education. Organize the participants into small groups and ask each group to develop a list of the areas of need. Give each group a stack of play money or a lottery ticket and have them determine which area of need the money or the proceeds from a winning lottery ticket should be used for. To complete the task each group should develop a prioritized list of needs. This activity will provide you with valuable insight into your school's/community's ability to identify and articulate its most pressing problems and educational needs.

This exercise can be done with community groups, teacher groups, student clubs and organizations, unions, or open sessions. You may want to ask groups to share their lists. Ultimately it is helpful if your school's advisory committee and/or teacher and parent groups come to an agreement on the top three or four problem areas that need to be addressed.

The next step is to capitalize on your teachers' and volunteers' interest in addressing these problems by having them brainstorm possible solutions. In fact, you can use the lottery tickets to promote interest. If one is a winning ticket, the group can use the proceeds to start solving the problem right away! The purpose of the brain-storming session is to identify unique, innovative, creative solutions that can be incorporated in a proposal to attract funding from a grantor who is interested in seeking educational change.

As you involve the entire school/community in taking responsibility for identifying problems and creating solutions, you may begin to see some very positive outcomes. Dr. Dennis Waitley in his book *The Psychology of Winning* suggests that individuals move in the direction of their dominant thought every moment of their lives. Therefore, if their dominant thought is negative, they will move in a negative direction. For example, if your school/community believes that problems in your school are hopeless and overwhelming, it will focus on these negative perceptions and the problems will get worse.

However, by using your school's potential for grant support to develop a prioritized list of problems and solutions that will reduce or eliminate them, you can change your group's entire focus to a positive, problem-solving perspective. In fact, groups sometimes believe so strongly in their solutions that they institute them even if they are not awarded a grant. In some cases the money is *found* by reallocating existing funds.

Actually, schools should be moving in these positive directions anyway and deserve to have more resources to do their job. But reality is harsh, and it is easy to get sidetracked and to focus on the negative. The bottom line is that by stressing the possibility of a grant and making your teachers and volunteers aware of the amounts of grant funds available for model and innovative projects, you can help your school/community focus in a positive direction.

Individuals invest their time and effort in the grants process for many reasons besides wanting to make a difference, and your grant system should allow for and foster these other reasons. When asked why they donated their time and effort to prepare a proposal, grantseekers often say they were motivated by:

- the *feeling that they were part of a team or group* (i.e., the social aspect of grantseeking).
- *recognition for their work.* (They liked seeing their names in school publications and the newspaper and were thrilled at being asked to make presentations at meetings to inform their peers about their project.)
- *a sense of achievement and fulfillment that came from using their talents and abilities.*

- *the feeling of power from controlling materials, equipment, and their own budget.*

The role of the principal in encouraging the grants process begins with an understanding of how grant funds can be used to address the problems in your school. Of course you must be honest with your staff and inform them that in the grants marketplace we are always working with a percentage of success, and that failure will occur. However, remind your potential grantseeker that:

1. By assessing your school's positive and negative aspects, you will be designing a plan for the future that capitalizes on your school's strengths and prioritizes its needs. In fact, you and your grantseekers will begin to view your school's problems as grant opportunities. (Assuming that your school personnel develop positive dominant thoughts, your school will continue to move in a positive direction.)
2. Grants success depends upon many factors, but motivation and a can-do, problem-solving spirit are two of the basic ingredients. If your grants system mirrors the system outlined in this book, your grantseekers can expect a success rate of around 50 percent or more. Because elementary and junior high schools have only recently begun to expand their grantseeking, detailed success rates are difficult to verify, but principals who have employed these concepts have reported a 50 percent success rate.
3. You can't win if you don't play the game. Of course there will be some work and some failure, but sitting around the faculty room complaining is a waste of time and energy.
4. A positive, proactive effort will provide your grantseekers with enough information to realistically assess their chances of success before they write the proposal. Their first step will *not* be to write a lengthy, detailed proposal. They will begin writing only after they have located an interested funder.
5. Grantseeking is not a last-minute, 72-hour miracle that produces heartburn and grantseeker burnout. Grantseekers who have a chaotic, reactive grants system waste time and money and do not meet their school's predetermined needs, goals, or objectives.

The positive and organized grants system outlined in the following chapters shows how you, the principal, can initiate and utilize the *grants opportunity.* The results of grantseeking can be far reaching, but the grants atmosphere is critical to your success.

One public school administrator I know set up a grants reward system that consisted of public recognition for grantseekers, an annual award dinner, plaques, and even small cash awards. And the system was funded on a grant! Yes, a foundation realized that a small grant to reward and thank grant writers could result in far more grant funds than it could ever distribute to the school. Be creative. You can provide staff with the proper environment to stimulate grantseeking.

When you visit a business or an organization that is striving to create the best atmosphere possible, take note of the motivational techniques it employs. When visiting a hotel, notice the plaques and pictures of the employees-of-the-month and find out what rewards employees received in addition to the public recognition.

As an administrator at a public school, I proposed the possibility of using a grant to address my district's prioritized list of needs. I provide this example because no matter what your list of priorities or needs is, I believe the possibility of procuring grant funds should be explored before you use your own budget and school funds to meet these needs.

In my district, a community advisory group and the elementary school teachers and staff determined that one of their priorities was to develop a health-education curriculum at the elementary level that would form the basis for the junior high school health-education program. The teachers were concerned about the risk-taking behavior and carelessness that had caused several students to be severely injured and wanted to explore how those behaviors related to health-related problems such as drug and alcohol abuse.

We formed an elementary health curriculum advisory committee and developed a proposal to submit to a government funding source. The teachers developed a model curriculum that included the scope and sequence of the objectives at each grade level. The proposal requested funds that would enable the teachers to preview and ultimately purchase the materials *they* felt comfortable using with their students. Parents were also involved. The parents' advisory committee developed a parents' education kit that included take-home sheets, suggested topics for home discussion, and follow-up activities.

The classroom leaders participating in the project met for 54 contact hours and were awarded graduate credit from a nearby university (they paid tuition fees) or in-service credits if they did not want or need the graduate credit.

The teachers were motivated and involved because they had control over what to purchase and how to use it. Getting a grant to buy the materials gave them additional incentive to get involved in creating the solution. This process of utilizing the grants system can be employed by other schools.

While several aspects of the principal's role in encouraging and supporting grantseeking could be explored, this book will highlight the *major* areas and provide the direction and insight that will promote grants success.

Ensuring Quality and Coordination

Another critically important aspect of the principal's role as the leader in the grants process is that of ensuring quality and coordination in the grants effort. Your school and the entire district will be judged by the quality of the proposal that you submit to the grantor. Foundation, corporate, or government officials will base their opinion of your entire school system and of your school in particular on the quality of your proposal, and you, the principal, are ultimately responsible for this quality. Your role in the grants process is to ensure that every proposal submitted represents your school's/community's *best effort,* and you must be willing to be judged on each proposal.

In summary, you are crucial in promoting a positive grants atmosphere in your school. Your role in supporting the process of proposal preparation will depend on your knowledge of and interest in the process of securing grants. The following chapters will provide you with information and techniques that will help you develop a dynamic grants system. Review the checklist that follows and evaluate the ways in which grants are utilized and grant winners recognized in your school. Make suggestions on how these methods can be improved. Your suggestions for change will provide the basis for your annual plan for grants success.

CHAPTER 1 CHECKLIST

Evaluation and Planning Worksheet

Complete this assessment to help develop your plan.

1. **Base Data: Grants Activity in 19 ___**

   \# of proposals submitted ____________

   \# of proposals awarded ____________

   \# of proposals rejected ____________

2. **Use of Grants Potential to Identify Problems/Opportunities:**

   a. Do you utilize a grants advisory committee? ____ yes _____ no

   b. If yes, who is it comprised of?

   _____ parents _____ staff _____ teachers
   _____ community _____ corporate leaders _____ experts
   _____ other (please list) ________________________________
   ____

3. **Recognition for Grantseekers (Please Check):**

   Press Releases for Committee Work _____

   External Recognition (Newspaper, Radio, TV, etc.) for:
   submittal of proposal _____ grants success rate _____
   award of grant _____

   Internal Recognition (Newsletter, Announcements, etc.) for:
   submittal of proposal _____ grants success rate _____
   award of grant _____

   Other Recognition Techniques:
   cash awards _____ special entitlements:
   plaques _____ privileged parking _____
   trophies _____ day off _____
   awards dinner _____ other entitlements:
   ____
   ____

4. **Education of Faculty, Staff, and Community on the Opportunities that Grantseeking Presents:**

   Citing of Grants to Other Schools _____ Other (please list)
   Publishing of Grants Facts in Newsletters _____ ______________________
   ____

CHAPTER TWO

$ Setting up a Successful Proactive Grants System In Your School

As you learned in chapter 1, you can utilize the possibility of attracting outside funding to focus on your school's needs. You, the school leader, can use grantseeking as a low-investment, high-return strategy that brings the community, teachers, parents, and students together to develop positive, action-oriented solutions to your school's problems.

In order to sustain interest, build upon this involvement, and create at least a 50 percent grants success rate, you need to develop an organized, proactive grants system. This task is not easy to accomplish in the changing environment of educational administration. Twenty years ago, your central office was responsible for seeking grants. Current circumstances, including site-based management, school/community involvement, and local empowerment, have altered your and your district's traditional roles in the grants system. This book will help you create the "right" system for your school and determine how your district's rules and procedures will affect your new system. If necessary, obtain permission from your central administration and push for policies and regulations that your district office needs to enact in order to avoid unregulated grants competition, poor image with funders, and problems in grants administration.

The techniques and strategies involved in setting up a success-based, proactive grants system are tried and proven. The more of these techniques you incorporate in your system, the higher will be your rate of success and the more motivated you will become to develop a positive, can-do atmosphere in your school. But these techniques must be coordinated with the grant efforts of your district's central office. Be aware that sometimes district grants policies and procedures have not kept pace with changes in school management.

1. Developing a Proactive Grants System for Your School

The first step in proactive grantseeking is to develop focus groups that identify and prioritize your school's needs, problem areas, and areas of excellence or programs you want to improve. The reason more schools do not use the grants marketplace to its full potential is that they view grantseeking as a reactive activity that is driven by grantors who publicize a program and a deadline that allows the grantseeker little or no time to prepare a proposal. This, in turn, causes the grantseeker to hastily develop an idea, write up a proposal, and put all the pieces together in a mad rush. The chaos of the final 72 hours of reactive grantseeking can turn people off to the entire process.

To make matters worse, funding sources or grantors can spot last- minute proposals, and when they do they wonder:

- Why didn't the grantseekers start earlier?
- Where are the letters of endorsement and the statements of support from the school board, the community, and the district?
- Why didn't the grantseekers contact us to discuss the best way to approach us?
- Are the potential grantees just out looking for money? Would they propose any idea that they thought would look good to a funding source?
- How does this project relate to their schools' stated mission and their predetermined goals and objectives?

No wonder teachers are not lining up to get involved in the grants process. You have to be sadomasochistic to want to be involved in a reactive grants system.

So what is the alternative? Grantseeking can be a positive process controlled by the grantseeker, which minimizes stress and last-minute herculean efforts.

The purpose of your grants system is not to "get the proposal out the door" but to fulfill the grantor's needs through your school's project, at a price the grantor can afford. In order to develop a fundable and interesting project, your grants system needs to focus on the needs and projects your school/community feels are important. When this has been accomplished, you should search for grant sources that are interested in the same educational change and improvement. When a grantseeker takes the proactive approach of developing project ideas first, he or she appears less like a grantseeker who will do anything for money and more like a grantseeker who wants funding only for projects that move the school toward its predetermined goals.

Proactive grantseeking affords your grantseekers the time to research the potential funder to discover who else it has funded and for what projects, so that they are reasonably sure that the funder will be interested in your project. With advance time and knowledge, grantseekers can also establish preproposal contact. In fact, many funding sources encourage grantseekers to talk with them before writing a formal proposal to be certain that the prospective grantee's approach meets the grantor's requirements. The chances of grants success are dramatically increased by making this contact! By knowing the grantor's funding pattern and discussing your school's approaches to the need with the grantor, you can begin to develop a sound basis for a productive grantor-grantee relationship.

If you are starting to get the impression that grantseeking is going to take up too much of your time, relax. You may not even be the best person to contact the grantor. In fact, your classroom leaders may not be the ideal choices, either. The best person to make preproposal contact is a volunteer who:

- is involved in the project (proposal),
- has donated her or his time,
- is a member of a school/community advisory committee,
- has paid her or his own way to see the grantor, and
- will not profit from the grant award.

Many grant applications require documentation of community involvement. Grantors may want to see minutes of meetings involving the individuals or families who will be affected by the award and implementation of the proposed project. By involving the entire school/community in the grantseeking process you will have the commitment and cooperation of the volunteers.

2. Developing Community Advisory Groups

I have suggested in the *Grantseeking Primer for Classroom Leaders* that teachers discuss with their principals the concept of developing focus groups or community advisory groups to address the problems facing their classrooms. This should be the first step in developing support for grantseeking. As the administrator, you have input that is critical in coordinating the development of these groups, for which the structure of your community may already provide the basis. Whether or not it does, it is important that the advisory group members who deal with grantseeking be selected very carefully. You may want to form a grants advisory group as a subcommittee of your larger focus groups. There is no "best way" to create the structure, as long as you keep in mind the skills that are needed and the types of individuals who can best carry out the tasks involved in successful grantseeking.

The following sample letters and worksheets will help you develop your grants advisory group and build a proactive, successful grants system. Naturally, the materials should be tailored to your particular school and situation. As previously stated, you could develop either several grants advisory groups or one grants advisory group and several problem-specific focus groups. The focus groups could provide the grants advisory group with suggestions for projects.

Worksheet for Planning a Grants Advisory Group (Fig. 2.1)

Use this worksheet to develop a tentative list of the individuals whom you may want to participate in your grants advisory group.

Avoid placing well-intentioned zealots on the committee. Although these outspoken individuals may be highly motivated, they can turn off the other committee members as well as potential funders because they often lack the listening skills needed to truly grasp what the grantor is looking for.

Look for individuals who will make the grantseeking process less work for you. Assess the skills and resources that the committee members will bring to the group.

Figure 2.1

WORKSHEET FOR PLANNING A GRANTS ADVISORY GROUP

Review the suggested categories of individuals to include and write down names.

Whom to Invite

_______ Parents

_______ Corporate Leaders

_______ Foundation Board Members

_______ College Professors/Educators

_______ Retired Teachers

_______ Wealthy/Influential People

_______ Others (Please Add)

Review the "Skills/Resources Needed" list below and write the underlined key resource description next to the possible committee members you have listed above. Avoid inviting volunteers who are overzealous about children but have no resources or contacts.

Skills/Resources Needed

- **Commitment** to children and education
- **Contacts** with people on foundation/corporate boards
- **Travel** to other areas of the state/nation where there are more funders
- Willingness to share **telephone credit card** for grant-related calls
- **Marketing/sales skills**
- **Budgeting** and financial analysis skills
- Access to equipment and materials necessary to produce **audiovisual** aids depicting need
- Other

Grants Resources Inventory Worksheet (Fig. 2.2)

The Grants Resources Inventory Worksheet lists some of the resource areas that will be helpful in grantseeking. The worksheet can be used in several ways. First, quickly reviewing the worksheet may trigger the names of potential members of the Grants Advisory Group (see fig. 2.1). Second, once you have identified potential participants you can ask them to complete the inventory by noting their own skills and abilities and also to list any other potential members next to the corresponding resource area. For example, if Sylvia Smith is filling out the inventory, she may indicate that she can provide sales skills. She might also indicate that an acquaintance of hers, John Doe, might be willing to provide computer programming services.

Once you have your group members selected, don't be overly concerned with rules regarding their attendance at committee meetings. If the member promises to provide the resources and skills needed, what difference does attendance make? For instance, sales people who travel a lot may not spend much time in their offices or at home. It may be easy for them to make preproposal contact with a grantor in another part of the state or country but difficult for them to attend meetings.

To offer an example, a very productive sales executive on one of my grants advisory groups never attended a meeting but was instrumental in procuring several grant awards. When he was in the same city as a potential grantor, I would fax all the pertinent information to him at his hotel. This would include a description of the proposed project and information on the grantor, such as their funding history or pattern. He would then set up an appointment with the grantor to discuss the project. After his meeting with the funding source he would fax

Figure 2.2

GRANTS RESOURCES INVENTORY WORKSHEET

Please put a check mark next to any resource area in which you can help. Use the section at the end of the worksheet to briefly describe the resources you could provide. If you are willing to contact funding sources, please list the areas of the United States that you visit frequently.

RESOURCE AREA

_______ Evaluation of Projects

_______ Computer Programming

_______ Computer Equipment

_______ Printing

_______ Layout and Design Work

_______ Budget Skills, Accounting, Developing Cash Flow, Auditing

_______ Purchasing Assistance

_______ Audiovisual Assistance (equipment, videotaping, etc.)

_______ Travel

_______ Long Distance Telephone Calls

_______ Searching for Funding Sources

_______ Sales Skills

_______ Writing Skills/Editing Skills

_______ Other Equipment/Materials

_______ Other

Description of Resources: ______________________________

Areas Frequently Visited: ______________________________

information back to me concerning the appropriate strategy to pursue in the proposal. He was highly successful at getting in to see federal and state grantors as well as foundation and corporate sources. In many cases, he was actually given preferential treatment over the grant and education professionals, who, after all, were *paid to be there.* My advisory group member was donating his time; he was actually being paid to be somewhere else. In reality, the preproposal visit was costing him money. Many grantors will respond favorably to such a committed volunteer.

You need advisory group members who are free to travel and who have skills or resources in marketing, budgeting, printing, computer programming, and so on. What could be more ideal than a finished proposal, produced by a committee member donating his or her office and secretaries, and having the budget checked by their finance department?

Worksheet for Initiating a Grants Advisory Group (Fig. 2.3)

Discuss your plan to develop a grants advisory group with the faculty and staff of your school and ask them to suggest names of people they would be willing to contact and co-invite with you to take part in the group. You will be amazed at how many excellent contacts they suggest. Don't bc surprised if you discover that the spouse of one of your long-time volunteers or staff members is the marketing director of a local corporation and that he or she would be happy to donate to your grants effort resources from graphics to preproposal contact!

Sample Letter to Potential Committee Member (Invitation to Participate — Fig. 2.4)

You will need to tailor this invitation to the individual and to the scope of the grants advisory group's work. For example, a small school may have one grants advisory group to assist in all grantseeking activities while a large school or a school with diverse and critical areas of concern may have several grants advisory groups, each focusing on one particular problem area (e.g., illiteracy, delinquency, dropout prevention, drugs, alcohol, AIDS education, and so on).

The important point to get across in this letter and in your phone conversation with a potential committee member is that you are hoping that this person will lend her or his brainpower and resources. You are not asking for money. You are not *fund-raising.* You are grantseeking. Grants are provided by foundations, corporations, and government agencies, and any help that your advisory committee member can give in setting up a meeting or even a telephone conversation with a possible funding source will increase your chances of success.

It is important that the potential committee know that \$94$^+$ billion in grants will be given away in 1993 and that you are asking their help in getting some of that grant money for your school. Reassure them that they will not be involved in asking for a friend's personal donation but only for foundation and corporate funds.

Remember, you establish the requirements for committee membership. Individuals may ask how long they must serve. I suggest that you leave it up to them.

Figure 2.3

WORKSHEET FOR INITIATING A GRANTS ADVISORY GROUP				
Potential Members	**Who Will Contact Them**	**When**	**Results**	**Skills/Resources You Expect**

SAMPLE LETTER INVENTORY OF LINKAGES AND RESOURCES (FIG. 2.5)

The timing of this letter is very important, and the quantity and quality of the linkages derived from it will most likely correspond to the prestige of the grants advisory group member who signs it. For that reason have your *most* distinguished group member both sign the letter and introduce the concept of linkages at your advisory group meeting. This will increase the likelihood that inventories and worksheets will be completed and returned.

Chapter 6 underscores the advantages of preproposal contact. Since your time, travel, and access to funders are limited, uncovering *who knows whom* makes contact more likely and at the same time increases your school's credibility through involving others in education. However, even in the best of situations you may not uncover a link to a potential grantor. Be assured that grants are made to credible schools with well-organized proposals and projects even though they have no connections or endorsements. But you will maximize your grants success and

Figure 2.4

SAMPLE LETTER TO POTENTIAL COMMITTEE MEMBER (INVITATION TO PARTICIPATE)

Note: *You may telephone potential committee members first and then send them this letter, or send them this letter and then telephone them.*

Dear ____________________:

The children in [name of school/classroom] invite you to become involved in developing and implementing solutions in their education. Your past work in _____________ demonstrates your commitment and concern for children, their education, and our community. We are in the process of deleting a grants advisory committee, which we would like you to be part of. Your commitment and concern have prompted this invitation to join with a select group of individuals in developing solutions and resources to education-related problems and needs.

I look at the problems associated with educating children as opportunities — to become involved in developing creative solutions to the problems that hold our children back from____

____

____

[Add pertinent statistics. For example, "National reading scores for fourth graders are . In our school ___ percent of fourth graders read below this level." Include some outcomes, such as, "Students who lack reading skills _______________."]

This letter is your invitation to do something about this problem. [number] of your fellow citizens are receiving similar invitations to join our informal group. The purposes of the group include:

- Brainstorming suggestions for improving our educational programs for _________________________, and
- Capitalizing on the group members' skills and contacts for getting our proposals in front of foundation, corporate, and government funding sources.

Last year corporations and foundations awarded over $13 billion in grant funds. Elementary and middle schools are receiving a growing portion of these funds as private funding sources become more concerned about our children's education. Our knowing whom *you* know may give us the advantage we need to share in this funding.

Please attend our meeting on [date] at [place] and learn how *you* can play an important role in our grants development process. A study in the *Grants Magazine* indicates that there is up to a 500% increase in grants success if the funding source has personal contact with the proposal developer before the proposal is written. A simple phone call to set up an appointment with a prospective funder may elicit a favorable response to our proposal, and *you* could provide this essential contact.

Please set aside the date of _________ to attend our first meeting. I know you will enjoy learning how we can work together to improve our educational system.

Sincerely,

Figure 2.5

SAMPLE LETTER
INVENTORY OF LINKAGES AND RESOURCES

Dear ____________________:

The problems/opportunities that we have discussed at our grants advisory committee meetings have solutions, but the implementation of the solutions costs money. We will seek this money through grant funds from foundations, corporations, and possibly state and/or federal sources.

Foundations and corporate sources granted over $13 billion last year, and this figure will climb to $14 billion this year. These funding sources make these awards every year, and every year the funds they distribute will increase. However, these grantors are limited in staff support. In fact, while there are 34,000 foundations, they employ only 3,200 individuals, and fewer than 1,000 have offices. Taking these factors into consideration, it is very important to carefully plan our approach, especially since research indicates that contacting the grantor before writing the proposal increases success by 500 percent.

That's where you come in. We are not soliciting you for money, nor do we want a list of all your wealthy friends. What we are asking is that you provide us with a list of your friends, associates, and relatives who have a relationship with grantors so that we will know who to call to help us get a foot in the door.

The attached "Foot-in-the-Door Worksheet" is aimed at gathering the information we need. This webbing and linkage information will help us to know when to ask you for your assistance in securing personal or telephone contact with a grantor. Your responses will be kept confidential, and the only person that will have access to this information is [name of individual]. While we are a neighborhood school, we can still reach out to a variety of funding sources, and the linkages you provide us will help us do so.

When our research indicates that we have developed a project that is particularly suited to a funder that you know, we will contact you to discuss the project, the funder, and your desire to assist us. We may just need a foot in the door, or you may want to accompany us on a visit to the potential funding source or even visit them yourself. In any event, we will not contact any of the sources you suggest without your prior approval.

In addition to your suggested sources, it is also very important that you let us know of any grant-related resources that you can provide or help us procure. For example, nothing makes a more powerful statement than a volunteer taking time out from a business trip or a vacation to make contact with a funder. Since the volunteer is not paid to make the visit, he or she has great credibility with the funding source. Remember, the use of resources like your travel itinerary, sales skills, and telephone credit cards for long-distance calls all demonstrate how cost-efficient our grant seeking and proposed solutions can be.

Please review and complete the attached Grants Resources Inventory Worksheet and the Foot-in-the-Door Worksheet before our next meeting on _________ so that we can work together to make a difference. If we do not receive the worksheets before this date, please expect us to call you to arrange to pick them up.

Sincerely,

minimize the time you spend grantseeking if you encourage committee members to use their contacts.

Corporate people know the value of contacts. Knowing who plays bridge, golf, or tennis with whom is worth its weight in gold, especially when you consider that most corporate proposals are funded locally. The grants value of contacts in the corporate arena is surpassed only by that in the foundation marketplace.

Consider the following facts: There are only about 3,000 employees working for 34,000 foundations, and fewer than 1,000 foundations occupy offices. Some of the larger foundations will talk to potential grantees on the phone, but 33,000 do not even have a phone. What each foundation does have is a board of trustees. In most cases, the board is comprised of from five to ten individuals who meet a few times a year to act on the requests of nonprofit organizations.

If your grants advisory group knows a board member or trustee, discuss your proposed project with him or her in advance of a board meeting. (You will learn more about developing preproposal contact with each specific type of funder in a later chapter.)

Foot-in-the-Door Worksheet (Fig. 2.6)

This worksheet will help you develop your links to individuals who may be able to assist your grantseekers. These links can often provide inside information on a grantor that will help you tailor your appeal to your school's needs and the funder's priorities.

You will establish more valuable connections if you provide an opportunity for your grants advisory group to review the needs, priorities, and projects that your focus groups have developed. Ideally, selected members of the focus groups should make a presentation to the grants advisory group emphasizing the process through which their groups assessed your school's problems and opportunities. This is essential to increasing the grants advisory committee's sense of involvement and to making them feel that they too have ownership of the solutions. The grants advisory group's involvement in the solutions is imperative. A lack of input from them will result in fewer links and may also result in their approaching potential funders with weak statements such as "The school I am working with has some grant ideas they want to discuss with you" instead of an attention-grabber like "We at the ____________ school have developed several solutions to our problem with ____________, and we would like to discuss them informally with you." The committee members' depth of commitment and the detail with which they complete the Foot-in-the-Door Worksheet will also depend on their involvement in developing solutions and the degree to which they feel part of the solutions. Naturally, if your grants advisory group members are also members of your community focus groups they will be actively involved in brainstorming and prioritizing the areas that need to be improved. The worksheets in chapter 3 will help you establish a list of needs and develop solutions to them.

Figure 2.6

FOOT-IN-THE-DOOR WORKSHEET

Name and Title: ______________________________

Home Address & Phone (Winter & Summer):

______________________ ______________________

______________________ ______________________

Business Address & Phone:

____

____

1. What foundation boards are you currently a member of?

______________________ ______________________

______________________ ______________________

2. What foundation boards are you a past member of?

______________________ ______________________

______________________ ______________________

3. What foundation boards do members of your family serve on?

Name of Relative	Relationship	Name of Foundation

4. What foundation boards do your friends and associates serve on?

Name of Friend/Associate	Name of Foundation

5. What corporations do you have a relationship with?

Name of Corporation	Relationship to Corporation

Figure 2.6 (continued)

6. What corporate relationships do relatives, friends, and associates have?

Relative/Friend/Associate	Corporation	Relationship to Corporation
______________	______________	______________
______________	______________	______________
______________	______________	______________

7. What federal, state, city/county funding agencies do you have contacts in?

Name of Agency (Department/Division/Program)	Name & Title of Contact
______________	______________
______________	______________
______________	______________

8. What contacts do you have with federal, state, and city/county elected officials who could influence education-related appropriations? If the federal official is a senator or representative, indicate what state he or she represents.

Name and Title: ______________

Federal/State/City/County? ______________

Which State? ______________

Which City? County? ______________

Name and Title: ______________

Federal/State/City/County? ______________

Which State? ______________

Which City? County? ______________

9. What other clubs, groups, or organizations are you a member of or have a consulting, advisory, or other relationship with?

Name of Organization	Nature of Your Relationship
______________	______________
______________	______________

When you and your most influential grants advisory group members feel that the other group members are ready to "buy into" and work for school change, discuss the concept of linkages with them and mail or hand out the Inventory of Linkages and Resources Letter (fig. 2.5) and the Foot-in-the-Door Worksheet.

How to Use the Information You Receive

In my first experience collecting information on linkages, I researched the data bases on possible funders, selected those that were close by and whose interests showed a strong match with my school's newly brainstormed projects, and then determined if we had any links to them. For instance, if the Smith Foundation appeared to be a likely prospect, I reviewed the advisory committee members' worksheets to find out if we had a contact who could get his or her foot in the door on behalf of our school.

Winning Links is an IBM or IBM-compatible software program designed to assist in the database development of contacts and linkages. It allows the user to retrieve information necessary to access foundations, corporations, and government funding agencies. For more information, call 1-800-662-6642.

Another way to use the information collected on the Foot-in-the-Door Worksheet is to review the data and research those foundations, corporations, government agencies, and service clubs that your people have connections with. Determine what types of efforts the potential grantors fund and compare these with your list of needs and brainstormed projects.

The Foot-in-the-Door Worksheet and the data gathered from your Grants Resources Inventory will provide you, the principal, with command of communication. You will know whom to ask to call those funding sources that you do not have access to.

Corporate and community leaders know the value of the linkage process and are surprised that schools do not use it more often. Although educators may want to believe that the best proposal will win, reality tells us that a well-prepared proposal, pushed to the top of the pile by a mutual friend, will get the most attention and will likely be funded.

The concept of developing a data base of linkages is so attractive to corporate leaders that you should consider submitting a proposal to a local corporation to fund the development of your system. Corporate representatives are keenly aware of the benefit/return ratio of their investments in nonprofit organizations. By funding you to develop and implement a linkage system, they will enable your school to attract funding from other sources, without increasing corporate taxes. That is a good investment!

When you discuss the possibility of funding your linkage system with a corporation (or a foundation), be sure to include in your grant request the cost of the following items:

- a computer,
- a laser printer,
- software, and
- data input expenses.

When I introduced this concept to a local family foundation, my office was funded for a $15,000 linkage system that included all of the above items plus a modem and a subscription to a grants data base. You would probably be happy with much less, and the smaller the amount you request, the greater your chances of getting it. By the way, my funding source remarked that she made the grant in honor of her father, who had become a millionaire through his amazing ability to remember who knew the people he needed to meet!

Use the following checklist to begin assessing your system's access to preproposal contacts, webbing and linkages, and grants advisory committees and to help you develop a plan for improvement.

CHAPTER 2 CHECKLIST

Evaluation and Planning Worksheet

1. Data: What percentage of the proposals submitted by your school in the past year have:

a. utilized preproposal contact? _____%

b. been developed at the last minute? _____%

c. been endorsed by a community advisory committee? _____%

2. Do you have a group or committee already in existence that could function as your grants advisory group?

_____ yes _____no If yes, what group?_______________________

If no, could you initiate a grants advisory group? _____yes ___no

3. Could your school's grants effort utilize a webbing and linkage system?

_____ yes _____no

4. If you answered yes to question 3, would you attempt to develop a webbing and linkage system for your school's grants effort?

_____ yes _____no

If yes, who would act as coordinator to introduce the concept? _____________

5. What other groups, committees, or booster clubs could produce more linkages for your school?

Club Names and Contact Persons:

Club Name: ____________________ Contact: ____________________

Club Name: ____________________ Contact: ____________________

Club Name: ____________________ Contact: ____________________

6. If you have any corporate contacts, review them and identify one or two individuals who might be interested in providing grant funds to support the development of your linkage system. Record the results of your discussions with them.

Linkage: ______________________________

Contacted on: ______________________________

Results: ______________________________

Linkage: ______________________________

Contacted on: ______________________________

Results: ______________________________

CHAPTER THREE

Helping Others Assess Needs and Develop Goals and Solutions

As the principal, you can bring substantial credibility and status to the grantseeking process. By involving yourself in the development and support of focus groups, grants advisory committees, and brainstorming sessions, you will promote an atmosphere of cooperation and problem solving that reaches far beyond grantseeking. A grants system that generates needed funds for your school, with few up-front costs and lots of voluntary participation, can be an exciting part of your leadership role.

We know that when classroom leaders have a negative attitude and want to be paid up front for every extra effort they make, it is difficult to get them excited about *anything*, let alone something that is not in their job description — like grant writing. However, grantseeking actually provides an opportunity to develop a positive attitude in teachers, staff, parents, and students. A proposal to fund two or three miniprojects can create a spark that ignites a desire for change. A small grant of $3,000 from a local foundation dispersed in three $1,000 awards to classroom leaders could help you identify those individuals who care enough to make an extra effort to try to improve the educational system.

It is not necessary to develop enthusiasm and motivation in your entire staff or school. A few parents, students, and teachers who want to improve education can start the ball rolling, especially when you establish a grants system that provides the assistance and guidance they need.

Most, if not all, grant awards are intended to change a situation. Few awards are made to continue a program in its existing form. Even when granting funds to a school for an existing exemplary educational program, the grantor's underlying motivation is to fund the expansion of the program or to make it qualitatively better. At first glance, it may seem easy to demonstrate the need to address the educational inadequacies and problems that you face each day. But whether you seek to expand a successful program or change an inadequate one, the needs section of a proposal is frequently the most underdeveloped. One reason for the inadequate development of the statement of need and of the data to adequately substantiate the problem lies in the fact that those who live with the deficient situation day after day see it so clearly that they think it will be obvious to the grantor too or that the grantor will at least take their word for it. The old adage "You can't see the forest because of the trees" seems to sum up grantseekers' inability to clearly define their school's problem to others.

In addition, grantseekers are sometimes reluctant to document the need more clearly because it is depressing and/or upsetting to them. Your task as the principal is to focus in a positive manner on those areas of need as well as of excellence that grant funds could impact.

The following formula may help you initiate discussions that will identify your school's needs and document their importance.

Figure 3.1

FORMULA FOR SUCCESSFUL GRANTSEEKING

Needs	+	Solutions	+	Commitment	=	Educational Advancement
of your students, classroom, community, and society		ideas and strategies to adapt change, strengthen the education system		the extra effort of you, your colleagues, and parents	∞	* New strategies, equipment, and materials to meet the challenges of education

*Grantseeking provides the catalyst in this equation. Change occurs at an increased rate.

Assessing the Need

Most focus groups and brainstorming sessions center too soon on developing solutions and do not pay enough attention to determining how they know a problem exists. Whether because of the reasons stated previously or because of a strong desire to improve the situation, these groups will often move too quickly from documenting the problem to the "what are we going to do about it" stage: Not assessing the need sufficiently impairs the groups' ability to motivate a grantor and causes the brainstormed solutions and projects to be inspired more by personalities and group dynamics than by a clear documentation of the need.

Gap Diagram

To help the group members focus on the present situation and the desired state of affairs, they should construct a Gap Diagram (see fig. 3.2) for each identified school/community need (limit the choices to five to determine the areas of highest priority). Each member of the focus group should then rank order the needs, labeling them 1, 2, 3, and so on, according to the order in which they should be addressed. The rank orders should be combined to form a prioritized list of needs. You may want to use play money or lottery tickets (see chapter 1) to help the group identify and prioritize the needs.

Figure 3.2

THE GAP

What exists now. What is real. What the present situation is. How many students are at this stage.	What could be. The goal. The desired state of affairs, level of achievement.

Needs Worksheet

The Needs Worksheet (fig. 3.3) will give you additional help in documenting the need. The first step is to determine which problem or need the group will focus on and to record it on the worksheet after "Problem Area."

Before the group brainstorms solutions, ask them to provide information that demonstrates the current state of affairs. Many individuals will enthusiastically give their opinions, and some will provide very compelling stories and case studies that illustrate the need. Record all these examples and their sources on the worksheet. While some grantors prefer statistics and facts, the human-interest quality of examples and stories is often effective in motivating a potential funding source.

Also, record any pertinent studies and/or facts and their sources. In many cases, the group will not have a total command of the facts. Maybe there has never been a formal statistical documentation of the problem — the group just *knows* that it exists! Brainstorm the ways you could provide better documentation of the problem, such as attendance records, grades, and so on.

In many cases, a grant of $3,000 to $5,000 to document the extent of a problem can be acquired from a small funding source in your community. Since many of these smaller grantors have limited funds, their motivation for making an award to your school to develop a needs assessment would be to increase your chance of attracting funds from outside the community. Accurate, timely data and established mechanisms for collecting baseline data would allow you to perform pre- and postproject evaluations, making your school more fundable.

Most groups want to move quickly to solutions and must be reminded of grantors' need to document the change that will occur as a result of funding your project. Often the lack of sound preliminary and preassessment data complicates the postassessment and evaluation required by certain funding sources. By taking the time now to carefully review *how you know* there is a need you will bring to light the indicators of change that can be built into the evaluation.

Devoting time to developing a clear assessment of need will also give your group a sense of common interest and the motivation to do something about the problem.

Needs Worksheet Sample

In the sample worksheet (fig. 3.4) the group focused on parental involvement in supporting constructive informal education. At their first meeting, the group members realized that while they all *believed* that a lack of support for school activities and unsupervised television viewing were detrimental to the behaviors elementary teachers wanted to be reinforced at home, they were lacking *facts.* Therefore, each group member was asked to bring documentation of the problem to the next meeting.

In the end, this group used data and studies from the United States Department of Education and other state and federal agencies to document the need for parental involvement in children's education. As you can see from the sample, the measurement indicators for change were suggested through the methods used to demonstrate the problem and the gap (i.e., hours of television viewing; visit/contact with child's classroom). The group could also have conducted an informal survey of their own students and parents. This would have provided interesting comparisons to the national study and may have shown that their local problem was as bad or worse than the national problem. A local study may also have made the group a better choice for a grant because it would have demonstrated its commitment in time and resources to documenting the baseline data that could be helpful in the posttest or final evaluation.

Establishing the Goals of Your Project

After establishing the data necessary to document the need, the group should establish the goals. To do this, the group members should ask themselves what would result if the needs outlined on the needs worksheet were addressed and the problem was solved.

Goals Worksheet

This worksheet (fig. 3.5) will help the group focus on the opposite end of the gap continuum — the desired state of affairs. Because of the critical and often negative outlook of our society, group members may excel at documenting the problem but falter when asked to reverse their perspective and identify positive outcomes that will result from eliminating it.

Completing the Goals Worksheet will give your group a clearer direction. It will also help the group members realize that although projects, programs, and research are meaningful ways of moving toward desired outcomes, they are *not* goals. They are techniques and strategies to close the gap between what is now and what ought to be.

Figure 3.3

NEEDS WORKSHEET

Completing this worksheet will help you step back from possible solutions and projects and establish that there is a gap between what is now and what should be.

Problem Area: ____

____

____

Documentation of the Need to Address This Problem:

What Exists Now — The Present State of Affairs (Studies, Facts, Surveys, Case Studies, etc.)	**Source of Data** (Organization) (Journal, Newsletter, Newspaper, etc.) (Date of Publication)

Note: *Consider performing a survey of your classroom, school, and/or community to document that the problem exists.*

Goals Worksheet Sample

In the sample goals worksheet (fig. 3.6) the problem has been identified as parents' lack of involvement in their children's education. The goal is for parents and teachers to work together as responsible partners to maximize children's educational achievement. This goal will never be fully attained, but it will provide direction and purpose for teachers and parents to work side by side.

It is best if the group can cite quotations from experts that validate and confirm the goal as well as studies that confirm that the goal is worth pursuing and that progress toward it is likely to produce results. You will note that in the sample several studies, articles, and quotations are cited.

Developing Solutions

Worksheet for Developing Solutions and Projects to Reduce the Problem

Use this worksheet (fig. 3.7) when brainstorming possible solutions, projects, programs, research, interventions, and protocols that may help you

Figure 3.4

NEEDS WORKSHEET
SAMPLE

Completing this worksheet will help you step back from possible solutions and projects and establish that there is a gap between what is now and what should be.

Problem Area: Parents' lack of involvement in their children's formal education and lack of support for constructive informal educational experiences.

Documentation of the Need to Address This Problem:

What Exists Now — The Present State of Affairs	Source of Data
4 out of 5 parents reported that they regularly discuss schoolwork with their children. Yet two-thirds of the children said their parents rarely or never talked about school with them.	Department of Education, Office of Educational Research and Improvement, Study reported in the *Wall Street Journal* on January 3, 1992. 25,000 middle school children surveyed.
Two-thirds of the parents claimed to place limits on television viewing. Two-thirds of the children said they had no limits on television viewing.	
The middle school group (8th graders) reported watching 21.4 hours of television per week, in comparison to spending 5.6 hours per week on homework.	
50% of the parents reported attending school meetings, but less than one-third had ever visited their child's classroom. 66% had never talked to school officials concerning their child's homework.	

Note: *You could include findings from surveys of your classroom, school or community; a consortium of classes; or a comparison to a classroom in Europe or another part of the world.*

reduce the problem and progress toward the stated goal.

When you are brainstorming, express all ideas for solutions without critique or in-depth analysis. Even those solutions that seem less than feasible should be stated since they may lead to other, more achievable solutions.

Jot down the suggested solutions on the worksheet. Give a copy of the worksheet to each member of the group. Then set a precise time limit to discuss each proposed solution.

Worksheet to Develop the Top Five Suggested Solutions to the Problem

After the discussion, have the members rank order the solutions and place the top five on the Worksheet to Develop the Top Five Suggested Solutions to the Problem (fig. 3.8). The members of the group should address

Figure 3.5

GOALS WORKSHEET

Problem Area: ____

____

____

____

If the needs documented on the *Needs Worksheet* were fulfilled and the problem was eliminated, what would result? What is the desired state of affairs? The ultimate end? The answer to these questions states the goal. The *Needs Worksheet* documents what exists now. The *Goals Worksheet* documents what ought to be. The goal provides purpose, direction, and motivation for grantseeking.

Goal: ____

____

____

____

Record studies, quotations, and research findings that document what ought to be. Provide sources and dates.

Studies — Quotations — Research Findings	**Source — Date**

Note: *This is not the place to list solutions. The means of closing the gap between what is now and what ought to be is the solution. The solution reduces the problem. It is discussed in Chapter 5.*

each of the issues on the worksheet to the best of their ability (e.g., estimate of the cost, cost per student/teacher, number of beneficiaries, drawbacks, and so on).

Sample Worksheet to Develop the Top Five Suggested Solutions to the Problem

This sample worksheet shows one group's preferred solutions to the problem of lack of parental involvement in children's education.

Figure 3.6

GOALS WORKSHEET

SAMPLE

Problem Area: Parents' lack of involvement in their children's formal education and lack of support for constructive informal educational experiences.

If the needs documented on the Needs Worksheet were fulfilled and the problem was eliminated, what would result? What is the *desired* state of affairs? The ultimate end? The answer to these questions states the goal. The Needs Worksheet documents what exists now. The Goals Worksheet documents what ought to be. The goal provides purpose, direction, and motivation for grantseeking.

Goal: Parents and teachers acting as responsible partners who work together to maximize children's educational achievement.

Record studies, quotations, and research findings that document what ought to be. Provide sources and dates.

Studies — Quotations — Research Findings	Source — Date
Students whose parents discussed their schoolwork recorded higher grades.	Dept. of Education Study *Wall Street Journal* 1/3/92
Television viewing restrictions tended to boost grades.	Dept. of Education Study *Wall Street Journal* 1/3/92
"Burden of education should not be on the teachers and schools alone." Education Department study says, "Parents have a major role to play."	Dept. of Education Study *Wall Street Journal* 1/3/92
Home-based guidance program in Rochester schools demonstrates educational improvement in low income students. Homeroom teacher acts as liaison between schools and parents. When teacher makes home visits, children do better in school.	Harvard University, 3-year study, *Democrat & Chronicle* November 28, 1991.
Preschool children from single-parent homes have better verbal skills than children from two-parent homes (more one-on-one communication).	Unpublished study 1989-90 Dierdre Madden, Baldwin Wallace College, Berea, OH, *Democrat & Chronicle* November 28, 1991.
Harrison, Arkansas — Students score in top 10% of the nation in test scores, yet Arkansas ranks 272 of 327 in education taxes. One of the lowest tax rates in the U.S. Money may not be the resource that makes the difference. Parents volunteer in their children's classrooms 100 hours per week. Duties include: making copies, grading papers, working with students, listening to students read. Basically, the parents save teachers time. Parents and teachers meet on school councils and determine the educational goals for next year. Each school reports progress toward goals in a newspaper advertisement. School system received 10 new computers donated by civic clubs. Parents made speeches at clubs.	*USA Today* 11/18/91 Study identifies good schools through "School Match" of Columbus, Ohio. "School Match" provides information to families moving to new areas.
Frank Newman, President of Education Commission, states, "They're saying parents are important and teachers are important and they should be part of running the schools."	

Note: *This is not the place to list solutions. The means of closing the gap between what is now and what ought to be is the solution. The solution reduces the problem. It is discussed in Chapter 5.*

Figure 3.7

WORKSHEET FOR DEVELOPING SOLUTIONS AND PROJECTS TO REDUCE THE PROBLEM

Problem: ____

____

____

____

List any and all proposed solutions. No discussions, please. Discuss the ideas after the allotted time for brainstorming has expired. Then request each participant to rank order the proposed solutions, with 1 being the favorite.

Rank **Proposed Solutions/Projects to Reduce the Problem**

-
-
-
-
-
-
-
-
-
-
-
-
-
-
-
-
-
-
-
-
-
-
-

Figure 3.8

WORKSHEET FOR DEVELOPING THE TOP FIVE SUGGESTED SOLUTIONS TO THE PROBLEM

Problem: ____

____

Describe the top five proposed solutions briefly and give a rough estimate of the cost of each. Also provide an estimate of the cost per student or teacher. Include the number of individuals who would benefit directly from each solution and the number who could benefit indirectly through duplication of the approach at other schools. List the drawbacks of each (i.e., those things that would impede its success).

Ask the following of each solution. Would you fund this idea with a grant? What is the extent of the benefits for the money expended?

Solution #1:

Solution #2:

Solution #3:

Solution #4:

Solution #5:

Figure 3.9

WORKSHEET FOR DEVELOPING THE TOP FIVE SUGGESTED SOLUTIONS TO THE PROBLEM

SAMPLE

Problem: Parents' lack of involvement in their children's education and lack of support for constructive informal educational experience.

Describe the top five proposed solutions briefly and give a rough estimate of the cost of each. Also provide an estimate of the cost per student or teacher. Include the number of individuals who would benefit directly from each solution and the number who could benefit indirectly through duplication of the approach at other schools. List the drawbacks of each (i.e., those things that would impede its success).

Ask the following of each solution. Would you fund this idea with a grant? What is the extent of the benefits for the money expended?

Solution #1: Develop a parent-teacher-student education contract that outlines each party's responsibility to support education. Review and renew every month on a three-part carbonless form.

Solution #2: Send home to the parents a short videotape of classroom and educational techniques and add a specific segment on the parents' child and her or his progress.

Solution #3: Require teachers to visit every student's home twice per year to report on the child's educational progress.

Solution #4: Allow taxpayers to lower their school taxes by volunteering/working at the school.

Solution #5: Send parents a newsletter each month with articles on how and why they should get involved.

CHAPTER 3 CHECKLIST

Evaluation and Planning Worksheet

1. **Does your school have a prioritized list of needs to be addressed?**
   _____ yes _____ no

2. **If the answer to question #1 is yes, and if you have a system for developing this prioritized list of needs, could the system be improved?**
   _____ yes _____ no

   If yes, how (techniques, changes, additions, etc.)?

   ____
   ____
   ____
   ____

3. **If you do not have a prioritized list of needs or a system for developing one, do you have any *existing* groups or committees that could develop this list?**
   _____ yes _____ no

   If yes, please list the groups and/or committees and the names of the appropriate contact people.

Group	Contact Person
____________________	____________________
____________________	____________________
____________________	____________________
____________________	____________________
____________________	____________________
____________________	____________________

4. **List the information, resources, and materials you could provide to your school groups to help them develop each of the following areas.**

   Problem Areas: ____
   ____
   ____

   Needs: ____
   ____
   ____

   Goals: ____
   ____
   ____

   Solutions: ____
   ____
   ____

CHAPTER FOUR

The Grants Marketplace – What A Principal Needs to Know

You need to have a conceptual framework of where the grant funds are and approximately in what amounts. Developing and encouraging effective grants strategies and decisions do not require that you abandon your other administrative duties to study grantsmanship full time. General knowledge, coupled with a theoretical decision-making strategy and links to a computer-based grants retrieval system, will dramatically improve your school's grant program and enhance your image as a top-notch administrator.

To increase your information about the grants marketplace at minimal cost, invite a college or university professor or administrator to become a member of your grants advisory group. Individuals from higher education are usually more familiar with the competitive grants mechanism and have access to the resources of their universities' grants offices including grants professionals and computer-based grant information retrieval systems. Your relationship with a representative of higher education will be mutually beneficial. Professors are usually eager to become involved with elementary and/or middle schools because these can provide teaching and research experience for their graduate students and also enable them to make money outside of their university positions. Your cooperation will provide your school with grants resources, help in performing third-party evaluations, and give you the status of having an individual with an advanced degree and a list of published articles on your side.

The following grants marketplace information is available through computers, but you need a basic knowledge of it in order to help your classroom leaders develop their grants strategy.

The grants marketplace can be broken down into the following basic elements:

- Federal Grant Opportunities
- State Grant Opportunities
- Large National General-Purpose Foundations
- Special-Purpose Foundations
- Community Foundations
- Family Foundations

- Corporate Foundations
- Large Corporate (Nonfoundation) Giving Programs
- All Other Corporations

A. The Grants Marketplace Quiz

In order to lead your school to grants success, you need to increase your "Grants I.Q." and that of your faculty, staff, and grants advisory group(s). The Grants Marketplace Quiz (fig. 4.1) will help you and your group develop a targeted, proactive, success-based, grantseeking effort based on knowledge of where the grants funds *really* are.

Use the quiz in a nonthreatening and relaxed way by asking the members of your group to take wild guesses at the answers, assuring them that the quizzes do not have to be signed. It is a good idea for you to take the quiz also and to share your answers with the group. Then display the correct answers on an overhead screen, board, or flip chart so that the members of your group can correct their quizzes. It is important for you to explain why the group's overall scores on the quiz may have been low. Point out that newspapers, journals, and newsletters focus on *exceptionally large* grant awards, causing people to believe that all grants are of the million-dollar variety. This is simply not the case.

Discuss how inappropriate grants strategies could evolve if the members of the group were to base their grantseeking on overinflated ideas about the grants marketplace. This is why it is so important to develop a realistic appraisal of the marketplace, which will also encourage the group members to think about the links they may have to potential funders.

The corporate representatives on your grants advisory group will particularly approve of approaching the grants area from a knowledge of where the funds are and how much is granted each year. These corporate individuals are comfortable with the idea of competition and want to know the chances of success.

You may wish to expand your discussion of the correct answers to the quiz (see fig. 4.2) by including the background information that follows the answer key.

Question 1 — The figure of 487,000 is somewhat misleading. There are actually many more 501(c)(3) tax-exempt organizations because *several* nonprofits may operate under one number approved by the I.R.S. For example, a university may have a center, an institute, and a museum, all operating under one number.

Question 2 — It is important to focus on the competition for grant funds that exists between all nonprofit organizations, and especially on the competition from other elementary and junior high schools. Keep in mind, however, that many of these schools have *never* applied for a grant, while others have applied for government funding only. Now is the time for your school to capitalize on the trend in the foundation and corporate grants

Figure 4.1

THE GRANTS MARKETPLACE QUIZ

1. How many 501(c)(3) tax-exempt charitable organizations are recognized by the Internal Revenue Service?

____

2. How many elementary schools, middle schools, and junior high schools are there in the United States?

____

3. How much money will the federal government grant through its 1,000+ granting programs this year?

____

4. What was the total amount of funds distributed to nonprofit groups through foundation grants, corporate grants, bequests, and individuals in the past year?

____

What percentage of total funds is granted by each of the following four sources?

Foundation Grants	________%
Corporate Grants	________%
Bequests	________%
Individual Giving	________%
	100%

FOUNDATIONS

5. Approximately how many grant-making foundations are there?

____

6. The business of approximately how many foundations is carried out in offices?

____

7. How many grants of more than $10,000 were awarded in the past year?

____

CORPORATIONS

8. How many corporations are there in the United States?

____

9. What percentage of corporations takes a deduction for charitable contributions?

____

10. Which of the following forms of corporate support to nonprofit organizations has experienced the greatest increase in the past five years?
    a. products
    b. cash
    c. securities
    d. loans

Figure 4.2

THE GRANTS MARKETPLACE QUIZ
Answer Key

1. How many 501(c)(3) tax-exempt charitable organizations are recognized by the Internal Revenue Service?
   487,000

2. How many elementary schools, middle schools, and junior high schools are there in the United States?
   71,887

3. How much money will the federal government grant through its 1,000+ granting programs this year?
   $75 billion

4. What was the total amount of funds distributed to nonprofit groups through foundation grants, corporate grants, bequests, and individuals in the past year?
   $122.7 billion

   What percentage of total funds is granted by each of the following four sources?

Foundation Grants	6.2%
Corporate Grants	4.9%
Bequests	6.2%
Individual Giving	82.7%
	100%

FOUNDATIONS

5. Approximately how many grant-making foundations are there?
   34,000

6. The business of approximately how many foundations is carried out in offices?
   1,000

7. How many grants of more than $10,000 were awarded in the past year?
   58,000

CORPORATIONS

8. How many corporations are there in the United States?
   3 million

9. What percentage of corporations takes a deduction for charitable contributions?
   35%

10. Which of the following forms of corporate support to nonprofit organizations has experienced the greatest increase in the past five years?
    ✓a. products
    b. cash
    c. securities
    d. loans

marketplace to award grants for early intervention to preschools and elementary and middle schools.

Question 3 — While the federal government will grant over $75 billion in 1993, far more than this will be appropriated to programs. For example, the Department of Education will not award all of its $30 billion appropriation in grants, because a large part of this sum must be used to pay for overhead, office space, and salaries and fringes for the program officers and staff. In other words, the amount *appropriated* to a program is not the same as the amount *awarded* by a program in the form of grants.

Your school's ability to access federal grant funds is a function of how your project is defined and who it is supposed to benefit. The Department of Education is only one source of federal funds. You can also apply for federal grant money that is distributed to your state as well as for funds from federal programs that focus on drug and alcohol prevention, the humanities, science, literacy, health, and many other related areas.

Question 4 — The total amount of nongovernment funding for nonprofits is calculated each summer for the previous year. The estimate for 1991 was $124.77 billion, a sum that may startle your grants advisory group members. Moreover, most individuals think that the portion of this money granted by foundations and corporations is much higher than it really is.

Once you reveal the correct percentages, some group members may express a strong desire to go after individual giving — 82.7 percent or $101.13 billion. That is, until you inform them that:

- 54.2 percent of individual giving is to religious organizations, and
- while that still leaves $50 billion, fund-raising techniques must be employed to access these funds, including special events, direct mail, telephone solicitation, and so on.

Seeking grants from foundations and corporations usually consists of preparing a well-targeted, two-page letter proposal. Compare this simple process with the stringent proposal requirements of government agencies, and the $14 billion in grants from foundations and corporations begins to look very good. Grantseeking in general is a better alternative to securing external resources than other traditional fund-raising techniques.

Grants advisory group members should be made aware that the federal government has far more financial resources than private agencies (foundations and corporations) do. Therefore, private agencies often prefer that potential grantees look to government sources first. This information will help your group understand why it is important to support federal as well as private grantseeking.

Question 5 — Highlight the differences between the 1,000-plus federal programs and the 34,000 foundations. Each foundation thinks of itself and the projects it supports as invaluable and unique!

Question 6 — No one knows exactly how many federal employees are involved in the grants area. If you include program officers, staff, and auditors, the number must be staggering.

Since foundations often have limited funds, they feel that the more staff they have, the fewer grants they can make. If they do not have an office, they need few, if any, paid staff. For this reason fewer than 1,000 foundations occupy offices.

The 34,000 foundations actually employ only slightly more than 3,000 individuals. Keep in mind also that some large foundations have 100 or more employees, while thousands of smaller foundations have none.

Armed with these facts, your grants advisory group members will clearly understand how important it is to utilize an informal webbing and linkage system in contacting foundation and corporate board members.

Question 7 — This information will help your group set realistic expectations based upon sound knowledge of the grants marketplace. Since only 58,000 grants in excess of $10,000 are reported to the Foundation Center, receiving a $100,000 foundation grant is an admirable achievement.

The positive aspect of this situation is that there are hundreds of thousands of grants for under $10,000. This is good news for classrooms and schools that can formulate interesting proposals for small requests to support programs or projects that can influence many students.

Question 8 — There are several reasons why many corporations are not deeply involved in philanthropy. The root of their lack of involvement goes back to the late 1930s, when it was actually illegal for corporations to make gifts to nonprofit organizations.

Question 9 — In reality, many more corporations make gifts than take deductions. Many do not report deductions for these gifts so as not to invite Internal Revenue Service audits. In addition, many owners and executives make contributions from their personal funds. Incorporate the following basic facts of corporate philanthropy into your school's strategy for grantseeking.

1. Corporations do not "give away" money. They "invest" it and expect a return.
2. Corporations invest where they live and where the children of their workers go to school.
3. Corporations value involvement. Many will not make a grant unless their employees volunteer time to the nonprofit applicant.

Do not make the mistake of thinking that only large corporations make grants. The research section that follows shows that it often pays off to approach smaller corporations. Especially keep in mind corporations that you have a link with; for example, smaller corporations with employees who are graduates of your school.

Question 10 — Gifts in the form of products may be less costly than cash, reduce inventories, provide a write-off for dated products, entice future purchasers, and lead to maintenance contracts or agreements. For all of these reasons, corporations like to donate products and equipment.

B. The Grantseekers' Matrix

Now that you have a basic idea of where the grant money is and how many billions of dollars are available, you need a systematic approach to identifying what types of organizations will be interested in funding the programs, projects, and equipment you need. The Grantseekers' Matrix (fig. 4.3) provides the basis for such an approach.

Column 1 of the Grantseeker's Matrix describes the various types of projects — demonstration, research, equipment, replication, consortia, and international. Columns 2 through 9 provide the grantseeker with insight into how the various categories of grantors view the major variables that determine grants success.

Column 1: Type of Project — There are six basic categories or types of grant proposals listed on the Grantseeker's Matrix. While your task may be to help your school's grantseekers focus clearly on a need and several methods to address it, this matrix will enable grantseekers to look at changes in approaches that would expand the number of potential funders and increase funding opportunities.

You can change the nature of your project from research to demonstration to international. The secret here is to practice the golden rule of grantseeking — the funder has the gold and therefore makes the rules. You are not going to convince funding sources to change their needs or rules, so you will have to adjust your approach to fit *their* desires.

A. Demonstration — In this category of grants the funder's interest is in developing models for change. The emphasis is on proving what works and on demonstrating change. The funder who awards demonstration grants prefers innovative approaches and ideas. For example, this type of funder would be enthused by the idea that a project could become a model for other classrooms, curricula, or schools.

B. Research —At first glance this category of grants may appear to be out of the question for your school. But give it a second look! By utilizing a link to a college or university you may be able to develop your school's ability to attract these funds. A demonstration or model project can become a research project if you incorporate a control group and a statistical analysis component in the project plans. The best part is that to do so your school does not need a vast computer system and experts in statistical design. These resources already exist at your local college or university.

C. Equipment — Sources that fund educational equipment directly are relatively rare. However, grantors want to fund projects that will make a difference.

To that end they will allow the purchase of a limited amount of equipment if it plays an integral part in the project.

Even when you solicit hardware from a computer equipment manufacturer, the manufacturer will want to know:

- why you want the equipment?
- who will use it?
- how many will benefit from it?
- what curriculum changes will occur?
- how will in-service training be used?

By the time you finish writing a proposal for equipment, you will realize that you have really developed a model project and that, in fact, your chance of success in attracting the equipment will depend on the quality of your plan or project and how it will influence change or educational advancement.

D. Replication — Funders of this category of grants do not want to be involved in discovering *what works* or *how and why* something works — the rather risky ventures of research and model projects. Rather, they want their grant money to be used to encourage others to use or replicate the techniques that have been proven, usually under someone else's grant funds, to have a positive effect.

E. Consortia — Funders of this type of grant are interested in a partnership of grantseekers, each of whom brings outstanding qualities to the proposal.

- an increased likelihood of success.
- a *sharing* of expensive resources and equipment rather than a duplication.

Any of the previously mentioned types of grants can be consortia grants. For example, you can develop a demonstration, research, equipment, or replication grant that is also a consortia grant. In many cases grantors will encourage consortia grants, and some will even mandate or require them.

Consortia proposals have been around for many years, but are just now coming into their own as a powerful and cost-effective mechanism to achieve the outcomes suggested in proposals. Successful grantseekers will enter the year 2000 knowing how to utilize consortium arrangements to maximize cost efficiency and improve their competitive edge. The remainder of this decade will be marked by larger problems and fewer resources. Those schools that make the most of the limited resources available to them will win the funding.

F. International — Many grantors have links to other parts of the world. The political and social changes in Europe and the former Soviet Union, as well as the increasingly international interests of governments and corporations, all point to a marked rise in the success rates for international proposals.

Figure 4.3

GRANTSEEKERS' MATRIX

Type:____________________

1 Type of Project	2 Geographic Need	3 Award Size	4 School's Image	5 Credentials of Project Director	6 Preproposal Contact	7 Proposal Content	8 Review & Decision	9 Proposal Information and Administration
Demonstration A								
Research B								
Equipment C								
Replication D								
Consortia E								
International F								

Changes in trade and tariff rules and the growing number of multinational corporations may mean that a local corporation has a vested interest in another country. Including an elementary school from that country in your project plan may dramatically improve your chances for funding. For example, one of the largest U.S.-based manufacturers of blue jeans has just constructed a large manufacturing facility in Poland. A proposal that encourages educational change or that focuses on capitalism or any other of a number of corporate concerns, *and* that promotes an educated work force in Poland, might be considered very attractive by the U.S.-based manufacturer.

Finding an international partner is not difficult, especially if your grantseekers submit the proposal and initiate the contacts in the United States.

Column 2: Geographic Need — In most cases, your school must demonstrate a considerable local need for the solution you propose. Some grantors are interested in projects that address that same need in other areas. For example, your solution to your school's need may have a national or international impact, and highlighting this aspect of your project in your proposal might improve your fundability. In other cases, however, the mention of a national and/or an international focus may have little or no or even a negative impact on your fundability, because the grantor might be interested only in projects that address local needs.

Column 3: Award Size — The amount of grant funds needed to implement your solution is a critical factor in determining which type of funding source to approach. It is possible to ask several different types of grantors to fund part of your project, keeping your request within each one's budget, and in so doing to obtain funds for a considerably larger project than any one grantor could support.

Column 4: School's Image — What is the image or reputation of your school? Must you be designated as an outstanding school to attract funding from certain types of grantors?

Column 5: Credentials of Project Director — Each type of funding source will have different criteria for what constitutes a credible project director. Local reputation will have a positive impact on some grantors, while others will value doctoral degrees, records of publications, and previous grant awards.

Column 6: Preproposal Contact — The value of preproposal contact (contact before the proposal is written) cannot be overemphasized. However, some types of funding sources will not allow it. The vast differences in this particular area have a lot to do with whether a funding source has a grants staff, program officers, an office, or board members who can be approached through linkages.

Column 7: Proposal Content — This column summarizes the preferred format for the proposal and the application procedures. The purpose of this column is *not* for your prospective grantseeker to ascertain which type of funding source has the shortest application. Just because a grantor does not require a lengthy, detailed proposal it does not mean that proposal preparation will be easy. In fact, creating a two-page letter proposal to a foundation or corporation with no guidelines or required format can be much more difficult than preparing a lengthy application to a government funding source.

COLUMN 8: REVIEW AND DECISION — Who reads and reviews your school's proposal; what their biases, background, and education are; how much time they will spend reviewing each proposal; and what scoring system they will use are important factors for you to consider in preparing a winning proposal. Naturally, your school's proposal should be written with the reviewer in mind. The use of educational jargon may be acceptable to one type of reviewer and unacceptable to another.

Having this information before submitting your proposal will enable your grantseekers to perform a preliminary mock review of the proposal and to prepare the best possible proposal.

COLUMN 9: PROPOSAL INFORMATION AND ADMINISTRATION — It is important to know what the funding source will expect after the grant is awarded. Each type of grantor will have different rules, regulations, and guidelines that you must comply with. This column gives you an idea of what will be required of you as a school administrator.

C. The Government Grantseekers' Matrix

Review the Government Grantseekers' Matrix to determine your general strategy for approaching this $75 billion marketplace or to help you evaluate a specific project's viability for government funding.

As you can see from Column Two, the need must often exist outside of your school and geographic area. The award sizes are generally well above $10,000 per year, and awards of $50,000 to $250,000 are not uncommon. Your school's credibility should be high, and the credentials of the project director fairly well established.

If after reviewing this matrix you know that you want to pursue a federal grant opportunity, you can go directly to chapter 5 for in-depth information on searching for government grants. But I suggest that you review *all* of the matrixes to familiarize yourself with the requirements of and differences between each type of funder and to acquire valuable information on which to base alternative grant strategies.

D. Foundation Grantseekers' Matrix

LARGE NATIONAL GENERAL-PURPOSE FOUNDATIONS

Large national general-purpose foundations prefer demonstration and model projects. It is estimated that almost 50 percent of their grants are aimed at developing models and projects that promote change in their particular fields of interest.

These larger foundations may look a bit like government grantors since they generally do not fund replication grants, offer larger grants, and prefer to fund well-credentialed project directors. These types of foundations generally occupy an office and have staff or paid reviewers (consultants) who are experts in the field to critically evaluate proposals.

In some cases, you may approach a local foundation or corporation for a small grant to develop preliminary data or test part of your model; then go to a larger foundation for a grant to develop your project further before you approach a federal grants source for funding the implementation of your program.

Special-Purpose Foundations

Although there are only a few hundred special-purpose foundations, they have a lot of impact on their areas of interest. They are motivated by a strong desire to effect *immediate* change in the area of special needs. Your ability to improve the problem is paramount in their minds, and the rules and requirements imposed on the special-purpose foundation's grantees are not as stringent as those of government and large foundation funding sources.

When submitting a proposal to these funding sources, it is less important to demonstrate an outstanding image and impressive credentials than it is to captivate and excite them with a novel and cost-effective approach to *producing change in the needs area they value.*

Community Foundations

Community foundations are excellent grant resources for schools. While not every community has one, they are the fastest-growing area in the founda-48 tions marketplace, with over 300 in existence today. If your area is fortunate enough to have a community foundation, you have a superb source for funding those projects that the previously discussed funding sources would not support (e.g., replication, needs assessment). While the size of a community foundation grant is usually small, the impact it can have on your students and on your ability to make your school appear more fundable to other grantors is impressive.

If your area does not have a community foundation you would do well to help initiate one. A community-minded lawyer and banker on your grants advisory committee could get the ball rolling, and your school could soon have a new and unique source for grant funds. Even if your school has initiated a school foundation, a local community foundation should not be viewed as competition. It is just one more funding source.

Family Foundations

In some ways family foundations resemble community foundations. Built into

Figure 4.4

GOVERNMENT GRANTSEEKERS' MATRIX

1.Federal grants to elementary and middle schools come from the Department of Education and other programs that have an interest in children and families. The Department of Agriculture, Health and Human Services, as well as the National Science Foundation and the National Endowment for Arts and Humanities, can all be considered as possible sources of grants. There are over 1,000 federal programs granting over $75 billion annually.

Type of Project	Geographic Need	Award Size*	School's Image	Credentials of Project Director	Preproposal Contact	Proposal Content	Review & Decision	Proposal Information and Administration
Model/Demonstration— Great variety of areas Curriculum (math, science, reading, etc.) Learning-disabled, at-risk youth	Local/Regional State National	Medium to large	National/ Regional	Well-known, plus; published or spoken at conferences, etc.	Write, phone, go see	Long, detailed forms	Peer review by experts	Must follow OMB curricular long and elaborate forms an financial requirements
Research—Areas: Teaching Learning Vocation Fed. Dropouts Gifted	Local/National	"	National	Experts must be involved—subcontract or consortium or consortium with colleges/universities	"	"	"	"
Equipment—For acquisition (not very common); allowed when integral part of model or research	Local	Small to medium	Regional	Not essential	"	"	"	"
Replication—Not common unless Feds want regional sites or to expand to target population	Local	"	"	Local/Regional expertise	"	"	"	"
Consortium—More common now—allows use of experts and facilities lower cost	Local/national/ schools of consortium partners	Medium to large	National/ Regional		"	"	"	"
International— Interested in understanding U.S. language and culture, capitalistic system	Local National International	"	"		"	"	"	"

*Size of award is provided as rough guideline. Small is under $5,000, medium is $5,000–$50,000, and large is $50,000 and up.

their board of directors is a strong geographic homing device that is reflected in their granting pattern. They fund what they like, and they like programs that enhance educational opportunities in the geographic regions they care about.

Research is not a top funding priority for them. Since they seek to have a more immediate impact, they gravitate toward replication, equipment, and targeted model projects.

Corporate Foundations

Education is the top priority of the 1,287 corporate foundations. Approximately 40 to 50 percent of their grants go to education, and elementary and junior high schools have been the recipients of an increasing percentage of these funds. The key to procuring corporate foundation funds is your school's proximity to corporate plants or offices, the number of corporate workers who are motivated volunteers at your school, and the visible return on the corporate foundation's investment.

E. Corporate Grantseekers' Matrix

Large Corporate Grantors

This group is interested in schools located close to their plants, distribution centers, and stores. Despite what grantseekers are apt to think, large corporate grantors are not particularly motivated by press releases that make them appear like good corporate citizens. Some corporations do not even want their grant awards to be publicized, since publicity could result in more requests for grants. Instead, large corporate grantors are motivated by projects that position their products with students and/or teachers, help them develop and improve products, or produce a better-educated work force.

All Other Corporations

Corporate grant making was not practiced until after a 1953 court case that upheld the legality of a corporate grant to a university. Thus the history of corporate support is short, and the practice is not as widespread as many believe. But do not let this hold back your grantseekers. Smaller corporations are still a very valuable resource for your school. Since they are local, they may have ties and linkages to your school, and they certainly have a vested interest in your community. If you approach this group properly, the results may exceed your expectations.

Your grants advisory group members from the corporate community will be your key to corporate grants. When a corporate peer approaches a small corporation, explains the project and the direction your school is taking, and then invites the corporation to make a grant, you will get results!

Corporations know that voluntary grant making to local schools is better than a tax increase. After all, they get recognition and a good feeling from voluntary giving but just a canceled check from the tax collector for

Figure 4.5

FOUNDATION GRANTSEEKERS' MATRIX

Large National General-Purpose Foundations

2. Large National and General-Purpose Foundations: Ford, Rockefeller, MacArthur, etc.

Type: While relatively few in number (fewer than 50) this group has a large percentage of the assets and makes the majority of grants. They fund both nationally and internationally on a broad area of interests. They have paid staff and offices.

Type of Project	Geographic Need	Award Size	School's Image	Credentials of Project Director	Preproposal Contact	Proposal Content	Review & Decision	Proposal Information and Administration
Model/Demonstration Projects—Variety of interests by subject area and outcomes	Local/Regional/ National	Varies, but this group funds large & medium $50,000+	Helps to have regional or national image	Need to have expertise in school district very important	Phone—write letter, make a personal visit.	Many have guidelines and specific forms and restrictions	Staff are experts in field and hire outside expertise to evaluate	Many have application instructions and forms. Some produce annual reports and newsletters. Many have program specialists and auditors who may make pre-award and post-award visits. Administration follows established CPA guidelines.
Research—Many prefer a systematic research approach with statistical design and evaluation—wants to know what works	"	"	Good to include a university	Very important Utilize higher education linkages to Ed.D., Ph.D., colleges/universities	Critical to proposal acceptance	Length varies but 10–20 pgs. common. May use a preliminary review of your concept (letter proposal/letter of inquiry) before you are invited to submit	"	
Equipment—Allowable as part of the project methodology, but most avoid funding just equipment alone	"	"	"	"	"		"	
Replication—Most prefer to fund a model and dissemination of the project—not replication	"	"	"	"	"	"	"	
Consortium—More interest today than in the past. Look at IRS 990 to assist in choosing a past grantee as a partner	"	Larger sizes	Images of both partner schools important	Need to have experience and degrees in both partners	"	"	"	
International—Growing interest in the world, but still want to help out at home—discuss a possible foreign site to provide a comparison—look at IRS 990 to locate countries or languages of interest	Local/Regional & International	Larger to accommodate travel expenses	"		May be difficult to get both partners together with with funder. Use conference calls & teleconferences	"	"	In addition to the above, these grantors may have overseas staff.

Figure 4.6

FOUNDATION GRANTSEEKERS' MATRIX

Special Purpose Foundations

3. Special Purpose Foundations: Exxon Education Trust, Carnegie Foundation

Type: This type of foundation has a narrow, rather specific focus. There are special-purpose foundations for education and for the different levels of education, but don't overlook special-purpose foundations that fund subject areas of interest to elementary and middle schools, such as music, art, literacy, literature, health, etc.

Type of Project	Geographic Need	Award Size	School's Image	Credentials of Project Director	Preproposal Contact	Proposal Content	Review & Decision	Proposal Information and Administration
Model/Demonstration Project—They prefer project grants that call attention to their field or cause	Special needs population in your area	Large and medium	Not as critical as your potential to make a difference in their special interest	Important but not critical	Contact by phone, write, go see	Varies, usually have a proposal format; some use a concept paper to approve you to submit full proposal	Staff may be experts in target area	Use annual reports and tax returns to learn what they like and what type of organization they prefer as a grantee
Research—Only in their special interest. Usually the larger foundations like some research. On average, 10–20% of grant money awarded for research	"	"	"	Very important	"		Use some outside reviews	"
Equipment—Some will fund equipment; others will allow it if it is necessary to carry out the project/research	"	"	"	Important but not critical	"	"	"	"
Replication—Not usually priority unless a model was very successful	"	"	"	"	"	"	"	"
Consortium—Interested if the alliance will have more impact on the special interest	Special needs population in your area and your partner's	"	"	"	"	"	"	"
International—Several are interested in international as well as national	"	"	"	"	"	"	"	"

Figure 4.7

FOUNDATION GRANTSEEKERS' MATRIX

Community Foundations

4. Community Foundations: This type of foundation is named after the geographical area of concern. All its grants must benefit the specific area and boundaries are to separate the designated area — The Cleveland Foundation, the San Francisco Foundation, etc. Even smaller cities have them — Utica, New York Foundation and some areas have a statewide foundation — the North Dakota Foundation. The community foundation exists to support that particular community and is not under political or government sponsorship. They provide an excellent source of funds for elementary and middle school grants, but usually in smaller amounts.

Type of Project	Geographic Need	Award Size	School's Image	Credentials of Project Director	Preproposal Contact	Proposal Content	Review & Decision	Proposal Information and Administration
Model/Demonstration Project—This type of grantor prefers to grant money to projects that are sure to make a difference.	Need in the specific geographic area of "community"	Small, grants up to $10,000, many in the $5,000 range	How well your organization is known in your community and specifically by the board members.	The local image of the project director and key individuals involved in the project.	Contact with the designated official of the foundation is recommended.	Usually a short 2–8 pg. proposal	Usually a process that involves the board. Key factor here is that the board is represen-tative of the community.	There are many with annual reports, and their 990 A.R. IRS tax return is very helpful. Since most do not have many staff or support personal follow-up is limited.
Research—Not an area they usually fund	Only concerned with local need, not field of education	"		"				
Equipment—They may fund small purchases that show a lot of use	"	"		"	"	"	Greater range in socio-economic status, more women and minorities on the board.	
Replication—This is a good area because they have proof that it worked someplace else	"	"	"	"	"	"		
Consortium—Interested if all partners are in the same geographic area.	"	"	"	"	"	"	"	
International—Not a good bet, maybe if there is a strong ethnic group in the community.								

Figure 4.8

FOUNDATION GRANTSEEKERS' MATRIX

Family Foundations

5. Family Foundations: Over 30,000 of this type. Most are small, have little or no staff and no office, and meet once or twice per year. They support their families' concerns and values, with an eye to the past and the family member who created the foundation. They represent a valuable resource to elementary and middle school education because you can provide them with a lot of results for a small grant and because you have access to children and thus to the future.

Type of Project	Geographic Need	Award Size	School's Image	Credentials of Project Director	Preproposal Contact	Proposal Content	Review & Decision	Proposal Information and Administration
Model/Demonstration Project—This type of project interests many family foundations. They fear long-range support, so project must show self-sufficiency or other support later.	This type of funder has a very specific geographic granting perspective, and the need and your project must be in their area.	Small, under $10,000 and even $5,000	The credibility of your school, the district, and any of your contact people (friends) make the difference.	The project director's image in the school or community is important.	Since staff is limited, most state no contact except by letter. Your only opportunity is through "friends" who have contact with the board members.	Most want a short 1–2 page Letter Proposal or Letter of Inquiry. Usually no attachments are allowed.	Usually read by board members. You write to the level of expertise of the board. They are often family members and close friends or business associates.	Most do not publish an annual report. Information on what they prefer to fund is in their IRS tax return. IRS return found at Foundation Center Regional Collections. Administration should follow standard business practices and establish CPA guidelines. Little or not audit, follow-up, or compliance issues.
Research—Most want to invest money in what works, not a lot of interest in research.	Local. Interest if family had/has a child with educational problem.	Some medium-size but relatively rare		Very important		you to submit full proposal		
Equipment—This area is popular, since they prefer tangible things Computer is better than teacher's aide.	Local		Letters of endorsement from community groups help also.					
Replication—This type is a good source for replicating a successful program	Local							
Consortium—OK, but only if both partners are in their area of concern.	Local		Local reputation important					
International—Not best funder unless there is an ethnic relationship.								

Figure 4.9

FOUNDATION GRANTSEEKERS' MATRIX

Corporate Foundations

6. Corporate Foundations—Corporate granting is divided into two major categories: those companies that use a separate private foundation to make grants and corporations that make grants directly from the corporation and have no foundation (#7 Grant Seekers Matrix). Of the 2.5 million corporations in the United States, 1,287 corporate foundations are included in the National Directory of Corporate Giving. These 1,287 foundations represent a significant portion of corporate grants, and the corporate foundation grantseeker has access to the Internal Revenue Service Annual Reports so you can verify your approach and the amount you are seeking. In general, this group spends more time reading your proposal than the family foundation.

Type of Project	Geographic Need	Award Size	School's Image	Credentials of Project Director	Preproposal Contact	Proposal Content	Review & Decision	Proposal Information and Administration
Model/Demonstration Project—This type of proposal interests corporate foundations, especially if it affects their products, profits, or workers. **Research**—Interested if it advances their interests. **Equipment**—Will support some equipment; best chance is for equipment the company produces. **Replication**—Some interest if there are proven results. **Consortium**—Great approach if your partner is also in same area as corporate interest. **International**—Could be a great component if corporation is owned overseas or has a plant there.	The need must fit their granting perspective. May have a national agenda or have a primary focus on needs in their field of corporate interest.	Medium, \$10,000 to \$50,000; and large, over \$50,000	The more well-known your school is, the better. A National rankings, scores, awards, etc, help.	Credentials nationally are important as is local image with corporate officials, plant managers, and sales representatives.	Phone, write, go see the funder to describe the project. Many have staff.	Some have guidelines and even an application form.	Review may be done by some staff with knowledge of education. Decision made by the board.	May have annual reports that provide information on grant interests. You can also review IRS tax returns. Administration follows established CPA guidelines, some site visits and audits.

Figure 4.10

CORPORATE GRANTSEEKERS' MATRIX

Large Corporate Grantors

7. Large Corporate Grantors—Of the 2.5 million corporations only 700,000 are reported to make grants to any nonprofit organization. Those grants total less than $6 billion. The large corporate grantors have such good public relations that most grantseekers think that there are billions more in corporate grants than there are. From the perspective of education, this type of grantor offers a large resource because estimates are that 40% of corporate grants go toward education. While higher education has traditionally received the greatest portion, elementary and middle schools are attracting increasing interest.

Type of Project	Geographic Need	Award Size	School's Image	Credentials of Project Director	Preproposal Contact	Proposal Content	Review & Decision	Proposal Information and Administration
Model/Demonstration Project—This type of project must have a direct or indirect benefit to the company. **Research**—Interest if the research will contribute to the field of interest and enhance product development. **Replication**—Some interest if there are proven results. **Equipment**—Will grant company products, especially if the grant will put them in a position to sell more products to school or to students or parents. **Consortium and International**—Depends upon where the company has other plants, facilities.	The need for the project must be prevalent locally, but the need must correspond to the values of the corporation.	Medium, $10,000 to $50,000; Some large, $50,000 and over	Your school should have a relationship with the company, not necessarily a record of receiving grant support. Should have company support in the form of loaned executives and employees as volunteers.	The project director should have regional image and credentials.	Contact sales people, plant managers, regional supervisors by phone and personal contact. Involve them in the project and work through them unless application has different instructions.	Some have an application form. Many prefer a 2-5 page letter.	Several have staff and a few may employ one outside reviewer.	Little to no verifiable information available. Most entries in published directories are not verified. Some site visits and very few audits.

Figure 4.11

CORPORATE GRANTSEEKERS' MATRIX

All Other Corporations

8. All Other Corporations: This group includes smaller and medium-sized companies and represents approximately 600,000 of the 700,000 corporations reported to make grants to any nonprofit organization. These corporate grantors have great concern for the community in which they live and work. They listen because of their concern for their workers and the education of their workers' children. Most of these corporations are not planning on opening a business in another country and want quality education in their community. Get a list of corporations from your local Chamber of Commerce. Try to involve them in your advisory committee. How many of the children of their workers are in your school? Remember, they still are concerned about their products and their profits. They are not as motivated by a burning desire to do "good things" as you may think. They want something back for their investment.

Type of Project	Geographic Need	Award Size	School's Image	Credentials of Project Director	Preproposal Contact	Proposal Content	Review & Decision	Proposal Information and Administration
Model/Demonstration Project—There is some interest in developing a model, but concern is for what works. **Research**—Little or no interest unless they have a product that could benefit. **Equipment**—May be interested in donating used equipment or the equipment they sell. **Consortium**—Sharing with other schools, public and private, would look good, maximize resources. **National/International**—Not interested unless they have investments other places.	Basic concern is where the company is located and how the project will affect their workers, children and that particular community.	Most are small up to $10,000; some medium, $10,000 to $50,000	Your record in receiving is not very important. Involvement and familiarity with your school is greatest asset.	Known locally is what matters. Not a need for regional or national image; in fact, this may detract from what you do locally.	Definitely make contact with corporate decision maker by phone and in person. employees Cold proposals have a bad success rate. Involve the corporation's employees on your committees and use your "friends."	Few have an application form or format. Most instruct you to write them a letter.	Most have no full-time staff and few have part-time. They meet a few times per year and may not even read all the proposals—unless they are looking for yours.	Little or no verifiable data available. Use "friends" to perform a credit check through Dunn and Bradstreet or some other review group. More profitable the better. Few rules, almost never an audit. Follow CPA guidelines.

Figure 4.12

Service Clubs and Organizations Grantseekers' Matrix

9. Service Clubs and Organizations—This group of nonprofit organizations includes service organizations, Hellenic groups, business and professional organizations. They are a ready and willing participant in making grants, providing the linkages to friends that you need, and in many cases raising money to grant to your school's projects, programs, and needs. The individuals who belong to these organizations understand that by donating computers, for example, they increase the quality of education locally but do not increase taxes. Many schools have utilized this valuable community resource to involve the community in the schools. NOTE: Make a list of your school/community's service clubs and organizations. When and where they meet is listed on a sign as you enter your community.

Type of Project	Geographic Need	Award Size	School's Image	Credentials of Project Director	Preproposal Contact	Proposal Content	Review & Decision	Proposal Information and Administration
Model/Demonstration—Not as much interest in developing and discovering what works.	Primary concern of this type of funder is local need: How will the grant change	Most are small—up to $10,000	Local perception of your school's ability to serve the community and how the school has implemented other grants is critical.	Local credibility is essential. Credibility based on caring about education and kids is more important than publishing.	Essential to phone, go see individuals. For many groups the entree is to speak at their meeting to inform them of what you are doing. Remember a volunteer from your grants advisory committee can do it.	Most have a simple 3–4 page application or suggest a letter proposal.	Some service clubs have a grants committee or a committee for education of youth that recommends the proposal to the main group for approval.	Some organizations produce an annual report that states what activities and groups they have supported. Best source is a linkage or friend who belongs to the group. Follow-up is usually not formal. You can ask to give a result speech one year later, etc.
Research—Little or no interest in studying why something works.	"	"						
Equipment—Interested in equipment when it shows good cost-benefit ratio and is used by teachers and students.	"	"	Concerned about image regarding access to programs and equipment. Concerned with record of theft and maintenance.	"	"	"	"	"
Replication—Interested in implementing what worked in another school.	"	"		"	"	"	"	"
Consortium—Some interest, but the larger the project the more the cost goes up.	"	"		"	"	"	"	"
National/International—Some groups have strong international ties to other countries. German, Polish, African groups might like to sponsor a second site.	"	"	"	"	"	"	"	"

nonvoluntary giving (tax increases).

E. Service Clubs and Organizations Matrix

You will get a much better response from service clubs and organizations when you ask them to fund a *specific* project or proposal rather than for money for general purposes. Since most of these groups exist to serve the community, they actually *need* projects and causes to get involved in. They sponsor fund-raising events not only to raise money but also to get their members motivated and involved and to demonstrate their community spirit. Naturally, a good public image helps them recruit new members.

Their involvement with your school provides you with the opportunity to have other citizens *tell your school's story* to the community. This grass-roots involvement of service clubs and organizations will have dramatic effects, but these groups need your faculty and advisory group(s) to provide them with specific projects for smaller amounts of money that they can take on as a challenge.

Chapter 5 will provide you with information on identifying service clubs and organizations and suggestions on how to approach them.

Review the following checklist. It will help you share concepts concerning

CHAPTER 4 CHECKLIST

Evaluation and Planning Worksheet

1. What existing opportunities do you have to increase the Grants I.Q. of your school/community? (Group gatherings, faculty meetings, speeches, luncheons, Parent Teacher Association meetings, and so on.)

20

$ Researching the "Best" Funder — Matching Projects to Grantors

Your "best" grantor is the funding source who values your project enough to fund it. Of course, to the grantseeker the "best" funding source may be the one that appears to offer the easiest, fastest, shortest road to the money. However, to be successful your grants system should include the ongoing process of developing and sustaining relationships. These mutually beneficial relationships are enhanced when your search for funders is based upon how you can meet their needs while meeting your school's needs at the same time. This beneficial relationship should be the basis for identifying and selecting potential grantors. The purpose of this chapter is to provide you with information that will enable you to home in on funders whose past granting patterns indicate that your project would be of interest to them.

1. Developing a List of Key Search Words

This chapter describes a variety of sources you can use to search for grantors. Whether you are searching in printed material or computer data bases, grant opportunities are generally accessed by *key search words.* For example, if your project is aimed at increasing the reading level of dyslexic children, your *list of key search words* might include *handicapped, learning disabled, reading, literacy, disadvantaged children,* and so on. Thus the first task of the group that generates the potential solutions is to relate the project to as many key search words as possible.

To help this group, provide them with the following worksheets: *Expanding the Universe of Grantors, Key Words for Government Grantseeking,* and *Key Words for Foundation and Corporate Grantseeking.*

Expanding the Universe of Grantors Worksheet

By increasing your list of key search words you will expand your universe of potential funders. At first glance, this may seem counter-productive because you are trying to narrow your list of potential funding sources to the "best" five or six. But your ultimate goal is to help your staff locate the grantor who is most likely to fund your school's project. By altering your project slightly, you can:

- expand your list of key search words,
- increase your list of potential funding sources,
- have a greater appeal to a particular funding source's values, and
- dramatically increase your grants success rate.

Key Words Worksheet for Government Grantseeking

This list of search words has been taken from key federal grant listings. Your grantseekers should review the list and circle the key words that they could use in their search for government funding sources.

Key Words Worksheet for Foundation and Corporate Grantseeking

This worksheet lists some of the key words that can be used to search for nongovernment or private funding sources. Before you begin your search, review this list and circle the words that relate to your project.

2. Searching for Government Grants

State Grant Funds

Many of the state grant funds for education come from the federal government. While the federal government has an organized, easy-to-track grants system, the states do not. You can find out about federal money to your state by using your key search words to uncover related federal grant programs and then checking to see if state education agencies are eligible recipients under the federal regulations. If the funds are distributed in a block grant or according to a formula, you need to talk to your state education department to locate the individual in charge of those funds. This approach will give your grantseekers a command of the federal grants process. Once they have acquired this, they will receive a good reception from your state granting officials. State granting officials will be impressed by a grantseeker who can say, "A search of federal grant programs related to our school's need in the area of ________________ has led us to the state, since the federal regulations stipulate you as the recipient of those funds under program ___________." In comparison, a novice grantseeker may lose credibility by telephoning the state and saying, "Hi. Do you have any grant funds for __________________?"

Contacting state granting officials may require coordination through your school's district grants office (if you have one). In fact, your district grants office may know of additional state funding opportunities.

Information developed through your webbing and linkage system may lead you to a state contact who can help you initiate your search

Figure 5.1

EXPANDING THE UNIVERSE OF GRANTORS WORKSHEET

1. **What is the subject area the project will impact?**
   - Preschool Education
   - Elementary Education
   - Middle School Education
   - Health Education
   - Reading Education
   - Science Education
   - Humanities Education
   - Music Education
   - Art Education
   - Social Studies Education
   - * ____________________
   - * ____________________
   - * ____________________

2. **What problem areas could your project be aimed at affecting?**
   - Alcohol
   - Adult Literacy
   - Computer Literacy
   - Disadvantaged
   - Drugs
   - Dropouts
   - Gifted and Talented
   - Handicapped
   - Homeless
   - Immigrants
   - * ____________________
   - * ____________________
   - * ____________________

3. **How does your project currently relate to the problem areas identified in question 2?**

   ____
   ____
   ____
   ____

4. **How could the project be changed to relate to other problem areas?**

   ____
   ____
   ____
   ____

5. **Geographic Considerations—How could the project be altered to appeal to funders who value:**

   - Local Problems/Solutions?
   - Statewide Problems/Solutions?
   - Regional Problems/Solutions?
   - National Problems/Solutions?
   - International Problems/Solutions?

Figure 5.2

KEY WORDS WORKSHEET FOR GOVERNMENT GRANTSEEKING

The federal government uses the following subject index in describing grant opportunities in education. Review the list and indicate the key words that relate to your project. You may find it helpful to make a brief notation of any significant ways you could change your solution to make it relate to that key word.

The following descriptors relate to federal programs dealing with the whole area of education.

Adult Education
Disadvantaged Education
Early Childhood Education
Elementary Education
Health Education
Humanities Education
Indian Education
International Education
Tools for Schools

The following descriptors relate to federal programs dealing with elementary education.

Elementary Education Arts
Elementary Education Bilingual
Chapter 1
Chapter 2
Computer Learning
Disadvantaged/Deprived
Drug-Free Schools
Gifted and Talented Students
Handicapped
Homeless Children
Immigrant Children
Impact Aid
Math/Science
Migrant Education
Elementary Education Minorities
Neglected and Delinquent
Physical Fitness
Private Schools
School Dropout Prevention
Talent Search
Upward Bound

for state funding. While the contact person may not be in a position to actually grant awards, he or she may know people in the office who do. This contact person may have an "inside" way to get the basic information you will need to compete for the funds.

Federal Grant Funds

These funds come from taxes and are therefore subject to

Figure 5.3

KEY WORDS WORKSHEET FOR FOUNDATION AND CORPORATE GRANTSEEKING

The following key words are utilized in many electronic data retrieval systems and printed reference books. Review the list and indicate the key words that relate to your project. You may find it helpful to make a brief notation of any significant changes in your solution in order to relate to that key word.

Adult/Continuing Education Programs
Alternative Modes/Nontraditional Study
Arts Education Programs
Bicultural/Bilingual Education Programs
Biological Sciences Education Programs
Business Education Programs
Career Education Programs
Children/Youth
Cognition/Information Processing
Communications Education Programs
Computer-assisted Instruction
Computer Science Education Programs
Computer Sciences
Conference Support
Early Childhood/Preschool Education
Educational Counseling/Guidance
Educational Reform
Educational Studies —Developing Countries
Educational Testing/Measurement
Educational Values
Elementary Education
Employment Opportunity Programs
Employment/Labor Studies
Energy Education Programs
English Education Programs
Environmental Studies Education Programs
Fine Arts Education Programs
Foreign Language Education Programs
Foreign Scholars
Gifted Children
Handicapped Education Services
Handicapped Vocational Services
Handicapped/Special Education Programs
Health Education Programs
Humanities Education Programs
Illiteracy
Information Dissemination
International Studies Education Programs
Journalism Education Programs
Learning Disorders/Dyslexia
Mathematics Education Programs
Minority Education Programs
Music Education Programs
Nutrition Education Programs
Opportunities Abroad
Parental Involvement in Education Philosophy
Philosophy of Education
Physical Education Programs
Physical Sciences Education Programs
Precollegiate Education — Arts Education Programs
Precollegiate Education — Bilingual Education Programs
Precollegiate Education — Economics Education Programs
Precollegiate Education — Humanities Education Programs
Precollegiate Education — Professional Development
Precollegiate Education — Science/Math Education Programs
Prizes/Awards
Professional Development
Professional/Faculty Development
Reading Education Programs
Remedial Education
Rural Education
Rural Services
Rural Studies
Teacher Education
Telecommunications — Education Materials
Vocational/Technical Education
Women's Education Programs — Business Management
Women's Education Programs — Science/Engineering
Women's Studies Education Programs
Youth Employment Opportunity Programs

"freedom of information" laws. Using your key search words, you can use several easily accessed data retrieval systems to locate government grant opportunities. The following information will tell you where the federal grants information is generated and what kinds of information can be accessed. If someone working in higher education is on your grants advisory committee, ask him or her to use your solutions worksheet and key words worksheets to carry out a grants search through the college grants office. Most colleges and universities are on-line users of the following data bases.

- **SPIN** — Sponsored Programs Information Network is a grants data base that lists most federal government programs and many foundation and corporate grant opportunities. You do not need to purchase the system if you can work through your local institution of higher education. SPIN was originally developed by the State University of New York's Research Foundation to help the approximately 60 colleges and universities in the New York State system search for grant opportunities. It has since been adapted and marketed to institutions of higher education throughout the United States.
- **IRIS** — You may have a link to someone at a college or university that utilizes the Illinois Research Information System (IRIS). This data base started the same way as SPIN and provides similar information.
- **DIALOG** — Many school and community libraries are connected to the DIALOG data base, which has hundreds of useful components. Among these is the ORYX data base, which has information on federal grants.

If you have free access to one of these data bases, you could begin your search immediately. But first you should know what kinds of data these retrieval systems contain and how the federal grants system operates.

Most grantseekers fear the federal grants process because they do not act *proactively.* They do not realize that grantseeking does not have to be last-minute, chaotic, and *reactive.* The best way to develop successful federal proposals and to deal effectively with the pressure of deadlines is to be knowledgeable about the federal grants process and to start early. After working with several school districts, I can assure you that elementary and middle school grantseekers can note several federal deadlines a year in advance and take advantage of all available resources to meet deadlines and even submit proposals early. In other words, your grantseekers can learn to develop a controlled approach to federal grantseeking that will allow them to carry out their regular responsibilities and still apply for federal funds.

The federal government grants over $75 billion each year in a strictly organized yearly cycle. I refer to this cycle as the *federal grants clock*.

Figure 5.4

THE $75 BILLION FEDERAL GRANTS CLOCK™

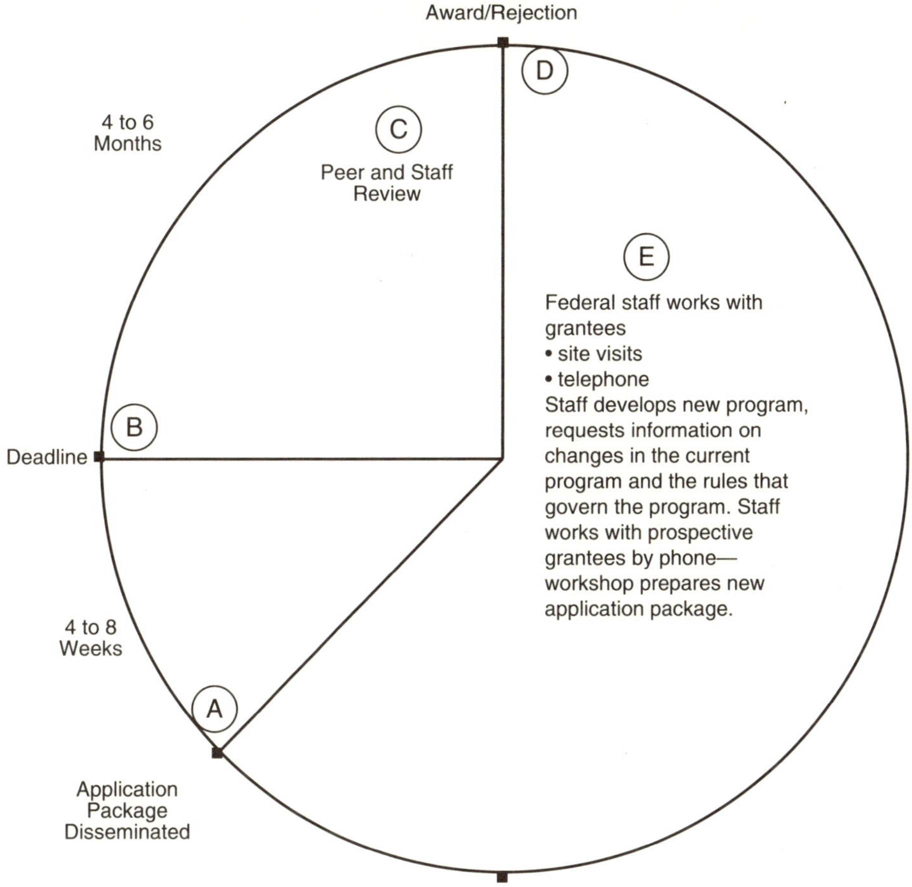

The clock operates 365 days per year. The federal government's year begins on October 1 and ends September 30.

Most federal grantseekers know that application packages are normally sent to prospective grantees four to eight weeks before the completed applications are due and that the grants are usually awarded four to six months after submission. The key to proactive government grantseeking is knowing *what else* occurs during this time and how your actions can dramatically increase your success rate and decrease the madness associated with trying to meet last-minute deadlines.

Do not wait until you receive an application package before you learn about grant opportunities and begin developing your school's proposal. *Start early!* To do so you need to have a working knowledge how the federal grants clock works.

1. The application package is disseminated.
2. Deadline — Most grantseekers do not begin their grants work until they receive the application package. This leaves only a short time to work on the proposal before the deadline occurs. The inflexible federal grants clock chimes the hour proposals are due, and submitting a proposal five minutes late delays consideration of it for *one year!*
3. Peer and Staff Review — Proposals are read, scored, and ranked.
4. Award or rejection notices are sent out.
5. During the final phase of the clock, the federal grants staff begins to get ready for another grants cycle and works with the current grantees.

If you understand the predictable and programmed nature of the federal grants clock you will be able to initiate your school's grantseeking long before the application packages are mailed. To start early, you also need to have a working knowledge of the basic federal grant information publications — *The Catalogue of Federal Domestic Assistance* (CFDA) and *The Federal Register.*

The Catalogue of Federal Domestic Assistance (CFDA)

The federal government produces a grants publication entitled *The Catalogue of Federal Domestic Assistance* (CFDA). Produced in the fall of each year, this catalogue lists the 1,225 programs that disseminate approximately $75 billion in grants annually and provides the grantseeker with all sorts of valuable information, including deadlines.

Where Can You Get the CFDA? You may purchase the CFDA from the Superintendent of Documents, U.S. Government Printing Office, Washington, D.C. 20402 (telephone 202-783-3238) for under $50.00. However, the CFDA is also provided free to at least two libraries in each congressional district. Your congressperson should know which libraries have been designated as Federal Depository Libraries. In addition to these designated libraries, most public libraries have a copy, as do college and university libraries and grants offices.

Why Should You Use the CFDA? First and foremost, the CFDA gives you access to $75 billion in grant funds. But even if you are planning to pursue only foundation or corporate grants, you should be knowledgeable about existing federal programs in your project area. Armed with this knowledge, you will be able to explain to a prospective private grantor why you are approaching them instead of a federal agency. For instance, if you know for certain that there are no federal funds designated for your project area or that federal funding is limited to three projects in your field across the entire country, it will be easier for you to demonstrate why private grant support is so necessary.

How Do You Use the CFDA? The most efficient way to locate the granting agencies that are your best opportunities is to compare the key search words you circled on your Key Words Worksheets to the indexes in the CFDA. The CFDA has five indexes.

- Deadline Index — This index is not very useful when you are searching for education-related grants because the Department of Education does not publish many program deadlines early in the federal year.
- Applicant Eligibility Index — This index allows you to determine which granting programs are restricted to state applicants and which are designated for local education agencies (L.E.A.s), such as your school district. If your project falls under a granting program restricted to state recipients, check with your state education department to determine how the previous year's funds were allocated.
- Agency Program Index — This index lists all programs in numerical order by five-digit codes. There are 164 Department of Education programs listed in this index.
- Functional Index — There are 20 basic functional categories of federal support and 176 subgroupings. Under education there are 23 subgroupings. Elementary/secondary education has two references.
- Subject Index — This is the most useful index for locating both Department of Education grant opportunities and those in other departments with an interest in education.

For example, assume that your school has a project idea related to the use of parent-teacher-student contracts and videotape feedback. When searching for federal grant opportunities for this project, your grantseekers could use "resource development" and "support for elementary education" as their key search words and look in the CFDA's indexes for program matches. By looking in the Functional and Subject indexes they could match your school's interests with several federal programs, including:

CFDA 84.201 School Dropout Demonstration Assistance

CFDA 84.212 First Family School Partnership

If your school changed the grant idea slightly and focused solely on math and science and parent-teacher-student contracts and videotape feedback, your grantseekers would find other matches, such as CFDA 84.168, the National Program for Math and Science Education.

Following are reproductions of CFDA 84.201 and CFDA 84.212 from *The Catalogue of Federal Domestic Assistance* to help you understand the federal grants system. The information contained in the CFDA is crucial to a proactive grantseeking system and in enabling you to start the grantseeking process early. It will also help you make preproposal contact with the appropriate funding agency.

CFDA 84.201
School Dropout Demonstration Assistance

In the first example, **CFDA 84.201 SCHOOL DROPOUT DEMONSTRATION ASSISTANCE—Dropout Prevention Program,** reader aids have been numbered in the left margin and underlined in the text.

1. Program Title: School Dropout Demonstration Assistance (Dropout Prevention Program)
2. Federal Agency: This informs you of the arm of the government that handles the program. While many grant programs are sponsored by the Department of Education, you may also apply to the National Science Foundation, the National Endowment for the Arts, and so on.
3. Authorization: This tells you the source of the funding.
4. Objectives: This section provides you with the first indication of the appropriateness of your idea in relationship to the funding program.
5. Types of Assistance: You must know what types of assistance are provided to determine if the federal program is interested in funding projects or research or if they fund on a formula basis that allocates the funds to eligible recipients through predetermined criteria.
6. User and Use Restrictions: User and use restrictions help you to further determine if the program is an appropriate source of funds for your project.
7. Eligibility Requirements:
    - Applicant Eligibility — This section tells you if your school is an eligible recipient. You are designated as a Local Educational Agency (LEA). If your school is not eligible for funding under this program, this section will provide you with the information you need to determine whom you should develop a relationship with so that you can submit your proposal through their organization.
    - Beneficiary Eligibility — This section tells you the type of individual or organization that is intended to benefit from the project.
    - Credentials/Documentation — The Office of Management

and Budget (O.M.B.) publishes several management booklets that outline the rules for requesting, spending, and documenting expenditures under a federal grant.

8. Application and Award Process:
   - Preapplication Coordination — This section outlines the O.M.B. requirements related to your state's review and knowledge of your proposal. If you have a district grants office, they will know who to contact in your state office concerning this matter.
   - Application Procedure — This describes the rules for submitting applications.
   - Award Procedure — This section informs you who will review and approve your proposal. Proposals submitted to this particular program will be reviewed by program staff based on the published criteria. Although experts will also read the proposals and assist the staff members, your grantseeker's writing style and level should be in accordance with the background of the staff.
   - Deadlines — Deadlines are published in *The Federal Register. The Federal Register* is explained immediately following the CFDA example.
   - Range of Approval/Disapproval Time — Period between submittal and notification of approval or disapproval. In this example, this information will be published in *The Federal Register.*
   - Appeals — In this case there is no procedure for appealing the grantor's decision. Some federal programs have a specific appeal procedure.
   - Renewals — This information is important when you are planning a project that may take several years.
9. Assistance Considerations:
   - Formula and Matching Requirements — This section outlines what portion of the project's costs will be borne by your school district. It is vital that you have a plan for the match and your school district's endorsement that it will commit this share. In this example, the recipient would need *at least* a 10 percent match in year one and a 25 percent match in year two.
   - Length and Time Phasing of Assistance — The length of the project period. In this case, approximately 12 months.
10. Post Assistance Requirements: Your district will be required to make reports and maintain records and may be subject to audits. Don't let this section scare you. Your business office will handle it.
11. Financial Information:
   - Account Identification — Account identification number

- Obligations — By reviewing this section you can determine if the program is slated to increase or decrease its funding level. Note: It is estimated that the future budget for this program will be $27,214,000, but this figure could be changed dramatically by Congress. In this example, program funds went up, then down.
- Range and Average of Financial Assistance — In 1991, the range was $250,000 to $1,500,000 with the average award being $694,000. This should tell you that this program is not your best choice if your project request is $25,000 per year.

12. Program Accomplishments: This section provides you with important information on previously selected grantees and on the number of awards made in the past. In this case, 89 awards were divided up by size of district in 1990. This section will also inform you if the program is being phased out. For example, it may say "no new awards."
13. Regulations, Guidelines, and Literature: This section outlines the rules and guidelines. Most of the rules mentioned pertain to your district personnel and business office. The only one that is relatively new is the Drug-Free Workplace and Campus rule. Compliance should be discussed with your district grants office or administration.
14. Information Contacts:
    - Regional or Local Office — Most regional offices were closed during the federal cutbacks of the early 1980s.
    - Headquarters Office — This section provides the contact name, address, and phone number you will need if you select this funder as a possible source.
15. Related Programs: This section lists the CFDA names and codes of other sources of funds that have similar target populations and/or objectives.
16. Examples of Funded Projects: This section provides a sample of the solutions that the grantor valued highly enough to fund.
17. Criteria for Selecting Proposals: This section lists the types of criteria that the agency will follow in its evaluation procedures. Each agency has its own criteria, and criteria may differ between programs. The criteria used in this example are EDGAR. See Chapter 9, page 162.

CFDA 84.212 First Family School Partnership

Review the second example, CFDA 84.212 FIRST FAMILY SCHOOL PARTNERSHIP (fig. 5.6). While this funding program's objectives look like a good match with the objectives of our example (parent, student, teacher involvement), a close scrutiny of the CFDA reveals that:

Figure 5.5

(1) 84.201 SCHOOL DROPOUT DEMONSTRATION ASSISTANCE (Dropout Prevention Program)

(2) **FEDERAL AGENCY: DEPARTMENT OF EDUCATION, OFFICE OF ELEMENTARY AND SECONDARY EDUCATION**

(3) **AUTHORIZATION:** Elementary and Secondary Education Act of 1965, Title VI, Parts A and C, as amended, Public Law 100-297.

(4) **OBJECTIVES:** To provide financial assistance to local educational agencies, educational partnerships and community-based organizations to establish and demonstrate effective dropout prevention and reentry programs.

(5) **TYPES OF ASSISTANCE:** Project Grants.

(6) **USES AND USE RESTRICTIONS:** Funds may be used for activities directly related to reducing the number of children that do not complete their elementary and secondary education. Not more than five percent of any grant may be used for administrative costs. Local educational agencies (LEAs) must not use Federal funds to supplant funds that would, in the absence of Federal funds, be made available from nonfederal sources for the activities that assistance is being sought. The Federal share of grants under this program shall not exceed ninety percent of the total cost of a project for the first year and seventy-five percent of the cost for the second year. The nonfederal share may be paid from any other source. Not more than ten percent of the nonfederal share may be from other Federal sources. The nonfederal share may be in-cash or in-kind.

(7) **ELIGIBILITY REQUIREMENTS:**

Applicant Eligibility: Local educational agencies, community-based organizations, and educational partnerships may apply.

Beneficiary Eligibility: Student dropouts, institutions of higher education, students at-risk of dropping out, students reentering school, local educational agencies, State educational agencies, community-based organizations, business organizations and nonprofit organizations will benefit.

Credentials/Documentation: Costs will be determined in accordance with OMB Circular No. A-87 for State and local governments. OMB Circular No. A-122, Cost Principles for Nonprofit Organizations, also applies.

(8) **APPLICATION AND AWARD PROCESS:**

Preapplication Coordination: The standard application forms as furnished by the Federal agency and required by OMB Circular No. A-102 must be used for this program. This program is eligible for coverage under E.O. 12372, "Inter-governmental Review of Federal Programs." An applicant should consult the office or official designated as the single contact point in his or her State for more information on the process the State requires to be followed in applying for assistance, if the State has selected the program for review.

Application Procedure: Applications must be sent to the Department of Education on or before the closing date. This program is subject to the provisions of OMB Circular No. A-110.

Award Procedure: Recommendations for the approval of applications are made by the program staff on the basis of published criteria, statutory considerations, and with the advice and assistance of a panel of expert reviewers. Applications are approved for awards by the Assistant Secretary for Elementary and Secondary Education, after completion of the competitive review.

Deadlines: Established by notice published in the Federal Register.

Range of Approval/Disapproval Time: The closing date will be published in the Federal Register.

Appeals: None.

Renewals: A grant recipient is eligible for continuation of its award for up to three additional years if it meets the criteria for continuation.

(9) **ASSISTANCE CONSIDERATIONS:**

Formula and Matching Requirements: The Federal share under this program shall not exceed 90 percent of the total project costs for the first year and 75 percent of the cost for the second year.

Length and Time Phasing of Assistance: Approximately twelve months.

(10) **POST ASSISTANCE REQUIREMENTS:**

Reports: Annual performance and financial reports are required in accordance with the provisions of EDGAR, Section 75.720.

Audits: In accordance with the provisions of OMB Circular No. A-128, "Audits of State and Local Governments," State and local governments that receive financial assistance of $100,000 or more within the State's fiscal year shall have an audit made for that year. State and local governments that receive between $25,000 and $100,000 within the State's fiscal year shall have an audit made in accordance with Circular No. A-128, or in accordance with Federal laws and regulations governing the programs in which they participate.

Records: In accordance with Education Department General Administrative Regulations, 34 CFR 74 and 75.

(11) **FINANCIAL INFORMATION:**

Account Identification: 91-1000-0-1-501

Obligations: (Grants) FY 90 $19,945,000; FY 91 est $32,600,000; and FY 92 est $27,214,000.

Range and Average of Financial Assistance: For fiscal year 1991, the range is estimated to be from $250,000 to $1,500,000; $694,000.

(12) **PROGRAM ACCOMPLISHMENTS:** In fiscal year 1990, 89 continuation grants were awarded: fourteen to local educational agencies (LEAs) and five to educational partnerships in LEAs with enrollments of 100,000 or more students; twenty-one to LEAs and eight to educational partnerships in LEAs with enrollments of 20,000 to 99,999 students; twenty-seven to LEAs and seven to educational partnerships with enrollments of less than 20,000 students; and seven to community-based organizations. New grants will be awarded in fiscal year 1991.

(13) **REGULATIONS, GUIDELINES, AND LITERATURE:** The Department of Education, General Administrative Regulations (EDGAR); 34 CFR 74, Administration of Grants, Part 75, Direct Grant Programs, Part 77, Definitions that Apply to Department Regulations, Part 79 (Intergovernmental Review of Department of Education Programs and Activities), Part 80 (Uniform Administrative Requirements for Grants and Cooperative Agreements with State and Local governments), Part 81 (General Education Provisions Act-Enforcement), Part 82 (New Restrictions on Lobbying), Part 85 (Governmentwide Debarment and Suspension (non-procurement) and Governmentwide Requirements for Drug-Free Workplace (grants) and Pact 86 (Drug-Free Schools and Campuses).

(14) **INFORMATION CONTACTS:**

Regional or Local Office: Not applicable.

Headquarters Office: Department of Education, Division of Educational Support, Office of Elementary and Secondary Education, 400 Maryland Avenue, SW., Mail Stop 624, Washington, DC 20202-6438. Contact: John R. Fiegel. Telephone: (202) 401-1342.

(15) **RELATED PROGRAMS:** None.

(16) **EXAMPLES OF FUNDED PROJECTS:** Grantees replicate or expand successful programs designed to: identify potential student dropouts, and keep them from dropping out; identify and encourage children that have already dropped out to reenter school; identify at-risk students in elementary and secondary schools; and establish model systems for collecting and reporting information. Typical activities include developing and implementing an extended day, or summer programs designed to address poor achievement, basic skills deficiencies, or course failures; establishing or expanding work-study, apprentice, or internship programs; training school staff; training parents in the use of community services; improving student motivation and the school learning environment; providing alternative classrooms and alternative schools, and other educational, occupational, and testing services intended to reduce the number of dropouts. Grantees will be required to cooperate with a national evaluation study. In fiscal year 1991, priority will be given to restructuring and reform projects and comprehensive targeted programs for at-risk youth.

(17) **CRITERIA FOR SELECTING PROPOSALS:** The Secretary evaluates applications on the basis of criteria required under

- the program's obligations have decreased from $4,443,000 to $927,000 and that
- the "Program Accomplishments" indicate that there are no new grants planned for 1993.

The CFDA provides the basic information that your school's grant effort must have in order to "play the grants game." These data can be found in most computerized grants information systems.

The Federal Register

The Federal Register can be described as the federal government's daily newspaper. A free copy can be found in your congressionally designated federal depository library. If you think that reading this publication will cause you a severe case of cognitive overload, you are correct. But wait — you should not be reading this publication on a daily basis, nor should your

Figure 5.6

84.212 FIRST FAMILY SCHOOL PARTNERSHIP

FEDERAL AGENCY: OFFICE OF ASSISTANT SECRETARY FOR EDUCATIONAL RESEARCH AND IMPROVEMENT, DEPARTMENT OF EDUCATION

AUTHORIZATION: Augustus F. Hawkins-Robert T. Stafford Elementary and Secondary School Improvement Amendments of 1988, Title III, Part B, Public Law 100-297.

OBJECTIVES: To increase the involvement of families in improving the educational achievement of their children in preschool, elementary and secondary schools.

TYPES OF ASSISTANCE: Project Grants.

USES AND USE RESTRICTIONS: Funds may be used to demonstrate family school partnership projects.

ELIGIBILITY REQUIREMENTS:

Applicant Eligibility: Local educational agencies eligible to receive Chapter 1 funds benefit.

Beneficiary Eligibility: Local educational agencies eligible to receive Chapter 1 funds benefit.

Credentials/Documentation: None.

APPLICATION AND AWARD PROCESS:

Preapplication Coordination: This program is eligible for coverage under E.O. 12372, "Intergovernmental Review of Federal Programs." An applicant should consult the office or official designated as the single point of contact in his or her State for more information on the process the State requires to be followed in applying for assistance, if the State has selected the program for review.

Application Procedure: Described in the application notice published annually in the Federal Register. Contact the headquarters office listed below for application packages containing the announcement, application, and assurance forms.

Award Procedure: The Assistant Secretary for Educational Research and Improvement approves the selection of applications for negotiation. The selection of applications is competitive, based on staff and nonfederal peer review according to the selection criteria contained in the regulation for the Family-School Partnership program (34 CFR 758), and the annual application notice published in the Federal Register.

Deadlines: Announced in an application notice published annually in the Federal Register. Contact the headquarters office listed below for further information.

Range of Approval/Disapproval Time: Approximately six months.

Appeals: None.

Renewals: Awards are made annually. Following an initial, competitively selected award of up to twelve months, two additional one-year non-competing continuation awards may be made for a total maximum term of three years.

ASSISTANCE CONSIDERATIONS:

Formula and Matching Requirements: None.

Length and Time Phasing of Assistance: Funds are awarded annually and may be for up to a three year period.

POST ASSISTANCE REQUIREMENTS:

Reports: A final financial status and performance report (ED 606) is due 90 days after termination of the grant.

Audits: In accordance with the Education Department General Administration Regulations in the Appendix to 34 CFR 80, State and local governments that receive financial assistance of $100,000 or more within the State's fiscal year shall have an audit made for that year. State and local governments that receive between $25,000 and $100,000 within the State's fiscal year shall have an audit made in accordance with the Appendix to Part 80, or in accordance with the Federal laws and regulations governing the programs in which they participate. Recipients that are not subject to the requirements of Part 80 must meet the requirements of EDGAR Part 74, subpart H, (34 CFR 74.61(h)).

Records: As required by EDGAR (34 CFR 74.20-25).

FINANCIAL INFORMATION:

Account Identification: 91-1000-0-1-501.

Obligations: (Grants) FY 90 $4,443,000; FY 91 est $3,611,000; and FY 92 est $927,000.

Range and Average of Financial Assistance: $50,000 to $200,000.

PROGRAM ACCOMPLISHMENTS: In fiscal year 1990, 31 new grants totalling $4.14 million were awarded. The projects were submitted by applicants from fourteen different States and addressed the needs of children in grades from preschool to twelfth. While all applications indicated a focus on at-risk students, several identified specific at-risk conditions including poverty, minority issues, limited English proficiency, and special education. Due to continuation costs for existing fiscal year 1989 and fiscal year 1990 projects, there will be no new awards for fiscal year 1991. No new awards are planned for fiscal year 1992 due to the planned phase-out of the program when its authorizing legislation expires in fiscal year 1993.

Figure 5.6 Continued

REGULATIONS, GUIDELINES, AND LITERATURE: Regulations in 34 CFR 758 and the Education Department General Administrative Regulations, 34 CFR 74, 75, 77, 78, 79, 80, 85, and 86.

INFORMATION CONTACTS:

Regional or Local Office: Not applicable.

Headquarters Office: Department of Education, FIRST, Office of Educational Research and Improvement, Washington, DC 20208-5524. Telephone: (202) 219-1496.

RELATED PROGRAMS: 84.211, FIRST Schools and Teachers; 84.215. The Secretary's Fund for Innovation in Education.

EXAMPLES OF FUNDED PROJECTS: One two-year project enables parent volunteers to work with students in the classroom to create student publications. After school workshops provide parents and students with special computer and desk-top publishing skills. One three-year project trains parents in how to enhance their effectiveness in community and school councils. Areas of training include policy, planning, conflict resolution, constituency representation, group interaction, budget fundamentals, school operations, and community resources. Another three-year project offers a Saturday drop-in program, follow-up home visits for at-risk families, English as a Second Language and General Education Development classes for parents, training for grandmothers who are the primary caretakers of the children, and a school orientation series for parents.

CRITERIA FOR SELECTING PROPOSALS: (1) Need for the project; (2) plan of operation; (3) quality of key personnel; (4) educational value; (5) budget and cost-effectiveness; (6) evaluation plan; and (7) national significance. For detailed criteria, see the regulations.

teachers. You only need to know the purpose of *The Federal Register* as it relates to federal grantseeking and how to use this publication to increase your knowledge of the grants cycle.

The Federal Register provides the government with a mechanism to announce new opportunities for federal funding and to invite comments on what the rules should be. If Congress and the president establish new grant programs for elementary and junior high schools, the first announcement will be in *The Federal Register* to invite comments on the rules that will govern the programs.

In addition, *The Federal Register* is used to announce deadlines and to solicit feedback on the grant rules that governed the previous year's grant solicitation and award process. It is not unusual for a federal agency to print last year's rules for granting funds in *The Federal Register* six months before the next deadline to solicit the public's opinions on the way the grants were awarded the previous year.

The public is usually given 30 days to comment on the rules. The agency reviews the comments and based on them may make changes in the rules. The public is then allowed another 30 days to comment on the changes before the final rules are printed. Since these rules will govern the program's priorities and the scoring or review system, they provide valuable insight into exactly what the agency is looking for. The important point is that the proactive grantseeker needs to have advance knowledge of the information in *The Federal Register.*

Now that you are aware of this process, you can give your

grantseekers a strong advantage over the competition. You now know that there is no need for them to wait around until they receive a formal application package. They can take the initiative and telephone a federal program officer to ask when information on the rules and the deadline was printed in *The Federal Register.* This information will provide them enough data to decide on the appropriateness of that grant program opportunity for their project ideas. If they decide that it is appropriate, they can begin to position themselves to receive a grant.

With information from the CFDA and *The Federal Register,* the principal is placed in the grants information loop. Before you or your grantseekers begin to write or telephone federal grant program officers listed in the CFDA and *The Federal Register,* read chapter 6, which contains information on making preproposal contact. The point to be made here is that there is no reason to wait until four weeks before the deadline to get started. Of greater importance to you, the principal, is that your decision on *which* grantors to approach and *how* to approach them will have a dramatic effect on your role in your grants system. If *your* name is placed on federal mailing lists, you must accept responsibility for the prompt and efficient forwarding of grant information to your staff. Finish reading this book to ensure that you select and incorporate into your grants plan the functions that best fit your administrative role and style.

You and your classroom leaders can use your new knowledge concerning the two most basic federal grants publications, the CFDA and *The Federal Register,* to look like "grants pros." For example, assume that your grantseekers have used their key search words and the CFDA indexes to determine that CFDA 84.201, the School Dropout Demonstration Assistance Program, looks like a likely funding source for your school's project. Your grantseeker or project director could contact John Fiegel, the information contact listed in the CFDA, to ask if the deadline has been announced yet, and if it hasn't, when he thinks it will appear in *The Federal Register.* They could also ask if any relevant notices have been published in the *Register* such as comments on the rules, and so on.

For example, suppose one of your teachers contacted Mr. Fiegel in December and was told that the notice to invite applicants was to be printed in January and that the application deadline was expected to be March. Clearly, you would gain both an advantage over your competitors and significant insight by consulting the January *Federal Register.* Review the following sample entry from *The Federal Register* and use the guide numbers on the left to help you understand this important publication.

Look for 10-7-91 notices

Figure 5.7

SAMPLE FEDERAL REGISTER ENTRY

(1) **[CFDA No. 84.201]**

(2) **School Dropout Demonstration Assistance Program; Notice Inviting Applications for New Awards for Fiscal Year (FY) 1992**

(3) *Purpose of Program:* To provide Federal financial assistance to demonstrate effective programs to reduce the number of children who do not complete their elementary and secondary education.

(4) *Eligible applicants:* The following are eligible for new awards under this competition: Local educational agencies (LEAs), community-based organizations, and educational partnerships.

(5) *Deadline for transmittal of applications:* March 26, 1992.

(6) Deadline for intergovenmental review: May 25, 1992.

(7) *Applications available:* February 10, 1992.

(8) *Available funds:* $10,000,000 is estimated for new awards in FY 1992.

(9) *Estimated range of awards:* $250,000 — $750,000.

(10) *Estimated average size of awards:* $500,000.

(11) *Estimated number of awards:* 20. **Note: The Department is not bound by any estimates in this notice.**

(12) *Project period:* Up to 36 months.

(13) *Applicable regulations:* The Education Department General Administrative Regulations (EDGAR) in 34 CFR parts 74, 75, 77, 79, 80, 85, and 86.

(14) *Description of program:* Title VI, parts A and C of Public Law 100-297, as amended by Public Law 102-103 (The School Dropout Demonstration Assistance Act of 1988) (20 U.S.C. 3241 *et seq.*) establishes a program of grants to eligible entities to pay the Federal share of the cost of authorized activities. This program supports AMERICA 2000, the President's strategy for moving the Nation toward the National Education Goals by seeking to develop effective programs to prevent students from dropping out of school and to encourage those who have dropped out to reenter school. It also seeks to collect key information on the reasons for dropping out and effective prevention strategies. National Education Goal 2 specifically calls for the high school graduation rate to increase to at least 90 percent by the year 2000. While your attention is called to the text of these provisions, which will be provided in the application package, the following is a summary of some of the pertinent parts of the authorizing legislation.

(15) *Purpose*

The purpose of the program is to reduce the number of children who do not complete their elementary and secondary education by providing Federal assistance to LEAs, community-based organizations, and educational partnerships to establish and demonstrate (1) effective programs to identify potential student dropouts and prevent them from dropping out; (2) effective programs to identify and encourage children who have already dropped out to reenter school and complete their elementary and secondary education; (3) effective programs for early intervention designed to identify at-risk students in elementary and early secondary schools; and (4) model systems for collecting and reporting information to local school officials on the number, ages, and grade levels of children not completing their elementary and secondary education and reasons why they have dropped out of school.

(16) *Funding Categories*

The Secretary will allot FY 1992 funds in four categories as follows: (1) LEAs administering schools with a total enrollment of 100,000 or more elementary and secondary school students (25 percent of the amount appropriated, or an estimated $2,500,000 for new awards in FY 1992); (2) LEAs administering schools with a total enrollment of at least 20,000, but less than 100,000 (40 percent of the amount appropriated, or an estimated $4,000,000 for new awards in FY 1992); (3) LEAs administering schools with a total enrollment of less than 20,000 (30 percent of the amount appropriated, or an estimated $3,000,000 for new awards in FY 1992); and (4) community-based organizations (five percent of the amount appropriated, or an estimated $500,000 for new awards in FY 1992). For category (3), grants may be made to intermediate educa-tional units and consortia of not more than five LEAs if the total enrollment of the largest of these LEAs is less than 20,000 elemen-tary and secondary school students. In addition, not less than 20 percent of the funds in category (3) will be awarded to LEAs administering schools with a total enrollment of less than 2,000 elementary and secondary school students.

(17) *Educational Partnerships*

In each of the first three categories mentioned under Funding Categories, the Secretary will allot not less than 25 percent and not more than 50 percent of the funds available to educational partnerships. An educational partnership in-cludes: (1) An LEA; and (2) a business concern, or business organization, or, if an appro-priate business concern or business organization is not available, one of the following: any community-based organization, nonprofit private organization, institution of higher education, State educational agency (SEA), State or local public agency, private industry council (established under the Job Training Partnership Act), museum, library, or educational television or broadcasting station.

(18) *Distribution of Funds*

The Secretary ensures that, to the extent practicable, in approving grant applications: Grants will be equitably distributed on a geographic basis within each enrollment size category; the amount of a grant to an LEA will be proportionate to the extent and severity of the local school dropout problem; not less than 30 percent of the available funds will be used for activities related to dropout prevention; and not less than 30 percent of the funds will be used for activities related to persuading dropouts to return to school and assisting former dropouts with specialized services once they return to school.

(19) *Limitation on Costs*

Not more than five percent of any grant may be used for administrative costs.

(20) *Federal Funds*

The Federal share of a grant under this program will not exceed 90 percent of the total cost of a project for the first year and 75 percent of the total cost in each succeeding fiscal year. The "non-Federal" share may be paid from any source except for funds under

Figure 5.7 continued

this program, but not more than 10 percent of the "non-Federal" share may be from other Federal sources. The "non-Federal" share may be cash or in kind.

Additional Information

21 Additional information concerning application requirements, program requirements, and allowable activities is contained in the application package and the authorizing statute.

Priorities:

22 *Absolute Priority*

Under 34 CFR 75.105(c)(3) and section 6005(c) of the statute (20 U.S.C. 3245(c), the Secretary gives an absolute preference to applications that meet the following priority. The Secretary funds under this competition only applications that meet this absolute priority:

Applicants must propose projects that both replicate successful programs conducted in other LEAs or expand successful programs within an LEA and reflect very high numbers or very high percentages of school dropouts in the schools of the applicant in each category described in section 6004(a) of the statute.

Competitive Priorities

Under 34 CFR 75.105(c)(2)(ii) and section 6005(d) of the statute (20 U.S.C. 3245(d)), the Secretary gives preference to applications that meet the following competitive priorities. An application that meets these competitive priorities is selected by the Secretary over applications of comparable merit that do not meet these competitive priorities. The Secretary will give competitive preference to applications that include:

(a) Provisions that emphasize early intervention services designed to identify at-risk students in elementary or early secondary schools: and

(b) Provisions for significant parental involvement.

Invitational Priority

Under 34 CFR 75.105(c)(1), the Secretary also invites applicants to propose projects that include activities designed to address the persistently high dropout rate among Hispanic Americans.

An application that meets this invitational priority does not receive competitive or absolute preference over other applications that do not meet this invitational priority.

23 *Federal evaluation:* The Department is conducting a national evaluation of projects funded under the School Dropout Demonstration Assistance Program. A contract has been competitively awarded to conduct the evaluation. The evaluation will assess all components of the project, including those paid for with other Federal, State, or local funds. Pursuant to 34 CFR 75.591, all grantees will be required to cooperate with the national evaluation that will consist of two parts.

The first part of the evaluation will be a descriptive evaluation that involves collection of data on (1) the students being served, including socio-economic background and attendance, achievement, and retention data; (2) the services provided and cost of providing those services; (3) extent of involvement of parents, business, and community groups and the social and economic environment in which the project operates; (4) coordination with other agencies; (5) staff training and qualifications; and (6) status of program implementation. All projects will be required to collect and report data for the descriptive evaluation in collaboration with the national contractor.

The second part will be an outcome evaluation that assesses the effects of the program. For the outcome evaluation, the Department is selecting a number of sites from grants awarded in FY 1991 for in-depth study. Each remaining site, including each new grant to be awarded in FY 1992, will itself contract with a local evaluator or use district evaluation staff to conduct an outcome evaluation. These evaluation plans will be implemented only upon review and approval by the Department of Education. The local evaluators will establish control or comparison groups and collect prior and current administrative records. Each site will provide outcome data and summaries to the national evaluation contractor for inclusion in national analyses and reports. Technical assistance will be available from the national contractor to local project directors and evaluators.

In the application, each applicant must submit an assurance that it will collaborate with the national evaluation in the collection of descriptive and outcome data, as required by 34 CFR 75.591.

Evaluation by the grantee: The Secretary reminds prospective applicants that the requirements for self-evaluation in 34 CFR 75.590 apply to this program. As part of its application, an applicant must submit a self-evaluation plan that will complement the activities conducted through the national evaluation. An applicant may propose additional local evaluation activities to meet local evaluation needs as well. These evaluation plans will only be implemented upon review and approval by the Department of Education. Once a grant is awarded, the grantee will be expected to submit to the Department a copy of the report from any local evaluation implemented as part of the dropout demonstration.

Selection criteria: In evaluating applications for funds under the School Dropout Demonstration Assistance Program, the Secretary will apply the selection criteria in 34 CFR 75.210(b).

Weighting for selection criteria:

Under 34 CFR 75.210(c), the Secretary is authorized to distribute an additional 15 points among the selection criteria in 34 CFR 75.210(b) to bring the total possible points for an application to a maximum of 100 points. For the purpose of this competition, the Secretary will distribute the additional points as follows:

Plan of operation. (§75.210 (b)(3)). Ten (10) additional points will be added for a possible total of 25 points for this criterion.

Evaluation plan. (§75.210 (b)(6)). Five (5) additional points will be added for a possible total of 10 points for this criterion.

For applications or information contact: John R. Fiegel, School Dropout Demonstration Assistance Program, U.S. Department of Education, 400 Maryland Avenue, SW., room 2049, Washington, DC 20202-6246. Telephone: (202) 401-1342. Deaf and hearing impaired individuals may call the Federal Dual Party Relay Service at 1-800-877-8339 (in the Washington, DC 202 area code, telephone 708-9300) between 8 a.m. and 7 p.m. Eastern time.

Program Authority: 20 U.S.C. 3241 *et seq.*

Dated: January 8, 1992.

John T. MacDonald,

Assistant Secretary for Elementary and Secondary Education.

[FR Doc. 92-1245 Filed 1-16-92; 8:45 am]

Billing Code 4000-01-M

1. CFDA No.: You now know that all 1,200-plus federal programs are referred to by a CFDA number.
2. Program Title and Purpose of the Notice: This section states the title of the program and whether the purpose of the notice is to invite applications, solicit comments, publish final rules, and so on.
3. Purpose of Program: This section gives a brief description of the aim of the program.
4. Eligible applicants: This section tells you of any changes that may have occurred since the comments on the rules were made. For example, if funding community organizations has proven disastrous in the past, the rules regarding eligibility may have changed, and in this granting cycle only local educational agencies may be eligible.
5. Deadline for transmittal of applications: This is the last date on which the current year's applications will be accepted.
6. Deadline for intergovernmental review: After your school submits its application to the federal government, a copy of it must be sent to your state's "single-point-of-contact" with a request that they send their comments to the federal agency by the deadline for intergovernmental review.
7. Applications available: This is the date when the application package will be available. You are already ahead of the game at this point, and the following chapters will have even more suggestions for getting further ahead.
8. Available funds: This is not a final figure, but it will give you a good estimate of the total amount of funding available. If the figure is significantly different from the one in the CFDA, you will know that the program is either in favor or falling out of favor. You can adjust your grants strategy accordingly.
9. Estimated range of awards: These "high" and "low" figures will help you select which of your solutions best matches the size of the expected award.
10. Estimated average size of awards: This information gives you more focus on the average size of awards. If you envision securing $25,000 for your project and the program's estimated average size of awards is $500,000, you need to discuss the appropriateness of your project with the program officer.
11. Estimated number of awards: This figure gives you insight into how intense the competition for funding might be. In the sample entry, 20 awards throughout the entire United States is not very many, but you will discover that other programs expect to make even fewer awards!
12. Project period: This is the time frame allotted for support.

In the sample entry, the project period is up to 36 months. Therefore, you would have to project your objectives and measurement indicators for a three-year period.

13. Applicable regulations: This refers to the Department of Education's grant policies that must be followed.

    (Note: Items 14 through 23 are usually repeated in the application package. But by having access to this information early, you can increase your ability to control your time and to use the federal grants clock efficiently. The data contained here are more detailed and more timely than those in the CFDA.)

14. Description of program: This section gives you background information that may be useful to reference in your proposal. For example, using our sample entry, you may want to mention America 2000 or the National Education Goal #2 in your project.
15. Purpose: This section provides a more detailed idea of the types of activities the funding agency believes will meet the program description.
16. Funding Categories: This section allows you to estimate how much of the total funds will be granted to your type of school. For example, if you have fewer than 2,000 elementary and secondary students, you might believe you don't stand a chance with CFDA 84.201. But look at the last few lines. At least 20 percent of the funds will be awarded to LEAs administering schools with a total enrollment of fewer than 2,000 elementary and secondary students.
17. Educational Partnerships: This gives you insight into who you might include in your project to increase your chances for success. In this example, collaboration with a business or community-based organization would be a good idea.
18. Distribution of Funds: This section highlights the target areas. Some programs may target a particular population or region. In this case, funds will be spread around.
19. Limitation on Costs: Here you will find a variety of information concerning what is *not* allowable. The most common limitation is a cap on overhead or administrative costs.
20. Federal Funds: This section outlines necessary matching or in-kind contributions and the rules on what is allowable as part of the match. In the sample entry, there must be a 10 percent match in year one and a 25 percent match each succeeding year, and only 10 percent or less of the nonfederal share may be from other federal sources. The nonfederal match may be in cash or in kind.

21. Additional Information: More information may be available in the actual application package.
22. Priorities: Absolute, Competitive, and Invitational: Review these priorities. They will help you select the solution that will obtain the highest ranking. In the sample entry, projects demonstrating early intervention in elementary and early secondary school and parental involvement will receive preference.
23. Federal Evaluation: It is important to review this section carefully. Make sure you are aware of how the points and weights are designated in evaluating the applications for funds. Review this section to determine whether extra points will be given for special priorities.

Computerized Searching of Federal Programs

Now that you are familiar with two CFDA programs, you are aware of the indexes and the manner in which all 1,225 federal programs appear in *The Catalogue of Federal Domestic Assistance.*

The CFDA is also available in electronic form. This speeds up the search for federal programs and makes the information more accessible to rural schools, which may be a considerable distance from a federal depository library.

The computerized version of the CFDA is known as the Federal Assistance Program Retrieval System, or FAPRS. You can usually initiate a FAPRS search by contacting the state agency that is designated to provide such searches. (You may or may not be asked to pay a small fee for this service.) To locate your nearest access point, write or call:

The Federal Domestic Assistance Catalogue Staff (WKU)
General Services Administration
Ground Floor, Reporters Building
300 7th Street, S.W.
Washington, DC 20407
Telephone 202-708-5126
Toll-Free Answering Service 1-800-669-8331

Several useful software programs are also available. You can purchase the FAPRS discs from the Catalogue staff for $140, but you may find that by paying slightly more you will get a more user-friendly version. For instance, GRANTSEARCH CFDA is available from Capitol Publications, Inc., P.O. Box 1452, Alexandria, VA 22313-2053, telephone 1-800-847-7772. This easy- to-use program was priced at $425 at the time of this printing.

Information on computer-search resources containing both federal and private funding sources (foundation and corporate) is contained in the bibliography.

3. Searching for Foundation Grantors

The U.S. Justice Department investigated foundations in the late 1960s and raised many questions concerning some foundations' policy of keeping information on their granting patterns secret from the public. One of the results of these investigations was a renewed effort on the part of foundations to provide timely and accurate data on their granting programs. In fact, foundation grants were utilized to initiate and support a network of library collections on foundation information. The Foundation Center's National Collections now offer the best available selection of information on foundation and corporate grants. The national collections are located in New York City, Washington, D.C., Cleveland, and San Francisco. To assist nonprofit organizations that are not able to access the national collections, cooperating collections have been established in libraries, community foundations, and even some nonprofit agencies throughout the United States. The organizations that house the cooperating collections do not get paid to do so, although they do receive the publications for free. Use the list in Figure 5.8 to locate the collection closest to you.

The Foundation Center publishes several popular reference materials on foundations, including *The Foundation Directory.* Available at your Foundation Center Regional Library, *The Foundation Directory,* published each year, is the most important single reference work available on grant-making foundations in the United States. The 1993 edition is the fourteenth. To be included in the *Directory,* a foundation must either have assets of over $2 million or make grants in excess of the same amount annually. Over 6,300 of the existing foundations have met one of these criteria and are included in the *Directory.*

The Foundation Directory, Part 2: A Guide to Grant Programs $50,000 to $200,000 is another very important publication. It lists over 4,500 foundations.

Both *The Foundation Directory* and *The Foundation Directory, Part 2* are indexed according to foundation name, subject area, geographic region, type of support, and key officials:

- Foundation Name — If you know the name of a foundation that may be interested in elementary or middle school education, you can locate it in the Directories using this index. The index entry itself will provide you with one crucial piece of information — the state in which the foundation is registered. You need to know this to locate the foundation in the Directories, since the entries are in alphabetical order by state.

Figure 5.8

THE FOUNDATION CENTER COOPERATING COLLECTIONS NETWORK

Free Funding Information Centers

The Foundation Center is an independent national service organization established by foundations to provide an authoritative source of information on private philanthropic giving. The New York, Washington, DC, Cleveland and San Francisco reference collections operated by the Foundation Center offer a wide variety of services and comprehensive collections of information on foundations and grants. Cooperating Collections are libraries, community foundations and other nonprofit agencies that provide a core collection of Foundation Center publications and a variety of supplementary materials and services in areas useful to grantseekers. The core collection consists of:

Foundation Directory 1 and 2
Foundation Fundamentals
Foundation Grants Index
Foundation Grants Index Quarterly
Foundation Grants to Individuals
Literature of the Nonprofit Sector
National Data Book of Foundations
National Directory of Corporate Giving
Source Book Profiles
User-Friendly Guide

Many of the network members have sets of private foundation information returns (IRS 990-PF) for their state or region which are available for public use. A complete set of U.S. foundation returns can be found at the New York and Washington, DC, offices of the Foundation Center. The Cleveland and San Francisco offices contain IRS 990-PF returns for the midwestern and western states, respectively. Those Cooperating Collections marked with a bullet (•) have sets of private foundation information returns for their state or region.

Because the collections vary in their hours, materials and services, IT IS RECOMMENDED THAT YOU CALL EACH COLLECTION IN ADVANCE. To check on new locations or more current information, call 1-800-424-9836.

Reference Collections Operated by the Foundation Center

The Foundation Center
8th Floor
79 Fifth Avenue
New York, NY 10003
212-620-4230

The Foundation Center
Room 312
312 Sutter Street
San Francisco, CA 94108
415-397-0902

The Foundation Center
1001 Connecticut Avenue, NW
Washington, DC 20036
202-331-1400

The Foundation Center
Kent H. Smith Library
1422 Euclid, Suite 1356
Cleveland, OH 44115
216-861-1933

ALABAMA

•Birmingham Public Library
Government Documents
2100 Park Place
Birmingham 35203
205-620-3600

Huntsville Public Library
915 Monroe St.,
Huntsville 35801
205-532-5940

University of South Alabama
Library Reference Dept.
Mobile 36688
205-460-7025

•Auburn University at Montgomery Library
7300 University Drive
Montgomery 36117-3596
205-244-3653

ALASKA

•University of Alaska
Anchorage Library
3211 Providence Drive
Anchorage 99508
907-786-1848

Juneau Public Library
292 Marine Way
Juneau 99801
907-586-5249

ARIZONA

•Phoenix Public Library
Business & Sciences Dept.
12 East McDowell Road
Phoenix 85257
602-262-4636

•Tucson Public Library
101 N. Stone Ave.
Tucson 85726-7470
602-791-4393

ARKANSAS

•Westark Community College Library
5210 Grand Avenue
Fort Smith 72913
501-785-7000

Central Arkansas Library System Reference Services
700 Louisiana Street
Little Rock 72201
501-370-5950

Pine Bluff-Jefferson County Library System
200 East Eighth
Pine Bluff 71601
501-534-2159

CALIFORNIA

Ventura County Community Foundation
Community Resource Center
1357 Del Norte Road
Camarillo 93010
805-988-0196

•Orange County Community Developmental Council
1695 W. MacArthur Blvd.
Costa Mesa 92626
714-540-9293

•California Community Foundation
Funding Information Center
606 S. Olive St., Suite 2400
Los Angeles 90014-1526
213-413-4042

•Community Foundation for Monterey County
177 Van Buren
Monterey 93942
408-375-9712

Riverside Public Library
3581 7th Street
Riverside 92501
714-782-5201

California State Library
Reference Services, Rm. 301
914 Capitol Mall
Sacramento 94237-0001
916-322-4570

Nonprofit Resource Center
Sacramento Central Library
Downtown Plaza South Mall
Sacramento 95812-2036
916-449-2131

•San Diego Community Foundation
101 W. Broadway, Suite 1120
San Diego 92101
619-239-8815

•Nonprofit Development Center
1762 Technology Dr., Suite 225
San Jose 95110
408-452-8181

•Peninsula Community Foundation
1700 S. El Camino Real
San Mateo 94402-3049
415-358-9392

Volunteer Center Resource Library
1000 E. Santa Ana Blvd.
Santa Ana 92701
714-953-1655

•Santa Barbara Public Library
40 East Anapamu
Santa Barbara 93101-1603
805-962-7653

Santa Monica Public Library
1343 Sixth Street
Santa Monica 90401-1603
213-458-8600

COLORADO

Pikes Peak Library District
20 North Cascade Avenue
Colorado Springs 80901
719-473-2080

•Denver Public Library
Sociology Division
1357 Broadway
Denver 80203
303-640-8870

CONNECTICUT

Danbury Public Library
170 Main Street
Danbury 06810
203-797-4527

•Hartford Public Library
Reference Department
500 Main Street
Hartford 06103
203-293-6000

D.A.T.A.
70 Audubon St.
New Haven 06510
203-772-1345

Figure 5.8 Continued

DELAWARE
•University of Delaware
Hugh Morris Library
Newark 19717-5267
302-451-2432

FLORIDA
Volusia County Library Center
City Island
Daytona Beach 32014-4484
904-255-3765

•Nova University
Einstein Library – Foundation Resource Collection
3301 College Avenue
Fort Lauderdale 33314
305-475-7497

Indian River Community College
Learning Resources Center
3209 Virginia Avenue
Fort Pierce 34981-5599
407-468-4757

•Jacksonville Public Libraries
Business, Science & Documents
122 North Ocean Street
Jacksonville 32206
904-630-2665

•Miami-Dade Public Library
Humanities Department
101 W. Flagler St.
Miami 33130
305-375-2665

•Orlando Public Library
Orange County Library System
101 E. Central Blvd.
Orlando 32801
407-425-4694

Selby Public Library
1001 Boulevard of the Arts
Sarasota 34236
813-951-5501

•Leon County Public Library
Funding Resource Center
200 W. Park Ave.
Tallahassee 32301
904-487-2665

Tampa Hillsborough County Public Library System
900 N. Ashley Drive
Tampa 33602
813-223-8866

Community Foundation of Palm Beach and Martin Counties
324 Datura Street
West Palm Beach 33401
407-659-6800

GEORGIA
•Atlanta-Fulton Public Library
Foundation Collection – Ivan Allen Department
1 Margaret Mitchell Square
Atlanta 30303-1089
404-730-1900

HAWAII
•Hawaii Community Foundation
Hawaii Resource Room
222 Merchant Street
Honolulu 96813
808-537-6333

University of Hawaii
Thomas Hale Hamilton Library
2550 The Mall
Honolulu 96822
808-956-7214

IDAHO
•Boise Public Library
715 S. Capitol Blvd.
Boise 83702
208-384-4024

•Caldwell Public Library
1010 Dearborn Street
Caldwell 83605
208-459-3242

ILLINOIS
Belleville Public Library
121 East Washington St.
Belleville 62220
618-234-0441

•Donors Forum of Chicago
53 W. Jackson Blvd., Rm. 430
Chicago 60604
312-431-0265

•Evanston Public Library
1703 Orrington Avenue
Evanston 60201
708-866-0305

•Sangamon State University Library
Shepherd Road
Springfield 62794-9243
217-786-6633

INDIANA
•Allen County Public Library
900 Webster Street
Fort Wayne 46802
219-424-7241

Indiana University Northwest Library
3400 Broadway
Gary 46408
219-980-6582

•Indianapolis-Marion County Public Library
40 East St. Clair Street
Indianapolis 46206
317-269-1733

IOWA
•Cedar Rapids Public Library
Funding Information Center
500 First Street, SE
Cedar Rapids 52401
319-398-5123

•Southwestern Community College
Learning Resource Center
1501 W. Townline Rd.
Creston 50801
515-782-7081, ext. 262

•Public Library of Des Moines
100 Locust Street
Des Moines 50308
515-283-4152

KANSAS
•Topeka Public Library
1515 West Tenth Street
Topeka 66604
913-233-2040

•Wichita Public Library
223 South Main
Wichita 67202
316-262-0611

KENTUCKY
Western Kentucky University
Helm-Cravens Library
Bowling Green 42101
502-745-6125

•Louisville Free Public Library
301 York St.
Louisville 40203
502-561-8617

LOUISIANA
•East Baton Rouge Parish Library
Centroplex Branch
120 St. Louis Street
Baton Rouge 70802
504-389-4960

•Beauregard Parish Library
205 S. Washington Ave.
De Ridder 70634
318-463-6217

•New Orleans Public Library
Business and Science Division
219 Loyola Avenue
New Orleans 70140
504-596-2580

•Shreve Memorial Library
424 Texas Street
Shreveport 71120-1523
318-226-5894

MAINE
•University of Southern Main
Office of Sponsored Research
246 Deering Ave., Rm. 628
Portland 04103
207-780-4871

MARYLAND
•Enoch Pratt Free Library
Social Science and History Department
400 Cathedral Street
Baltimore 21201
301-396-5320

Carroll County Public Library
Government and Funding Information Center
50 E. Main St.
Westminster 21157
301-848-4250

MASSACHUSETTS
•Associated Grantmakers of Massachusetts
294 Washington Street
Suite 840
Boston 02108
617-426-2608

•Boston Public Library
666 Boylston St.
Boston 02117
617-536-5400

Western Massachusetts Funding Resource Center Campaign for Human Development
65 Elliot St.
Springfield 01101
413-732-3175

•Worcester Public Library
Grants Resource Center
Salem Square
Worcester 01608
508-799-0655

MICHIGAN
•Alpena County Library
211 North First Avenue
Alpena 49707
517-356-6188

University of Michigan — Ann Arbor
209 Hatcher Graduate Library
Ann Arbor 48109-1205
313-764-1148

•Battle Creek Community Foundation
One Riverwalk Centre
34 W. Jackson St.
Battle Creek 49017
616-962-2181

•Henry Ford Centennial Library
16301 Michigan Avenue
Dearborn 48126
313-943-2330

•Wayne State University
Purdy-Kresge Library
5265 Cass Avenue
Detroit 48202
313-577-6424

•Michigan State University Libraries
Reference Library
East Lansing 48824-1048
517-353-8818

•Farmington Community Library
32737 West 12 Mile Road
Farmington Hills 48018
313-553-0300

•University of Michigan — Flint Library
Reference Department
Flint 48502-2186
313-762-3408

•Grand Rapids Public Library
Business Dept.
60 Library Plaza NE

Figure 5.8 Continued

Grand Rapids 49503-3093
616-456-3600

•Michigan Technological University Library
1400 Townsend Dr.
Houghton 49931
906-487-2507

•Sault Ste. Marie Area Public Schools
Office of Compensatory Education
460 W. Spruce St.
Sault Ste. Marie 49783-1874
906-635-6619

MINNESOTA

•Duluth Public Library
520 W. Superior Street
Duluth 55802
218-723-3802

Southwest State University Library
Marshall 56258
507-537-7278

•Minneapolis Public Library
Sociology Department
300 Nicollet Mall
Minneapolis 55401
612-372-6555

Rochester Public Library
11 First Street, SE
Rochester 55902-3743
507-285-8000

St. Paul Public Library
90 West Fourth Street
Saint Paul 55102
612-292-6307

MISSISSIPPI

Jackson —Hinds Library System
300 North State Street
Jackson 39201
601-968-5803

MISSOURI

•Clearinghouse for Midcontinent Foundations
Univ. of Missouri
Block School of Business
5110 Cherry St., Suite 310
Kansas City 64112
816-235-1176

•Kansas City Public Library
311 East 12th Street
Kansas City 64016
816-221-9650

•Metropolitan Association for Philanthropy, Inc.
5585 Pershing Avenue
Suite 150
St. Louis 63112
314-361-3900

•Springfield —Greene County Library
397 East Central Street
Springfield 65801
417-866-4636

MONTANA

•Eastern Montana College Library
1500 N. 30th Street
Billings 59101-0298
406-657-1662

Bozeman Public Library
220 East Lamme
Bozeman 59715-3579
406-586-4787

•Montana State Library
Reference Department
1515 E. 6th Avenue
Helena 59620
406-444-3004

NEBRASKA

•University of Nebraska
106 Love Library
14th & R Streets
Lincoln 68588-0410
402-472-2848

•W. Dale Clark Library
Social Sciences Department
215 South 15th Street
Omaha 68102
402-444-4826

NEVADA

•Las Vegas – Clark County Library District
1401 East Flamingo Road
Las Vegas 89119-6160
702-733-7810

•Washoe County Library
301 South Center Street
Reno 89501
702-785-4012

NEW HAMPSHIRE

•New Hampshire Charitable Fund
One South Street
Concord 03302-1335
603-225-6641

•Plymouth State College
Herbert H. Lamson Library
Plymouth 03264
603-535-2258

NEW JERSEY

Cumberland County Library
800 E. Commerce Street
Bridgeton 08302-2295
609-453-2210

The Support Center
17 Academy Street, Suite 1101
Newark 07102
201-643-5774

County College of Morris
Masten Learning Resource Center
Route 10 and Center Grove Rd.
Randolph 07869
201-328-5296

•New Jersey State Library
Governmental Reference
185 West State Street
Trenton 08625-0520
609-292-6220

NEW MEXICO

Albuquerque Community Foundation
6400 Uptown Boulevard N.E.
Albuquerque 87105
505-883-6240

•New Mexico State Library
325 Don Gaspar Street
Santa Fe 87503
505-827-3824

NEW YORK

•New York State Library
Cultural Education Center
Humanities Section
Empire State Plaza
Albany 12230
518-474-5355

Suffolk Cooperative Library System
627 North Sunrise Service Road
Bellport 11713
516-286-1600

New York Public Library
Bronx Reference Center
2556 Bainbridge Avenue
Bronx 10458
212-220-6575

Brooklyn in Touch
One Hanson Place
Room 2504
Brooklyn 11243
718-230-3200

•Buffalo and Erie County Public Library
Lafayette Square
Buffalo 14202
716-858-7103

Huntington Public Library
338 Main Street
Huntington 11743
516-427-5165

Queens Borough Public Library
89-11 Merrick Boulevard
Jamaica 11432
718-990-0700

•Levittown Public Library
One Bluegrass Lane
Levittown 11756
516-731-5278

SUNY/College at Old Westbury Library
223 Store Hill Road
Old Westbury 11568
516-876-3156

Adriance Memorial Library
93 Market Street
Poughkeepsie 12601
914-485-3445

•Rochester Public Library
Business Division
115 South Avenue
Rochester 14604
716-428-7328

•Onondaga County Public Library at the Galleries
447 S. Salina Street
Syracuse 13202-2494
315-448-4636

•White Plains Public Library
100 Martine Avenue
White Plains 10601
914-422-1480

NORTH CAROLINA

•Asheville-Buncomb Technical Community College
Learning Resources Center
340 Victoria Rd.
Asheville 28802
704-254-1921 ext. 300

•The Duke Endowment
200 S. Tryon Street, Ste. 1100
Charlotte 28202
704-376-0291

Durham County Library
300 N. Roxboro Street
Durham 27702
919-560-0100

•North Carolina State Library
109 East Jones Street
Raleigh 27611
919-733-3270

•The Winston-Salem Foundation
310 W. 4th St., Suite 229
Winston-Salem 27101-2889
919-725-2382

NORTH DAKOTA

•North Dakota State University
The Library
Fargo 58105
701-237-8886

OHIO

Stark County District Library
715 Market Avenue North
Canton 44702-1080
216-452-0665

•Public Library of Cincinnati and Hamilton County
Education Department
800 Vine Street
Cincinnati 45202-2071
513-369-6940

Columbus Metropolitan Library
96 S. Grant Avenue
Columbus 43215
614-645-2590

•Dayton and Montgomery County Public Library
Grants Information Center
215 E. Third Street
Dayton 45402-2103
513-227-9500 ext. 211

•Toledo – Lucas County Public Library
Social Science Department
325 Michigan Street
Toledo 43623-1614
419-259-5245

Ohio University – Zanesville
Community Education and Development
1425 Newark Road
Zanesville 43701
614-453-0762

Figure 5.8 Continued

OKLAHOMA
•Oklahoma City University Library
2501 North Blackwelder
Oklahoma City 73106
405-521-5072

•Tulsa City – County Library System
400 Civic Center
Tulsa 74103
918-596-7944

OREGON
Oregon Institute of Technology Library
3201 Campus Dr.
Klamath Falls 97601-8801
503-885-1772

•Pacific Non-Profit Network
Grantsmanship Resource Library
33 N. Central, Ste. 211
Medford 97501
503-779-6044

•Multnomah County Library
Government Documents Room
801 S.W. Tenth Avenue
Portland 97205-2597
503-248-5123

Oregon State Library
State Library Building
Salem 97310
503-378-4277

PENNSYLVANIA
Northampton Community College
Learning Resources Center
3835 Green Pond Road
Bethlehem 18017
215-861-5360

•Erie County Public Library
3 South Perry Square
Erie 16501
814-451-6927

Dauphin County Library System
101 Walnut Street
Harrisburg 17101
717-234-4961

Lancaster County Public Library
125 North Duke Street
Lancaster 17602
717-394-2651

•The Free Library of Philadelphia
Logan Square
Philadelphia 19103
215-686-5423

•University of Pittsburgh
Hillman Library
Pittsburgh 15260
412-648-7722

Economic Development Council of Northeastern Pennsylvania
1151 Oak Street
Pittston 18640
717-655-5581

RHODE ISLAND
•Providence Public Library
Reference Department
150 Empire St.
Providence 02903
401-521-7722

SOUTH CAROLINA
•Charleston County Library
404 King Street
Charleston 29403
803-723-1645

•South Carolina State Library
Reference Department
1500 Senate Street
Columbia 29211
803-734-8666

SOUTH DAKOTA
Nonprofit Grants Assistance Center
Business and Education Institute, East Hall
Dakota State University
Madison 57042
605-256-5555

•South Dakota State Library
800 Governors Drive
Pierre 57501-2294
605-773-5070
800-592-1841 (SD residents)

Sioux Falls Area Foundation
141 N. Main Ave., Suite 500
Sioux Falls 57102-1134
605-336-7055

TENNESSEE
•Knoxville –Knox County Public Library
500 West Church Avenue
Knoxville 37902
615-544-5750

•Memphis & Shelby County Public Library
1850 Peabody Avenue
Memphis 38104
901-725-8877

•Public Library of Nashville and Davidson County
8th Ave. N. and Union St.
Nashville 37203
615-259-6256

TEXAS
•Community Foundation of Abilene
Funding Information Library
500 N. Chestnut, Suite 1509
Abilene 79604
915-676-3883

Amarillo Area Foundation
700 1st National Place One
800 S. Fillmore
Amarillo 79101
806-376-4521

•Hogg Foundation for Mental Health
University of Texas
Austin 78713-7998
512-471-5041

•Corpus Christi State University Library
6300 Ocean Drive
Corpus Christi 78412
512-994-2608

•Dallas Public Library
Grants Information Service
1515 Young Street
Dallas 75201
215-670-1487

•Pan American University
Learning Resource Center
1201 W. University Drive
Edinburg 78539
512-381-3304

•El Paso Community Foundation
1616 Texas Commerce Building
El Paso 79901
915-533-4020

•Texas Christian University Library
Funding Information Center
Ft. Worth 76129
817-921-7664

•Houston Public Library
Bibliographic Information Center
500 McKinney Avenue
Houston 77002
713-236-1313

Lubbock Area Foundation
502 Texas Commerce Bank Building
Lubbock 79401
806-762-8061

•Funding Information Center
507 Brooklyn
San Antonio 78215
512-227-4333

UTAH
•Salt Lake City Public Library
Business and Science Dept.
209 East Fifth South
Salt Lake City 84111
801-363-5733

VERMONT
•Vermont Dept. of Libraries
Reference Services
109 State Street
Montpelier 05609
802-828-3268

VIRGINIA
•Hampton Public Library
Grants Resources Collection
4207 Victoria Blvd.
Hampton 23669
804-727-1154

•Richmond Public Library
Business, Science, & Technology
101 East Franklin Street
Richmond 23219
804-780-8223

•Roanoke City Public Library System
Central Library
706 S. Jefferson Street
Roanoke 24016
703-981-2477

WASHINGTON
•Seattle Public Library
1000 Fourth Avenue
Seattle 98104
206-386-4620

•Spokane Public Library
Funding Information Center
West 906 Main Avenue
Spokane 99201
509-838-3364

Greater Wenatchee Community Foundation at the Wenatchee Public Library
310 Douglas St.
Wenatchee 98807
509-662-5021

WEST VIRGINIA
•Kanawha County Public Library
123 Capital Street
Charleston 25304
304-343-4646

WISCONSIN
•University of Wisconsin — Madison
Memorial Library
728 State Street
Madison 53706
608-262-3242

•Marquette University Memorial Library
1415 West Wisconsin Avenue
Milwaukee 53233
414-288-1515

WYOMING
•Laramie County Community College Library
1400 East College Drive
Cheyenne 82007-3299
307-778-1205

Teton County Library
Community Resource Library
320 S. King St.
Jackson 83001
307-733-2164

AUSTRALIA
ANZ Executors & Trustees Co. Ltd.
91 William St., 7th floor
Melbourne VIC 3000
03-648-5764

CANADA
Canadian Centre for Philanthropy
1329 Bay St., Suite 200
Toronto, Ontario M5R 2C4
416-515-0764

Figure 5.8 Continued

ENGLAND
Charities Aid Foundation
114/118 Southampton Row
London WC1B 5AA
71-831-7798

JAPAN
Foundation Library Center of Japan
Elements Shinjuku Bldg. 3F
2-1-14 Shinjuku, Shinjukuku
Tokyo 160
03-350-1857

MEXICO
Biblioteca Benjamin Franklin
American Embassy, USICA
Londres 16
Mexico City 6, D.F. 06600
905-211-0042

PUERTO RICO
University of Puerto Rico
Ponce Technological College Library
Box 7186
Ponce 00732
809-844-8181

Universidad Del Sagrado Corazon
M.M.T. Guevarra Library
Correo Calle Loiza
Santurce 00914
809-728-1515 ext. 357

U.S. VIRGIN ISLANDS
University of the Virgin Islands
Paiewonsky Library
Charlotte Amalie
St. Thomas 00802
809-776-9200

Participants in the Cooperating Collections Network are libraries or nonprofit information centers that provide fundraising information or other funding-related technical assistance in their communities. Cooperating Collections agree to provide free public access to a basic collection of Foundation Center publications during a regular schedule of hours, offering free funding research guidance to all visitors. Many also provide a variety of special services for local nonprofit organizations, using staff or volunteers to prepare special materials, organize workshops, or conduct library orientations.

The Foundation Center welcomes inquiries from libraries or information centers in the U.S.A. interested in providing this type of public information service. If you are interested in establishing a funding information library for the use of nonprofit agencies in your area or in learning more about the program, please write to: Anne J. Borland, The Foundation Center, 79 Fifth Avenue, New York, NY 10003.

- Subject Area — Your Key Words Worksheet will provide you with the words you need to access this index and find the foundations interested in your particular area. Remember that elementary education is becoming an increasingly popular target of funding.
- Geographic Region — This index will help you find foundations in your area that share your interests.
- Type of Support — Many foundations have severe restrictions on the types of funding they will provide. This index allows you to quickly discover this important information.
- Donor, Trustees, and Officers (Key Officials) — This index provides you with information that may be useful in developing linkages with foundations.

All of the indexes refer to the foundations by a four-digit number that appears above each foundation's name. As already mentioned, the foundations are arranged in alphabetical order according to the state they are incorporated in.

The following fictitious sample is set up like a real entry in *The Foundation Directory.*

Sample Entry
The Foundation Directory

2762
The Sebastian Jessica Foundation
2604 Northstar
Chicago 60604 (312) 896-8360

Incorporated in 1926 in IL.
Donor(s): Vastell Jessica, Mrs. Sebastian Jessica
Foundation type: Independent
Financial data (yr. ended 6/30/92): Assets, $150,444,176 (M); expenditures, $6,488,200; qualifying distributions, $6,400,200 including $4,488,200 for 126 grants (high: $300,000; low: $200; average: $10,000-$50,000). $85,200 for 65 employee matching gifts and $1,200,200 for 7 foundation administered programs.
Purpose and activities: Dedicated to enhancing the humane dimensions of life through activities which emphasize the theme of improving the quality of teaching and learning. Serves precollegiate education through grant making and program activities in elementary and secondary public education.
Types of support: Consulting services, technical assistance, special projects.
Limitations: No support for colleges and universities (except for projects in elementary and secondary education). No grants to individuals, or for building or endowment funds, or operating budgets; no loans.
Publications: Annual report, informational brochure (including application guidelines), financial statement, grants list.
Application information: Grant proposals for higher education not accepted; fellowship applications available only through participating universities.
Application form not required.
Initial approach: letter
Copies of proposal: 1
Deadline(s): None
Board meeting date(s): May and Nov., and as required
Final notification: 4 weeks
Write: Dr. Stefan Ross, Pres.
Officers: Vastell Jessica, Chair; Ann Jessica, Vice-Chair. and Secy.; Stefan Ross, Pres.; Winifred L. Boser, V.P.; Franz Kirshbauer, Treas.; Bilal Ali, Prog. Dir.
Trustees: John R. Bige, Alice S. Romano, Donald C. Crowne, Jr., Charles Power, George Gaylin, P. John Passitty.
Number of staff: 4 full-time professionals; 1 part-time professional; 4 full-time support.
Employer Identification Number: 679014579

In an effort to find a funder for our example project in involving parents, teachers, and students in responsible education, we turned to our key words and the subject index in *The Foundation Directory*. We were able to determine that the (fictitious) Sebastian Jessica Foundation has an expressed interest in elementary education. From the entry, we were also able to ascertain that our request will fall within the foundation's average grant size of $10,000 to $50,000. However, we are still not ready to write a proposal or even to telephone the foundation.

We need to learn more about the Sebastian Jessica Foundation. For example, what do they *really* value? What types of projects did they fund in 1992? What types of organizations did they make their awards to? Since *The Foundation Directory* entry does not state that the foundation limits its giving to any one geographic area, we are also interested in knowing where they have awarded their grants in the past.

Another popular Foundation Center publication, *The Foundation Grants Index,* can provide us with much of this information. *The Foundation Grants Index,* published annually, lists approximately 58,000 grants made by 840 of the largest independent corporate and community foundations. The twenty-first edition (1993) indexes grant awards of $10,000 or more. *The Foundation Grants Index* is divided into six sections.

Section 1 — Grants Listing

This is an alphabetical listing by state of the foundations included in the publication. Each grant of $10,000 or more awarded by the foundation is listed under the foundation's name. Each grant has a grant identification number. In our example, to locate a listing of the grants awarded by the Sebastian Jessica Foundation, we would go the Section I index, locate Illinois (the state of incorporation), and follow the alphabetical order until we reach Jessica.

Section II — Grant Recipients

This is an index of grant recipients (grantees) presented in alphabetical order by recipient name. The recipient name, state, and grant identification number are provided in each entry. This information allows you to trace the entry to the grantor by locating the grant identification number in Section I.

Section III — Subject Index

This index lists subject areas (key words) in alphabetical order. Under each subject area is a list of grant identification numbers. These numbers identify the grants that were awarded in that particular subject area. Again, the grants in Section I can be located by using their identification numbers.

Section IV — Type of Support/Geographic Area

This section is an alphabetical index by type of support (e.g., annual campaigns, building, equipment, and so on) and subject categories (e.g., education, science/social science, youth development, and so on). The grants in each subject area are listed by state and identification number. This enables analysis of geographic granting patterns as related to types of support and subject areas.

Section V — Recipient Category Index

This index provides an alphabetical listing by type of recipient organization (e.g., schools, youth development organizations, and so on). Each recipient category is further broken down by type of support awarded and the state where the recipient organization is located.

Section VI — Foundations

This is an alphabetical listing of the foundations included in the publication. It includes each foundation's address and any geographic restrictions of their giving program. By using this index, you can determine what state a particular foundation is located in and can easily find its description in Section I of the publication.

The following shows a fictitious entry as it might appear in Section I of *The Foundation Grants Index.*

Sample Entry — Section I

The Foundation Grants Index

The Sebastian Jessica Foundation

No support for colleges and universities (except for projects in elementary and secondary education). No grants to individuals or for building or endowment funds or operating budgets; no loans.

2713. Association of Indiana School Administrators, South Bend, IN. $25,000, 1991. For Reorganization of Schools Project. 9/14/91.

2714. Association of Michigan School Administrators, Detroit, MI. $14,000, 1991. For Consortium for Schools of the Future. 10/21/91.

2715. Association of California School Administrators, Fresno, CA. $15,000, 1991. For Reorganization of Schools Project. 10/10/91.

2716. Hazelnut School District, Hazelnut, MO. $12,500, 1991. For individualized alternative program for at-risk students. 7/9/91.

2717. Kids in Between, Kansas City, MO. $10,000, 1991. For educational program for teachers working with children of divorce and their parents. 10/15/91.

2718. Platterton School District, Agnes Middle School, Alexandria, VA. $13,000, 1991. For staff development activities related to Marginal Learners/Responsive School Project. 7/15/91.

From this list we can see that the Sebastian Jessica Foundation appears to exhibit values compatible with those of our example project. It appears that a grant of $25,000 would be the Foundation's upper limit and that a proposal for $10,000 to $15,000 might stand a better chance of being funded.

Besides having many excellent books on foundation funding, your Foundation Center Regional Library has two other references you should be familiar with — Internal Revenue Service Foundation Tax Returns and Grant Guides.

- **The 990 Internal Revenue Service Foundation Tax Returns** — The Internal Revenue Service requires private foundations to file income tax returns each year. The 990-PF returns provide fiscal details on receipts and expenditures, compensation of officers, capital gains or losses, and other financial matters. Form 990-AR provides information on foundation managers, assets, and grants paid and/or committed for future payment. The Foundation Center's National Collections in New York City, San Francisco, Washington, D.C., and Cleveland have the past three years, tax returns of all private foundations on microfiche. Each of the Cooperating Collections has returns of private foundations located in its state and sometimes in surrounding states.
- **Grant Guides** — Published by the Foundation Center, these computer-produced, customized guides to foundation giving provide descriptions of hundreds of foundation grants of $10,000 or more recently awarded in specific subject areas. There are currently 30 guides available in subject areas ranging from aging to women and girls, including guides in the subject areas of children and youth, elementary and secondary education, and health programs for children and youth.

State foundation books, which many states have, are also useful research tools. These are publications describing the granting patterns of foundations located in a particular state. These books derive their data from the annual reports of foundations and from Internal Revenue Service tax returns. They are usually available at Foundation Center Cooperating Collections.

4. Searching for Corporate Grantors

If the corporation has a foundation, you will be able to locate its 990-AR I.R.S. tax return. However, many corporations that have foundations also make grants directly through the corporation. Because grants made through a corporate foundation are subject to public scrutiny (the 990-AR I.R.S. tax return), many corporations make grants that they do not wish to be made public through their corporate giving program.

The current federal I.R.S. rules allow a corporation to take up to 10 percent of its gross profits as a tax deduction when this amount is given as grants to nonprofit organizations (501(c)(3)s). However, not many corporations give this much. The national average is approximately 2 percent of gross profits.

Corporate stockholders have strong opinions concerning who should and should not receive their hard-earned grant dollars. This is another reason why many corporations make grants through both a corporate foundation and a corporate giving program. When grants are made through a corporate giving program, the data are confidential, because not even a stockholder can get a copy of the corporation's tax return. In addition, when a corporation perceives that a potential project will bring it commercial benefit (e.g., enhance marketplace positioning or product testing) it will often make the grant through its marketing department and usually will not take a write-off against taxable profits. Again, this type of grant will not show up on any grant list or in any research tools unless the company voluntarily supplies the information. The inability to verify corporate support accounts for the inaccuracy and lack of specificity that characterize the corporate grants marketplace.

What motivates corporations to make grants? What benefits can they receive by funding your school? By reviewing the values of corporate funders, we can see that their motivation comes from a concern for:

- their workers and the children of their workers
- product development
- product positioning

In the example project to increase responsible educational behavior in parents, students, and teachers, the method or solution calls for the possible use of videotaping to provide a link between parent and teacher and the student's level of performance and responsible educational practices. Companies in the area with employees whose children attend the local school may be interested in the project; and companies that make, sell, or distribute video recorders, players, and tapes may be interested, even if they are outside the area. If the model project were to result in an educational change, these companies would benefit. In addition to the benefits related directly to education, a company producing video equipment would also come out ahead by being able to position its products with parents and students — future consumers.

So there are many reasons for companies to support grant projects. But remember, they are not simply interested in doing nice things for education and your school. They want, and expect, a return.

How can your grantseekers locate the companies that will be most interested in your school's project and its potential benefits? Your public library or local college library should have several helpful resources available. In addition, if you are near a Foundation Center National Collection or a Regional Cooperating Collection you and your grantseekers will have access to many resources, including two of the Foundation Center's primary corporate research tools — *The National Directory of Corporate Giving* and *Corporate Foundation Profiles*.

- *The National Directory of Corporate Giving* — This directory provides information on 1,500 corporate foundations as well as 600 direct corporate giving programs. It also has an extensive bibliography and six indexes to help you target funding prospects.
- *Corporate Foundation Profiles* — This publication contains detailed analyses of 247 of the largest corporate foundations — grant makers who give at least $1.25 million annually. An appendix lists financial data on hundreds of additional corporate foundations that hold assets of $1 million or give at least $100,000 in grants annually.

Since companies define themselves in terms of markets and products, it would be helpful for your grantseekers to look at those funding prospects that might value your school's project because of its potential impact in their marketplace. *The Standard Industrial Classification Code Book* is an excellent tool to find out who makes what products. It is available at your public library. Once you have determined the companies that manufacture the product your school is interested in, you or your grantseekers can telephone the local sales representative or phone or write the company's corporate offices to ascertain their level of interest in your school's project.

One crucial fact to remember is that corporate grants decrease as profits go down. A look at *Dun and Bradstreet's Million Dollar Directory* will tell you how 160,000 of the largest U.S. businesses stand financially. A company that is financially weak is *not* a prime target for a grant request.

Obtaining Corporate Grants From Companies in Your Community

Corporations in your area are another good bet for grant support. Find out what these companies are and if your school serves the children of their workers. If it does, you are more likely to receive a positive response, since some of the company's future workers may come from your school.

While corporations give where they live, they still expect a professional approach from their potential grantees. Just as companies are judged by the quality of their sales representatives, your school will be judged by the quality of the individual who approaches the company. Your grantseekers should always check with you and possibly a district administrator before approaching a company for grant support. Since many elementary and middle schools do not have a formal grants system, many classroom leaders have taken their proposals to corporations themselves and have been quite successful. In fact, corporate support for elementary and middle schools is increasing.

Chambers of Commerce usually produce an annual listing of all the companies in their area. The listing rank orders the companies by number of employees and payroll and often gives product information. This listing is an excellent research tool. You should have several members from the corporate world on your grants advisory group. One of them should be able to procure this invaluable list for your school.

Since most corporations make grants out of their profits, knowing which local companies are profitable will be a big help. If there is a stockbroker on your grants advisory committee he or she can find out which companies in your area are paying increasing stock dividends because of increased profits. Another advantage to including business leaders in your grants advisory group has to do with the fact that corporations are always concerned with their customers' credit ratings. How companies pay their bills is a reflection of their fiscal situation and profitability. Hence, companies subscribe to several services that keep close tabs on their customers. Request information on what services the corporate members of your grants advisory group subscribe to and ask them to provide you with a report on the companies your school is planning to approach. The more you know about these companies, the more respect they will have for you.

Make sure your grantseekers do not overlook smaller companies and independently owned businesses in your area. While individual companies or businesses in this group may not be able to fund a grant idea on their own, several could band together to fund one project. Many small companies in the same type of business will belong to associations or groups that might sponsor your project. Whether auto dealers or funeral directors, there is usually a larger group to which they belong. Just because a company or business does not employ hundreds of individuals does not mean it is not concerned about quality education. But small or large, for-profit companies will expect to see a sound business plan as part of your school's proposal. (More on this in a later chapter.)

E. Obtaining Grants from Service Clubs and Organizations

The service clubs and organizations that are closest to you are the most likely to make a grant to your school. This will not be a donation of cash for general use. These groups need a proposal and a project that they can see themselves sponsoring.

As an example, one of my seminar participants from a nonprofit organization in Alaska raised over $2,000 from service clubs and organizations to sponsor her attendance at a grants workshop of mine held in Washington, D.C. She reported that she actually had fun seeking funds for the seminar and that contact with her local service clubs and organizations allowed her to develop lasting relationships with them. The clubs and organizations that sponsored her saw the benefits of sending her to a grants workshop. They realized that once she developed expertise in grantseeking, her organization's clientele would begin to benefit from improved and expanded programs made possible though her acquisition of external resources.

Following the step-by-step system outlined on the next few pages and completing the accompanying worksheets will help you match your school's projects to the "best" service club or organization in your community. A service club or organizations's funding interests can be determined from the areas of support and espoused values they describe in their statement of purpose and from the projects and groups they have supported in the past.

The Foot-in-the-Door Worksheet in chapter 2 requests information on links with service clubs and organizations. This webbing and linkage information will be of great help to you when you are soliciting support from these groups. Most service clubs and organizations have a contact person or corresponding secretary. Make direct contact or use any links you may have to these individuals.

In general, service clubs and organizations prefer to support projects that require smaller amounts of grant funds. In addition, they are motivated by a tight focus on the target population. A grant for equipment that will be used by many students and be made accessible to parents or other members of the community is a good example. Whether they are financing after-school programs or computer equipment, service clubs and organizations want to feel that they are making a difference in the community.

The pragmatic nature of these organizations and the fact that many of the members are businesspeople lead them to an analysis that usually includes information about the number of students or beneficiaries that will be affected, what they will be able to do, and at what price or cost per student beneficiary. Have your grantseekers complete the target population worksheet in figure 5.9. This will help them focus on the types of data your local service groups will respond to.

Figure 5.9

TARGET POPULATION WORKSHEET

What school/youth population do you currently serve?

- Target Age Group(s)
- Number of Youth Currently Served, by Age, Grade Level, Special Needs Population, and so on
- Geographical Area Served (School Boundaries, Open Enrollment, Population, Daily Attendance)
- Number of Programs Currently Provided by Your School (You may choose to focus your response on the target population)

From Your Needs Worksheet, list those studies, examples, and articles that document the local need for this project and the target population that will benefit from it.

Select an affordable ($1,000 to $10,000) solution from the Solutions Worksheet and describe how it would change the local situation. (Remember your Service Clubs and Organizations Matrix here. These funding sources are not usually interested in research. They want to fund what works.)

Understanding Service Clubs and Organizations

As you and/or your grantseekers intensify your search for these potential grantors, remember that they will make grants and adopt and support projects based on their perception of and past experiences with the grantee. In your case, the grantee is your school. It is important to realize that the members of the clubs and organizations may have a totally different view of education than you. I was once rebuffed by a local service club dedicated to supporting projects related to literacy and at-risk students, even though I was asking for a grant to support library resources. Why? Because the individuals I met with from the club never used the research section of our public school library. In fact, one member of the service club's education committee had never used the library at all because he had been thrown out of it as an eighth grader. Changing our grant to support funding for a conversational library and including reference books and manuals on everything from herb gardening to snowmobile and motorcycle repair resulted in our project being met with much greater enthusiasm and financial support.

Step 1 — Service Clubs and Organizations Worksheet

Review the Service Clubs and Organizations Worksheet (fig. 5.10) and identify those groups that are in your area. Your public library

Figure 5.10

SERVICE CLUBS AND ORGANIZATIONS WORKSHEET

Place a checkmark next to those service clubs and organizations that may be interested in sponsoring your project. Record contact's name and phone number and the club's/organization's areas of interest and values. Add to the list of clubs and organizations.

Check	Club/Organization	Contact/Phone	Areas of Interest/Values
____	Rotary Club	____________	____________
____	Junior League	____________	____________
____	Kiwanis Club	____________	____________
____	Zonta Club	____________	____________
____	Jaycees	____________	____________
	Hellenic Groups:		
____	____________	____________	____________
____	____________	____________	____________
	Fraternal Groups:		
____	____________	____________	____________
____	____________	____________	____________
____	Masons________	____________	____________
____	Knights of Columbus	____________	____________
	Church Groups:		
____	____________	____________	____________
____	____________	____________	____________
	Other:		
____	____________	____________	____________
____	____________	____________	____________
____	____________	____________	____________
____	____________	____________	____________
____	____________	____________	____________

may have a list of local service clubs and organizations, and the telephone book can be of great help. There may even be a sign as your enter your city, town, or village that lists the service organizations and the places and times of their meetings.

The Service Clubs and Organizations Worksheet is not intended to be a complete list. Feel free to add more groups to it. For example, there are many Hellenic, fraternal, and social groups and societies that will help your school.

Step 2 — Approaching Potential Service Clubs and Organizations

The following section provides you with sample letters and checklists to help you tailor your approach to service clubs and organizations. Types of contact include:

1. Letter to Introduce Your School and Its Need
2. Telephone Call
3. Personal Visit

While the standard approach is to write, telephone, and make personal contact, any combination of these is appropriate. However, the most effective approach is personal contact. A study published in *Grants Magazine* in 1989 substantiates the importance of personal contact in appealing to foundations, corporations, and government agencies by citing a 500 percent increase in success if the funding source is contacted *before* the proposal is written. This positive effect also results from personal contact with a service club or organization whom you want to sponsor your project. Personal contact works because it enables your grantseekers to gather valuable information about the service club or organization face to face, information that will allow them to tailor their approach to the funding source's values as well as to the size of its pocketbook. If personal contact cannot be made, then you must find information about prospective funding sources through other means before writing to them.

Figure 5.11

OUTLINE FOR CONSTRUCTING A LETTER TO SERVICE CLUBS OR ORGANIZATIONS

Tailor Your Letter

1. What information do you have on the service club's or organization's purpose and values or the programs it has supported in the past? (Focus on this information in the letter.)

____

____

____

____

2. What contacts or friends do you have in the service club or organization? (Mention these contacts/friends in the letter so that the club or organization can confirm your legitimacy through them.)

____

____

____

____

3. List any past positive experiences that your school and/or educational programs have had that the service club or organization may have knowledge of (e.g., awards, commendations, and so on). (You may want to remind them of these in the letter and thank them for their past support, if applicable.)

____

____

____

____

Figure 5.12

SAMPLE LETTER TO SERVICE CLUBS OR ORGANIZATIONS

Dear ________________:

The work of the [name of club or organization] and your concern for __________________ lead me to contact you with an important project. Your support of [an organization, program or project they have funded in the past] indicates your care and concern for __________________.

The [school, school district, etc.] shares your concern and is dedicated to [statement of your purpose; be brief]. The need for our program here in [geographic area] is demonstrated by [cite studies, statistics, case studies, etc.].

Just as your club [or organization] is faced with many requests for assistance, we too face the reality of continuing a program for __________________, as well as relentlessly seeking funds to add more programs to serve __________________.

I am asking you, as business and community leaders, to consider this request of $ ___________ to ____________________________________.

I have enclosed detailed information on our project and our budgeted costs. [Number] groups and organizations have already contributed to this project including __________________. [If your project has partial support from your school district, or other grant funds, mention them here.] I will be happy to report back to your club [or organization] on the benefits of the project.

I will telephone you to discuss this opportunity to maximize your club's [or organization's] investment in our school, our children, and our community.

Sincerely,

OTHER RESEARCH TOOLS

This chapter has provided information on grantseeking materials. Many of these materials are inexpensive or free. In addition to the resources already mentioned, you may be interested in newsletters in the education/grants field. There are many, including those listed below. Contact the publishers for a free sample and subscription information.

- *Education Grants Alert, Education Daily, Foundation and Corporate Grants Alert, and Federal Grants and Contracts Weekly* — All published by Capitol Publications, Inc., 1101 King Street, PO Box 1453, Alexandria, VA 22313-2053, 800-327-7203
- *Education Funding News* — Government Information Services, 1611 N. Kent Street, Ste 508, Arlington, VA 22209, 703-528-1082

The bibliography notes other resources.

Figure 5.13

TELEPHONE CHECKLIST

Most communities have a directory of service clubs and organizations. Telephone the individual listed as the contact person in your community's directory.

1. If you have written to the organization, ask if they received your letter. Tell them you know of the good work their club/organization does and why you selected them to contact.
2. Ask if they are interested in having you or one of your grants advisory committee members speak or present your request at a meeting.
3. Ask for their thoughts regarding your request.
4. Inform them of the time frame under which you are operating.
5. If appropriate, ask for an appointment to meet with them or their committee to discuss the project.
6. Ask them what other information you could provide to help the organization make a decision.

Keep an accurate log of your phone calls to the organization and their responses.

Organization	Contact Person	Phone #	Response	Follow-up

Figure 5.14

PERSONAL CONTACT/VISIT CHECKLIST

1. Dress in the same style as the group or individual you will be meeting with.
2. Never bring more than two people to represent your school. A grants advisory committee member or other volunteer is better than a paid staff person.
3. Start the conversation with a comment about the service club/organization, not with your school's need. For example, you could begin by commenting on the community projects the club/organization has sponsored in the past. This will break the ice and also show that you have done some research on the club/organization.
4. Be brief and to the point.
5. Use photographs or examples (e.g., case studies) of your students and programs to educate them about the need.
6. Record your personal contacts. Keep a record of thank-you letters sent, follow-ups, and results.

Date	Individual Contacted	Results/Follow-Ups	Thank You

CHAPTER 5 CHECKLIST

Evaluation and Planning Worksheet

1. Have you contacted your district's central office for a list of available grant research services, materials, and so on?

_____ yes _____ no

2. The following resources will be helpful to your grantseekers. List where they can be found and the volume number and/or date of publication, when applicable.

Key Search Word Worksheets ______________________________

____

Computer-based Searches ______________________________

____

Catalogue of Federal Domestic Assistance ______________________________

____

Federal Register ______________________________

____

Foundation Directory ______________________________

____

Foundation Grants Index ______________________________

____

State Foundation Directory ______________________________

____

Foundation Center Regional Collection ______________________________

____

List of Corporations in District ______________________________

____

In addition to these basic resources, provide your grantseekers with a list of your local service clubs and organizations and the names of any school-related individuals affiliated with these groups.

____

____

____

3. List any linkages you or your grants advisory group members have with college or university grants offices that could provide access to grants research. Include their names and a brief description of their relationship with the college/university grants office.

____

____

____

____

____

____

____

____

CHAPTER SIX

Using Your Research to Make Preproposal Contact

The key to grants success is knowing how to use the valuable research tools outlined in chapter 5 to develop a plan for making preproposal contact with the grantor most likely to be interested in your project and in the benefits it will extend to your school, students, and community.

Developing District Endorsement for Your Preproposal Contact Program

Follow your district's guidelines for coordinating contact with prospective grantors. If your district requires notification or permission to seek grant funds from outside sources, submit a letter to the appropriate office stating why your school should approach this particular grantor. Use your research to show how your project matches the funder's values.

If your district does not have any rules governing contact with funders, you may want to prevent any possible trouble by submitting a letter to your central office advising them that you or your grantseekers will be contacting the grant sources listed in the letter unless you are instructed otherwise.

The purpose of district guidelines in this area is to protect the image of your school system. When a grantor receives 25 proposals from your district and intends to fund only one, it would like to know the priority or importance that your school system places on each of them. In other words, the grantor needs assurance that the proposal they select for funding will move the particular school and the district toward its predetermined goals, objectives, and mission.

A district grants procedure also helps preserve the image of the school system by ensuring that communication with a grantor, be it preproposal contact or a completed application, reflects the highest quality possible. When a principal contacts his or her district office before making preproposal contact to get the endorsement of the school system, the district grants office knows that the principal understands successful grantseeking and that the school's approach to grantseeking is credible.

Assure the grants office that you are requesting permission to make preproposal contact only to confirm the grantor's potential interest in your school's project and to discuss strategy and the possibility of developing a proposal. Since most grantors will require district signatures and in some cases school board endorsement, let your district office know that the final proposal will be in *early* for sign-off and that it will have already passed a mock review to ensure that it is of the highest quality.

No matter what your district grants system, you will find that sign-off on your proposal goes more quickly if you have employed a preproposal or early-warning system. This team approach will also help in cases where the grantor requires a matching or in-kind commitment.

By promptly alerting your central administration to a fiscal commitment, you will have a much better chance of procuring final signatures. Since many grants call for a decrease in grantor support over several years, you will have time to discuss with your district your plans for increased school commitment through budget reallocation, support from the community, or a grant from a local source.

Your school's grantseekers must notify *you* that they are interested in contacting a potential grantor for the same reasons that you must notify your district's central office. Despite your best efforts to keep up with what is going on in your school, it is quite possible that an overzealous grantseeker will forget to inform you of her or his plans to contact a funder.

Develop a grantseekers sign-on system that includes the requirement that no one initiate contact with a funding source without prior permission in writing from either you or your designated representative. For example, you may decide that the chairperson of your grants advisory committee should review all ideas proposed by your grantseekers and have the sole responsibility of signing the necessary forms or that the chairperson should review the proposed ideas and then take the requests to the entire grants advisory committee for final approval.

In any event, you must have a system in place that assures that any contact with grantors follows sound grantseeking principles and has school and/or district approval. Having a standard procedure and form will make your grantseekers aware of your school's guidelines on:

- how to contact the different types of grantors,
- who should contact them,
- what individuals should bring to preproposal meetings,
- how they should dress, and
- what information they should obtain to develop a quality proposal.

Your system should include giving each potential proposal a tracking number. This will help you periodically evaluate your grants system to determine how many of the proposed ideas actually resulted in a submitted proposal, an awarded grant, a rejection, and so on.

When and how the rules are publicized will vary according to what you and your grants advisory committee require, but they could be included in your teacher handbook or presented at orientation meetings, teacher workshops, in-service sessions, and so on.

Review the following School Grantseekers Preproposal Endorsement Worksheet for possible inclusion in your grants system.

Preproposal Contact — The Principal's Role

How can a busy principal integrate preproposal contact into an already packed schedule? The key is the proper use of your grants advisory group, volunteers, and teachers. You need not be the one who makes the contact. In fact, the best person to make contact may be a volunteer. If you mobilized your grants effort through a grants advisory group, you may already have a volunteer with a sales and marketing back-ground who would be happy to meet with a potential funding source.

Why is preproposal contact so important? Contact with grantors in advance of writing a proposal allows grantseekers to:

- confirm their research
- learn about changes, additions, and new grantor interests
- avail themselves of valuable information that will help them prepare their proposals. Whether in the form of copies of successful grants, newsletters, or priority statements, this information can be incorporated into the project and proposal.
- understand the proposal review process and how they can become a reviewer

Why Most Grantseekers Avoid Preproposal Contact

I ask many grantseekers why they avoid preproposal contact. While their answers vary, there is one consistent theme: Most people would rather write a proposal and place it in the mail than risk having their ideas rejected in a face-to-face meeting with a prospective grantor.

Whatever their reasons are for avoiding preproposal contact, you must help your grantseekers put them aside. Point out that preproposal contact will be less intimidating if they do their "grants homework" and know enough about the prospective grantor to ask intelligent questions that reflect their knowledge rather than expose their ignorance.

Contacting Grantors

First, encourage your grantseekers to review the appropriate Grant-

Figure 6.1

SCHOOL GRANTSEEKERS PREPROPOSAL ENDORSEMENT WORKSHEET

In order to ensure that you receive maximum benefit from your school and central office's grant development services, please submit this form to your school principal when you begin to consider seeking grant funds from nondistrict resources.

- Grantseekers Name : ______________________
  Phone: ______________________
- Area to Be Addressed through Grants:
  ____
  ____
- How the Need to Address This Area Was Identified:
  ____
  ____
  ____
- Brief Documentation of the Need:
  ____
  ____
  ____
- If potential solutions have been developed, please provide a summary of each.
  ____
  ____
  ____
  ____
  ____
- Please suggest key personnel to be involved in:
  1. The Development of the Proposal
  2. Implementing the Project if Funded (Include % of Time)
- List the resources that may be required to implement and maintain the project if the school and district support it.
  1. School Space Requirements (Sq. Footage, Special Needs)
  2. Equipment
  3. Supplies, Materials
- Will any matching or in-kind contributions be required of the school or school district?
  _____ yes _____ no

If you have already conducted a search for potential grantors, please attach your list of prospects this worksheet. By reviewing your list of potential funding sources, we will be able to determine whether any of these grantors are currently being contacted to support other school or district projects. This will minimize the chances of a potential conflict.

Permission to continue your search for funding will be evaluated. If granted, you will be required to follow the school's grants system to ensure a quality product.

seekers' Matrix to refresh themselves on the values and interests of the *type* of funder they have decided to approach. Second, have them review the research collected on each *specific* grantor. Naturally, any procedural information gathered on a particular funding source should be followed. In general, however, the following suggestions will be helpful.

1. How to Contact Government Grantors

Letter — Contact government agencies by letter, phone, and in person, when possible. The first step is to send the agency a letter requesting program information and to be put on the agency's mailing list. When appropriate, use the Sample Letter to a Federal Agency Requesting Information and Guidelines (fig. 6.2).

Telephone — Next, call the agency on the telephone. *The Catalogue of Federal Domestic Assistance* (CFDA) may give the program officer's name and the agency's phone number. Keep in mind, however, the possibility that no one in the agency has ever heard of the individual.

Tell the person who answers the phone that you are calling for

Figure 6.2

SAMPLE LETTER TO A FEDERAL AGENCY REQUESTING INFORMATION AND GUIDELINES

Date

Name
Title
Address

Dear [Contact Person]:

I am interested in the grant opportunities under [C.F.D.A. #], [Program Title]. Please add my name to your mailing list to receive information on this program. I am particularly interested in receiving application forms, program guidelines, and any existing priorities statements.

Please also send any other information that could help me prepare a quality application, such as a list of last year's successful grant recipients and reviewers. I am enclosing a self-addressed envelope for your convenience in sending these lists.

I will be contacting you when it is appropriate to discuss my proposal ideas. Thank you for your assistance.

Sincerely,

Name/Title
Phone Number

information concerning a grant program and identify the program by CFDA reference number and name.

It usually takes one or two referrals to get the correct person and program. Introduce yourself and ask to speak to the program officer or to someone who can answer a few questions.

Through research, you should have collected a considerable amount of information about the potential grantee and should use this opportunity to validate it. For example, the deadline dates and appropriations printed in the CFDA can be checked for accuracy.

Tell them what you want! Remember, there are more support staff involved in the government grants process than in the foundation or corporate process, and the rules governing freedom of information must be adhered to in tax-supported grant making. Staff members are generally willing to provide information.

Your objective is to discuss your school's approaches to solving the problem. Ask if you could:

- Fax the grantor a one-page concept paper and call after the grantor has had time to review it,
- be put on the grantor's mailing list to receive guidelines, application information, newsletters, and so on.

Review the following diagram of the Proactive Grantseeker's $75 Billion Federal Grants Clock and then ask where the agency is in the grants cycle.

Federal Register — Has the agency published information about its rules in *The Federal Register?* If so, request the date of publication and page number.

Past Grantees — Request a list of last year's grantees. This list of grant winners will help you determine whether your school even stands a chance as an applicant or whether you would be better off developing a consortium with other districts, joining with your intermediate district, or becoming part of a college or university's grant. The list of grantees will also tell you who got how much grant money.

Past Reviewers — Ask the agency official for information on the agency's peer review system. While *The Federal Register* may have information on the points that the reviewers award for each section of a proposal, you need to know who reads the grant applications. Knowing the types of reviewers and the reviewers' backgrounds will help you decide what writing style to use and how to construct your proposal. In addition, you should ask the program officer how you could become a reviewer.

Visit — The best strategy is for you, the principal, to visit the

THE PROACTIVE GRANTSEEKER'S $75 BILLION FEDERAL GRANTS CLOCK

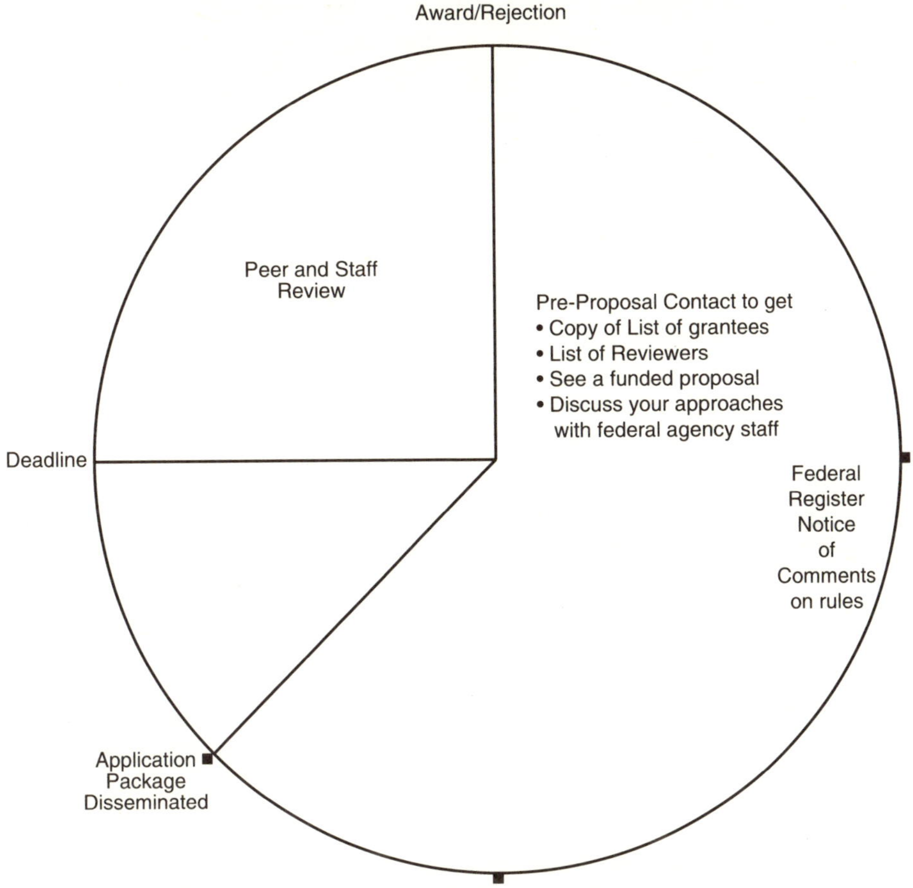

The clock operates 365 days a year. The federal government's year begins on October 1 and ends September 30.

federal agency in Washington. In two or three days you can contact possible funders for several different projects.

Some federal programs actually require a preproposal meeting. These agencies want potential grantees to submit the best proposals even if they are unable to fund them. Good proposals and frequent requests for funds prove that their program is needed.

You could also invite the funding official to visit your school to observe the problem firsthand. She may come if you ask her to present an informative session on the agency's grants to other schools and districts.

You may also ask the program officer if she plans to attend an education conference or professional meeting being held in your area in the near future. If she is, you, one of your teachers, or one of your grants advisory committee members may be able to meet with her there.

- *Who should represent you at the meeting?* If you cannot attend the meeting, send a volunteer or advocate from your grants advisory group. Ideally, you and your advocate will go to the meeting together. Two is the magic number when it comes to representation.
- *What should the representative(s) wear?* Federal program officers generally dress quite conservatively. However, program officers at the National Endowment for the Humanities usually dress more casually than those in the Department of Education. Generally, the older the bureaucrat, the more conservative the dress.

  Dress for Success by John T. Malloy has a section on how to dress for meeting with government bureaucrats. Although many individuals in the world of education are offended by the notion that people are judged by how they are dressed, it is worthwhile to look at this book. Malloy's work was originally funded by an education grant. The purpose of the grant was to determine whether classroom leaders' style of dress had an impact on students' learning and retention. The results of the research indicated that classroom leaders' clothing style did indeed affect learning outcomes. While very few educators ever read the research findings and fewer still improved their dress habits because of them, the important point is that your representatives will be judged by what they wear, so they should dress accordingly.
- *What should the representative(s) bring to the meeting?* Bring materials that help demonstrate the need. These may include photographs and short audiovisual aids (three to five minutes long), such as filmstrips, videotapes, and slide presentations.

  In addition, representatives may bring information on your community, school district, school, and/or specific classrooms. Although they can leave this information with program officers, they should *never* leave a proposal.

  Your representatives may also want to bring, or better yet, commit to memory, a list of questions to ask the program officer.

Recording Federal Research and Preproposal Contact

Be sure to keep copies of all the information gathered on a prospective government funding source and to record all contacts and correspondence on the Federal Research Worksheet (fig. 6.3). In addition, record all information collected on agency personnel on the Federal Funding Staff History Worksheet (fig. 6.4).

Figure 6.3

CFDA No. ____________________ **Deadline Date(s):** ___________

Program Title: ____________________ **Gov't. Agency:** ___________

Federal Research Worksheet

Create a file for each program you are researching and place all the information you gather on this program in the file. Use this Federal Research Worksheet to:

* keep a record of the information you have gathered
* maintain a log of all telephone and face-to-face contacts made with the government agency
* log all correspondence sent to and received from the agency

---

Agency Address: Agency Director:

Telephone Number: Program Director:

Fax Number: Name/Title of Contact Person:

Place a check mark (√) next to the information you have gathered and placed in the file for the foundation.

_____ Program Description from CFDA

_____ Letter Requesting to be put on mailing list

_____ Sent for _____ Received

_____ List of last year's grantees

_____ Sent for _____ Received

_____ List of last year's reviewers

_____ Sent for _____ Received

_____ Application package — expected availability date

_____ Sent for _____ Received

_____ Comments on rules/final rules from Federal Register

_____ Notice of rules for evaluation from Federal Register

_____ Grant Scoring System — Point allocation for each section

Source: ____

_____ Sample funded proposal

_____ Federal Funding Staff History Worksheet

_____ Written summary of each contact made

_____ Grantor Strategy Worksheet

Record of Face-to-Face and Telephone Contact:

Date Contacted	Contacted by	Foundation Contact	Results	Action

Record of All Correspondence Sent and Received:

Date of Correspondence	Purpose of Correspondence	Results/Action

Figure 6.4

CFDA No. ____________________

Program Title: ____________________

Gov't. Agency: ____________________

FEDERAL FUNDING STAFF HISTORY WORKSHEET

1. Name: ____________________
2. Title: ____________________
   (Agency Director, Program Director, Program Officer, etc.)
3. Business Address: ____________________
4. Business Telephone: ____________________
5. Birthdate: ____________________ Birthplace: ____________________
6. Marital Status: ____________________ Children: ____________________
7. College/University: ____________________
8. Degree(s): ____________________
9. Military Service: ____________________
10. Clubs/Affiliations: ____________________
11. Interests/Hobbies: ____________________
12. Board Memberships: ____________________
13. Other Philanthropic Activities: ____________________
14. Awards/Honors: ____________________
15. Other: ____________________

Notes:

2. Contacting Foundation Funding Sources

Sending for Information and Guidelines

Many foundations will mail you general information, grant application guidelines, annual reports, and newsletters upon your request. The Sample Letter to a Foundation Requesting Information and Guidelines (fig. 6.5) can be used with:

Figure 6.5

SAMPLE LETTER TO A FOUNDATION REQUESTING INFORMATION AND GUIDELINES

Date

Name
Title
Address

Dear [Contact Person]:

My research on your foundation indicates that you provide application guidelines to prospective grantees. My organization is preparing a proposal in the area of [topic] and I would appreciate receiving these guidelines at your earliest convenience.

I would also appreciate any other information you may have that could help us prepare a quality proposal. Please add us to your mailing list for annual reports, newsletters, priority statements, program statements, and so on.

Since both of our organizations are committed to [subject area] I believe you will find our proposal idea of interest.

Sincerely,

Name/Title
Phone Number

- National General-Purpose Foundations
- Special-Purpose Foundations
- Community Foundations
- Family Foundations

However, it cannot be used with *all* of the foundations in these categories. Use the letter to contact only those foundations that have application guidelines published in a resource like *The Foundation Directory,* since these foundations are likely to have directors and staffs.

Note that this is an inquiry letter for information only. It is not a proposal to the foundation. If there is no response to it, a telephone call to the foundation is justified.

Telephoning Foundations

Fewer than 1,000 of the 34,000 foundations have offices, so telephone contact is very often impossible. In addition, many of the entries in foundation resource directories do not give telephone numbers. Even if a phone number is listed in an entry or on an I.R.S. tax return, do not call the foundation if the description of the foundation clearly states that there should be no contact except by letter.

If you have not gotten a response to your letter, and you are not aware of any instructions prohibiting telephone contact, by all means telephone the foundation and try to arrange a personal visit. If a face-to-face meeting is not possible, use the phone call to ask the same kind of questions you would have asked at a meeting.

Ask the foundation official if you can fax a one-page summary of your ideas to him. Also ask if you can call him back to discuss the ideas. Arrange a mutually convenient time to call.

Steps for Contacting Foundation Grantors

Telephone — If permissible, call the contact person. The principal's dilemma is deciding who should establish a relationship with the funder — an administrator or a grantseeker. Since many educators are reluctant to make preproposal contact, you may want to just get your grantseekers started and then step back. (The caller may find it helpful to review the needs data first as a reminder that she is calling on behalf of your school, students, field of education, and so on, rather than for any private motive. This may help alleviate nervousness.)

The caller should introduce herself and state the purpose of the call. (If a secretary or administrative assistant is reached, ask to talk to the foundation director or to a staff person best able to answer questions.) As with government grantors, one purpose of the call is to validate the information already gathered on the foundation. The caller's questions should reflect knowledge of the foundation's granting pattern and priorities. Then ask questions that will help ascertain the foundation's interest in your approaches to the problem or in increasing educational opportunities for elementary and middle school children.

It is important to demonstrate that you are different from other grantseekers. Show them that their foundation has been purposefully selected by asking questions that reflect your research. For example, "I am contacting the Sebastian Jessica Foundation because it has demonstrated its desire to see expanded parental involvement in elementary and middle schools. My research shows that 40 percent of your funds in recent years were committed to this area."

As with government grantors, tell the foundation funding source what you want. For example: "I would appreciate five minutes of your time to ascertain which of the two or three approaches I have developed for the XYZ School would elicit your foundation's greatest support and appeal to your board." Note: You may use the fax approach here to maintain their interest.

Remember, you are presenting the funder with an opportunity to meet *their* needs. You are not begging. They are looking for good programs to support and you have one!

Visit — Your first choice is for you or your representative to meet face to face with the funder to discuss your grant approaches. You can either go to their location, or they can come to visit you at your school. By visiting your school they can observe your students and see the needs population or problem firsthand. In either case, the funder will expect to pay their way to visit you and will expect you to pay your way to visit them.

- *Who should be your representative(s)?* Whether you visit the foundation funder or they come to you, your team should be small — usually no more than two. Select an active and concerned volunteer from your grants advisory group who is *donating* his or her time to your proposed project/solution. The other person may be yourself or your classroom leader/grantseeker.
- *What should the team wear?* The team's style of dressing should be similar to that of the foundation official. Again, your research will come in handy here, as well as the book *Dress for Success* by John T. Malloy. It is important to remember that your goal is to project the "appropriate" image to the prospective funding source. This is not the time to register your objections or state your values.

  But don't go overboard. Your team should dress in clothes they are comfortable in. The most important outcome of the visit is that the grantor hear your ideas.
- *What should the representative(s) bring to the meeting?* What you bring to the meeting is extremely important. Focus on your objective. What do you expect to accomplish in a person-to-person visit with the potential grantor? You want:
  - agreement on the need or problem to be addressed
  - to induce the prospective funder to discuss their interest in your solution
  - information on the grants selection process so that you can tailor your approach
  - to validate your research and, in particular, ascertain the appropriateness of the size/amount of your potential grant request

  To avoid the common mistake of jumping directly to the money issue, concentrate on bringing material that solidifies agreement on the need or the problem. In many cases, the grantor has difficulty seeing the problem through the eyes of a student or an educator. Use the following techniques to help the funder develop insight into the problem. Your materials should be aimed at educating, rather than convincing, the grantor.

Videotapes/Slides — A short (three to five minutes) videotape or slide show, especially one produced by students as a class or school project, can demonstrate the problem very effectively. Whether it is about alcohol abuse or zoology, a short video or slide program tells a compelling story because it enables the funder to *see* what the need is.

Picture Book — A picture book that documents the need may provide the starting point for a discussion of the problem. Again, the objective of meeting with the grantor is to first establish agreement on the need for your project and then to ascertain the funding source's interests and to discuss several approaches or solutions.

Recording Foundation Research and Preproposal Contact

The purpose of preproposal contact is to validate your research on the funding source and to add to that knowledge so that you develop a grant-winning strategy. You want your grantseekers to be organized and to take advantage of every possible time-saving technique. Therefore, your grantseekers should keep a file on each grantor they are researching and thinking about approaching. Keep these files together in alphabetical order. This will be a great start toward achieving an organized grants effort.

Fill out the Foundation Research Worksheet (fig. 6.6) for each foundation that is a possible source of funds. The worksheet will help you keep an up-to-date record of the information and materials you have gathered. It will also serve as a log of all contact with each potential funding source.

In addition to information on a particular foundation, it is also important to collect as much information as possible on foundation officers, board members, and trustees. This information can help you and your grantseekers figure out strategies to deal with any preferences and biases you may encounter in your contact with a foundation. It will also help you pinpoint links between the foundation, your school, a volunteer on your grants advisory group, and so on.

Use the Foundation Funding Staff History Worksheet (fig. 6.7) to record the information you collect. Keep the worksheet in the

Figure 6.6

Foundation: ______________________ **Deadline Date(s):** ____________

Foundation Research Worksheet

Create a file for each foundation you are researching and place all the information you gather on this foundation in the file. Use this Foundation Research Worksheet to:

* keep a record of the information you have gathered
* maintain a log of all telephone and face-to-face contact with the foundation
* log all correspondence sent to and received from the foundation

---

Foundation's Address: Name of Contact Person:

Telephone Number: Title of Contact Person:

Fax Number:

Place a check mark (√) next to the information you have gathered and placed in the file for the foundation.

_____ Foundation description from *The Foundation Directory* or other source such as DIALOG, SPIN, etc.A.
Note Source: ____

_____ List of Grants from I.R.S. Form 990 or *The Foundation Grants Index*
Note Source: ____

_____ Application Information/Guidelines

_____ Sent for _____ Received

_____ Foundation's Annual Report

_____ Sent for _____ Received

_____ Foundation's Newsletter/Other Reports

_____ Sent for _____ Received

_____ Foundation Funding Staff History

_____ Written Summary of Each Contact Made

_____ Grantor Strategy Worksheet

appropriate file.

3. How to Contact Corporate Grantors

Steps for Contacting Corporate Grantors

Letter — If your research reveals a corporate contact for grants information, you may decide to begin the grants process by writing to that person for information and application guidelines. The Sample Letter to a Corporation Requesting Information and Guidelines (fig. 6.8) can be sent to those corporations that actually have a grants staff and a preferred proposal format or application form.

Telephone — Before you telephone the corporate grantor, review

Record of Face-to-Face and Telephone Contact:

Date Contacted	Contacted by	Foundation Contact	Results	Action

Record of All Correspondence Sent and Received:

Date of Correspondence	Purpose of Correspondence	Results/Action

Figure 6.7

Foundation ______________________

FOUNDATION FUNDING STAFF HISTORY WORKSHEET

1. Name of Director/Board Member: ______________________

2. Title: ______________________

3. Residence Address: ______________________ Phone ______________

4. Business Telephone: ______________________ Phone ______________

5. Linkages/Contacts (Mutual Friends/Associates who can contact Director/Board Member for you): ______________________

   ____

   ____

   List any data you have uncovered that might help you:
   - determine ways to deal with any of contact's preferences and biases
   - locate other possible linkages between this individual and you/your school/a volunteer on your Grants Advisory Group, etc.

6. Birthdate: ______________ Birthplace: ______________________

7. Marital Status: ______________ Children: ______________________

8. Employer: ______________________ Job Title: ______________________

9. College/University: ______________________ Degree(s) ______________

10. Military Service: ______________________

11. Clubs/Affiliations: ______________________

12. Interests/Hobbies: ______________________

13. Other Board Memberships: ______________________

14. Other Philanthropic Activities: ______________________

15. Awards/Honors: ______________________

16. Other: ______________________

Notes:

Figure 6.8

SAMPLE LETTER TO A CORPORATION REQUESTING INFORMATION AND GUIDELINES

Date

Name
Title
Address

Dear [Contact Person)]

My research on your company's grant support indicates that we share a concern for children and the importance of positive educational experiences.

[At this stage, mention your linkage if one exists]. John Smith, your sales representative, suggested I write to request your company's proposal guidelines and requirements for funding a project I believe you will find very interesting.

In an effort to promote the most efficient investment of both our organization's time, I would appreciate receiving any information relative to your company's funding priorities.

Sincerely,

Name/Title
Phone Number

the reasons why you think the company would value your project and how your project relates to its products. If you do not know who the corporate contact is, ask whomever answers the phone who would best be able to answer your questions about the corporation's grants process. The person you are referred to may be a local plant manager or a salesperson.

As with foundation and government granting sources, state the reason for your call; for instance, "I am calling to discuss the opportunity of working together on a grant that has mutual benefits to both the XYZ School and the ABC Corporation." Request five minutes of their time to answer your questions and suggest that you fax or mail them background information. The purpose of sending them background information is to solicit comments from them so that you can tailor your proposal to their needs. Be sure to let them know that you are not presenting your proposal to them at this point.

Summarize the research that has led you to contact this particular company. Let the corporate contact know that you are not approaching 100 corporations but only a select group.

Visit — Corporations may actually spend more time reviewing grants than foundations do. One possible reason for this is that they have employees and offices, even though employees who act as corporate grants contacts may have several other job responsibilities. This makes it possible for you to meet with the corporate grantor in person.

You may even want to invite the corporate person to visit your school to see the problem firsthand and to discuss the corporation's interest in the approaches you have developed to reduce the problem.

- *Who should represent your school?* While you may think that you, the principal, would be the best representative to meet with a corporate contact, a volunteer might be better. This is because while you are being paid by your district to represent it and your school, a volunteer is donating his or her time and may even be losing income to represent your school. Corporations will be impressed by the quality, commitment, and number of volunteers that your school can mobilize.

  But don't overwhelm the corporate funder with a massive team. Two well-chosen and carefully instructed representatives will be most effective.
- *What should the representative(s) wear?* Although clothes do not make the person, remember that first impressions count. Dress as much as possible like the people you will be meeting with and strive to project a serious, businesslike look.
- *What should the representative(s) bring to the meeting?* Bring information on the need for the project. As with other funding sources, you are advised to include one of the following:
  - a short videotape that documents the need. Include facts and, if possible, a testimony or case study for human interest.
  - a slide-audiotape presentation on the problem or need
  - pictures, charts, statistics, and so on

  Since corporations have their own style and vocabulary, it might be a good idea to ask a member of your grants advisory group from the corporate sector to make a short, corporate-style presentation to the funding source. This presentation might include colored charts and transparencies.

Recording Corporate Research and Preproposal Contact

As with foundations, you should create a file for each of your corporate prospects. The corporate files should be kept together in alphabetical order. Again, this will help organize your grants effort.

Fill out the Corporate Research Worksheet (fig. 6.9) for each of your most likely prospects for funding. The worksheet will help you keep an up-to-date record of the information you have gathered.

Figure 6.9

Corporation: ______________________ **Deadline Date(s):** ____________

Corporation Research Worksheet

Create a file for each corporation you are researching and place all the information you gather on the corporation in the file. Use this Corporation Research Worksheet to:

* keep a record of the information you have gathered
* maintain a log of all telephone and face-to-face contact with the foundation
* log all correspondence sent to and received from the foundation

---

Corporation's Address:	Name of Contact Person:
Telephone Number:	Title of Contact Person:
Fax Number:	Address of Corporate Contact

Place a check mark (√) next to the information you have gathered and placed in the file for the foundation.

_____ Description of Corporate Giving Program from *The National Directory of Corporate Giving, Corporate Foundation Profiles,* or other source.
Note Source: ____

_____ Required Proposal Format, Grant Application/Guidelines

_____ Corporate Foundations 990 I.R.S. Tax Return

_____ List of Corporate Officers, Sales Representatives
Note Source: ____

_____ Corporate Product Information (the Standard Industrial Classification Code)

_____ Profits/Dividends Information—Financial Status of Corporation from *Dun and Bradstreet's Million Dollar Directory,* Credit Rating Service, or other source.
Note Source: ____

_____ Corporate Funding Staff History

_____ Information obtained from Chamber of Commerce (number of employees, payroll, etc.)

_____ Written Summary of Each Contact Made

_____ Grantor Strategy Worksheet

Update the worksheet as additional information and materials are obtained. The worksheet will also be a record of all contact your grantseekers have had with the corporation.

Just as it is important to gather personal data on foundation officers, board members, and trustees, it is also important to gather personal data on corporate executives and contributions officers. You can uncover some information on corporate executives by examining various corporate resource materials such as *Standard and*

Record of Face-to-Face and Telephone Contact:

Date Contacted	Contacted by	Foundation Contact	Results	Action

Record of All Correspondence Sent and Received:

Date of Correspondence	Purpose of Correspondence	Results/Action

Poor's Register of Corporations, Directors and Executives.

The more information you collect, the better your chances of developing an approach that will appeal to the funding source. In addition, your chances of identifying more linkages to the corporation will increase. However, please note that you should not rule out a particular corporation as a funding prospect simply because you are unable to gather personal data on the corporation's funding officials.

The Corporate Funding Staff History Worksheet (fig. 6.10) should be used to record the information collected. The worksheet should be stored in the appropriate corporation's file.

The Grantor Strategy Worksheet

Complete the Grantor Strategy Worksheet (fig. 6.11) for each funding source your grantseekers are planning to submit a proposal to. This worksheet will help you tailor both your approach to each funding source and your school's proposal to each funder's viewpoint.

Every attempt should be made to analyze the funding source's granting history. Even if preproposal contact is not possible, you must at least make sure that the amount you are requesting fits the funding source's granting pattern.

Think about who might collaborate with you on your proposal and what other groups might submit proposals that better fit the funder's requirements.

If at all possible, find out who will read and evaluate your school's proposal. For example, will your proposal be read by staff members? board members? program personnel? outside experts/ reviewers? Besides helping you write the proposal, this information will be vital to performing a mock review.

The prospective funding sources should be rank-ordered by prospect potential. At this point, do not spend much time writing the proposal. Instead, your grantseekers should be investing their time "analyzing" their best prospects for funding.

Although some pieces of vital information will probably be missing, devise the best strategy you can, based on what you know.

Figure 6.10

Corporation ________________________________

CORPORATION FUNDING STAFF HISTORY WORKSHEET

1. Name of Funding Executive: ________________________________

2. Title: ________________________________
   (contributions officer, etc.)

3. Residence Address: ____________________ Phone ____________

4. Business Telephone: ____________Phone ________ Fax: __________

5. Linkages/Contacts (Mutual Friends/Associates who can contact Funding Executive/Corporation for you): ________________________________

   ____

   ____

   List any data you have uncovered that might help you:
   - determine ways to deal with any of contact's preferences and biases
   - locate other possible linkages between this individual and you/your school/a volunteer on your Grants Advisory Group, etc.

6. Birthdate: ______________ Birthplace: ____________________

7. Marital Status: ____________ Children: ____________________

8. College/University: __________________ Degree(s) ____________

9. Military Service: ________________________________

10. Clubs/Affiliations: ________________________________

11. Interests/Hobbies: ________________________________

12. Board Memberships: ________________________________

13. Philanthropic Activities: ________________________________

14. Awards/Honors: ________________________________

15. Other: ________________________________

Notes:

Figure 6.11

Potential Grantor: ____________________ **Priority #:** ____________

Deadline: ______________________________________

GRANTOR STRATEGY WORKSHEET

A. Strategy Derived from Granting Pattern

1. $_____ Largest Grant to Organization Most Similar to Ours
2. $_____ Smallest Grant to Organization Most Similar to Ours
3. $_____ Average Grant Size to Organizations Similar to Ours
4. $_____ Average Grant Size on Our Area of Interest
5. $_____ Our Estimated Grant Request
6. Financial Trend in Our Area of Interest Over Past Three Years
   Up __________ Down __________ Stable __________
7. If your proposal is a multiyear proposal, how popular have these been with the funding source in the past three years?
   ______ Many Multiyear Proposals Funded
   ______ Some Multiyear Proposals Funded
   ______ Few Multiyear Proposals Funded
   ______ No Multiyear Funding
   ______ Not Applicable
8. Financial Data on Funding Source: Obligation Levels for Last Three Years for Grants
   19 _____ $_______ 19 _____ $_______ 19 _____ $_______

B. Based on preproposal contact, which solution strategies are the most appropriate for this funding source?

____
____
____
____

C. Proposal Review System

1.Who evaluates submitted proposals? ____________________
____

2.What is the background and training of the evaluators? __________
____
____

3.What point system will be followed? ____________________
____
____
____

4. How much time will be spent reviewing each proposal? __________
____
____

D. Use this space to note anything "special" that will affect proposal outcome.

____
____
____
____

CHAPTER 6 CHECKLIST

Evaluation and Planning Worksheet

1. **Does your district have guidelines on contacting potential grantors?**
   _____ yes _____no
   If yes, do you have a copy of the guidelines?
   _____ yes _____no
2. **Are there unwritten rules regarding contact with grantors?**
   _____ yes _____no
   If yes, what are they?
   ____
   ____
   ____
3. **Do you have a standard form or letter that you use to apprise your central office of the funding sources you intend to approach for a grant?**
   _____ yes _____no
4. **Have you developed a guide for your grantseekers outlining your school's preproposal contact system and your role in assisting with preproposal contact?**
   _____ yes _____no
   - preproposal endorsement worksheet
   - list of services available
   - worksheets to help the grantseeker focus on the key components of proposal development
   - rules on how to contact the various types of funding sources
   - assistance in becoming a reviewer
   - a grants strategy that pulls all the data together

CHAPTER SEVEN

Helping Your Grantseekers Develop A Proposal Strategy, Create a Plan, And Justify the Budget

The keys to a successful grants strategy include:

- selecting the right grantor — one who is interested in the project and values the outcomes
- choosing a strategy or solution that the grantor wants to support
- providing the grantor with evidence that your school and the proposal developers are credible partners worthy of their grant funds and the affiliation and endorsement that grant funding brings to the grantee

Your school's proposals must stand out over the competition and command the respect of prospective grantors. You will establish your school's image as a source of exemplary proposals by submitting only those that reflect a comprehensive, organized approach to grantseeking. An interested grantor wants to believe that your school has a plan to support the proposed solution and reduce the gap between what exists and what could be for the target population. Overzealous grantseekers may get caught up in the excitement of implementing the proposed project and lose sight of the fact that the proposed project must have a detailed and complete plan. Even a grantor who rejects a proposal from your school should still believe that a quality proposal is guaranteed by your signature on your school's application.

A quality proposal is based on an easily understood plan that provides the rationale for the proposed activities and expenditures. Some grantors require that this plan be described in a budget narrative form. Other funding sources prefer to see the plan visually displayed on a spreadsheet. Even when it is not required by the grantor, your grant writers should complete a spreadsheet that provides the detail necessary to prepare and negotiate a budget. When you suggest developing this detailed plan to your grantseekers, they will most likely give a negative response. They will tell you that developing a spreadsheet takes too much time, and besides, if it isn't required by the grantor, why do it? The answer is simple — a spreadsheet will help them create a well-developed plan, provide the detail necessary to prepare and negotiate a budget, and be the basis for the job description and evaluation of the project personnel.

Not only are you, the principal, instrumental in developing and submitting proposals, but you are also responsible for putting the proposed plans in place and measuring the results. Indeed, your credibility and the reputation of your school rely on your successful completion of the grant-funded project. The reason you should be a moving force in developing a detailed grants plan is that your credibility and that of your school are tied to *each* grant proposal that is submitted for funding. The work does not stop when the funding is obtained. The moment of euphoria when you receive notice of the award is quickly replaced by the feeling of responsibility for implementing an error-free plan.

While you, the principal, may be closely involved in a *few* grants, you will play the roles of initiator, enabler, and facilitator for *many* other grant-funded programs. The farther removed you are from a grant-funded program, the more nervous you will be about spending the funds and meeting the expectations of the grantor. This is why you need a project management system that allows you to track each project's progress, locate the equipment purchased under each grant, and maintain your school's credibility within your district and outside it. Many principals complain of their inability to control and expend grant funds that were accepted by the district but never made available to their school and the project director who wrote the proposal. Situations like this can be avoided by employing an effective project management system.

Up to this point in your proactive grants system, your grantseekers should have documented a problem, come up with several possible solutions for addressing it, and decided which solution will most appeal to the potential grantor. Their research on the prospective funding source and their preproposal contact should have helped them choose the solution or approach that will most likely offer the prospective grantor what they want. Now the real work of proposal development begins.

Your grantseekers' research on the prospective funder may have included procuring a copy of a proposal the grantor has funded in the past. Any examples of what the grantor thinks are good proposals will give you an idea of the types of objectives, methods, and format the funder prefers.

Research on the grantor should have at least uncovered the funder's range of grant awards. If your school's proposal requires more funds than a single grantor is likely or able to invest, you will need a project plan that identifies several prospective grantors and the amount of funds needed from each. The plan should also clearly delineate which parts of the project each grantor will fund.

As your grantseekers become more and more involved in developing your school's proposal, it is important for you to remind them to try to view the proposal through the eyes of the potential funding source and to make every effort to tailor each proposal to each prospective grantor. By doing this, you will be reinforcing the values-based approach to grantseeking. Remember, the funder may not "see" the methods, budget, or grant request the same way you and your grantseekers do. In fact, each type of grantor will view the proposal parts differently. For example, government grantors prefer longer, well-organized proposals that allow them to easily identify matching or in-kind contributions and may require a written description linking each budget expenditure to a method. In contrast, most corporate and foundation funders operate under an entirely different set of expectations. They prefer a short letter of proposal and utilize a business approach that relies on cost analysis of each step in your plan.

Irrespective of the *type* of funding source, *all* grantors require that you have a clearly defined plan. Just as you require teachers to have well-developed lesson plans, funding sources require grantees to have well-developed plans before they give them access to their funds. The Project Planner will help your grantseekers format their grants plan. (The Project Planner (fig. 7.1) is presented here with permission from the American Council on Education.)

The Project Planner

Think of the Project Planner as a lesson plan or spreadsheet. The proposed plan is finalized when the project developers determine the solution or approach preferred by the prospective grantor. The plan must show the percentage of time and effort the key staff spends on the project, the use of consortium arrangements, and any matching or in-kind contributions your school will provide.

The Project Planner will help your proposal developers develop a clearly defined proposal methodology, plan, and budget. Once completed, the Project Planner will allow the proposal developers to define and refine several aspects of the project, including:

1. An adequate staffing pattern that describes who is needed to do what tasks when. (This will help ensure that your job descriptions match the tasks that must be accomplished.)
2. An easily scanned overview of the prescribed activities and how they relate to costs and the attainment of the objectives.
3. A logical framework on which to evaluate the tasks performed by consultants.
4. A detailed analysis of the materials, supplies, and equipment related to each objective.
5. A defensible budget and cash forecast.
6. An efficient way to keep track of in-kind or matching donations.
7. A basis for dividing costs among multiple funders.
8. A working document that helps you assess the involvement of multiple organizations and the responsibilities of consortium participants and subcontractors.

A Project Planner will appeal most to those funding sources who are familiar with and use spreadsheets in their work (i.e., corporations). In fact, the Project Planner has become a recent addition to government proposals. Today more than at any other time in history, federal program officers and their grant and contract officers are trying to pinpoint inflated budget items and will push grantees to agree to carry out their entire proposal for less than originally requested. The federal grantor may refer to this process of reducing the grant total or award as *negotiating the budget.* However, while negotiation requires some give and take, most grantseekers are apt to take what the federal grantor will give!

Standard federal budget forms utilize broad budget categories. These general budget groupings make it difficult to demonstrate to the funder how an objective will be compromised by a reduction in funds. By completing a Project Planner, the grantee can show how a reduction in funds will impede specific methods or activities and therefore negatively affect the proposal's objectives. This link between cause and effect is crucial to negotiating the final award because the achievement of a proposal's objectives is directly related to bringing about the change desired by both the grantee and the funder. The Project Planner will allow the grantseekers to present a clear picture of the relationship between project personnel, consultants, equipment and supplies, and the accomplishment of your school's proposal.

If you and your grantseekers are not familiar with spreadsheets, the Project Planner might seem a bit overwhelming. But remember, there are many ways to complete a project planner, and the only real mistakes one can make on a spreadsheet are mathematical (i.e., incorrect addition, multiplication, and so on).

Look at the Project Planner as a tool that helps your grantseekers identify the costs of carrying out the methods and activities in the proposed plan and how those costs will be divided among each partner in the agreement. Your grantseekers decide how detailed the Project Planner's breakdown of activities needs to be. The more detailed the breakdown of the steps involved, the easier it is to document the costs assigned to each activity and to defend them in budget negotiations.

The basic purpose of the Project Planner is to provide a clear plan that results in the educational change described in the project objectives. Therefore, we must look at how to develop objectives before we examine the general guidelines for filling out the Project Planner.

Objectives

This book's companion book for teachers, *The Grantseeking Primer for Classroom Leaders,* devotes an entire chapter to developing measurable project objectives. The principal needs to remind the proposal developer of the importance of developing objectives that demonstrate the *type* of changes that the *grantor* will value. The purpose of the proposed plan is to meet or exceed the educational change that is defined in the objectives. My rule is: no objectives, no need for a proposed plan — no grant, no need to bother a grantor!

A well-constructed objective tells the funding source *what will change* and *how much* as a result of the funds they provide. While your graduate training gave you experience in setting affective, cognitive, psychomotor, and behavioral objectives, many grantseekers do not understand the difference between an objective and a method. Some actually write objectives that focus on the approaches or methods that will be used to bring about the change. This confuses the issue of *what* will be accomplished with *how* it will be accomplished. Objectives deal with *what* will change; activities and methods tell *how* this change will be brought about.

Make sure your grantseekers develop well-constructed objectives. Review their objectives to determine if there is more than one way to achieve each one. If the objective in question suggests that there is only *one* possible approach, then you are dealing with a solution, not an objective. A well-developed objective focuses on an outcome, implying that there is more than one strategy that could be used to reach that outcome. If your grantseekers are confused about the differences between objectives and methods, ask them why they are performing a particular activity. Their reply may give them a clear sense of *what* will be measured as they close the gap in the area of need.

An objective provides a measurable way to "see" how much change will occur by the conclusion of the project. A method tells *how* this change will be accomplished. In short, *objectives* tell *what* you want to accomplish, and *methods* tell *how* you will do it. Being aware of this distinction will result in a dramatically strengthened proposal.

Developing objectives may appear to be tedious, especially when your grantseekers are eager to move on to the proposed solution and to write their proposal. But keep in mind that well-written objectives that focus on the measurable change to be created will:

- make the proposal more interesting and compelling to the funder,
- enable the grantseekers to measure the changes the proposal suggests, and
- increase your school's reputation as a source of excellent proposals.

The following guidelines may help your grantseekers develop objectives. More detailed guidelines are provided in *The Grantseeking Primer for Classroom Leaders.*

In general, an objective has the following components:

1. an action verb and statement,
2. a measurement indicator,

3. a performance standard,
4. a deadline, and
5. a cost frame.

1. Action Verb and Statement — What Will Change as a Result of the Successful Completion of the Project

The direction of the change to be accomplished is based upon the information provided on the Needs and Goals Worksheets. Remember, you and your grantseekers are not suggesting or promising that the goal *will* be met or that the gap will be entirely eliminated by funding the proposal. You are suggesting that a measurable part of the gap will be closed by means of the prescribed actions, methods, and activities. You are not *certain* that your proposed solution, model project, or research proposal will be *100 percent successful.* However, you are *proposing* a solution that will benefit the field of education by at least partially closing the gap and expanding our knowledge of what works.

For instance, in the example of the project to promote educationally responsible behavior in parents, teachers, and students, it is unlikely that the proposed approach will result in closing the gap *entirely.* The proposal writers suggest that the project will *increase* educationally responsible behavior in parents, teachers, and students. (This does not mean that the project is intended to *eradicate* irresponsible behavior in *all* parents, teachers, and students.)

When you ask your grantseekers what will change as a result of their project, you may find that some of their answers fall in the realm of knowledge and others in the realm of values and feelings. In the example concerning educationally responsible behavior in parents, teachers, and students, some outcomes might be in the area of cognition or knowledge and others in the area of attitudes and feelings. Because of the complexity of this issue, it might be useful for your grantseekers to ask for help from the college and/or university faculty members on your grants advisory committee when constructing objectives.

2. Measurement Indicator — How to Measure the Area You Are Attempting to Change

Just as there are many ways to accomplish the objectives, there are often several strategies by which to measure the change in the area of need. Your grantseekers should begin by asking themselves *what students will do differently* after experiencing the methods aimed at solving the problem and how the change in students' behavior can be measured. Are there standardized tests or evaluation instruments for this purpose? If not, can a way of measuring the desired change be developed?

In the sample project to increase educationally responsible behavior in parents, teachers, and students, the reduction in the gap between what exists now and what ought to be can be measured in a variety of ways. For instance, we could look for behavior we believe is indicative of a developing sense of responsibility in the education process, such as:

- improved grades
- decrease in absenteeism
- increase in the number of students who successfully complete their grade
- increase in time spent on homework
- increase in the number of teacher/parent contacts
- increase in parent/child educational discussions
- decrease in hours spent watching television

We might even develop an Educational Responsibility Scale that contains questions aimed at surveying many of the points outlined above.

3. Performance Standard — Amount of Change Necessary to a Successful Project

A grantor will look at the objectives, note the size of the grant requested, examine the measurement indicators, and compare the amount of the request with the expected amount of change.

In dealing with a multiyear project, your grantseekers may want to create objectives stating a one-year goal for change and increase the amount of expected change over subsequent years. For example, in the educationally responsible behavior project, the objective could be to achieve a 25 percent increase in one year and a 40 percent increase by the end of year two.

4. Deadline — Time Needed to Accomplish the Desired Degree of Change

Most government grants are for one year because of the way the federal budget appropriation cycle currently operates. However, there is a movement in Washington to allow multiyear awards because it is difficult to demonstrate behavioral change in just 12 months. In addition, it often takes a good part of the year just to develop and conduct pretests that provide the baseline data for posttests.

Thus far in our discussion, the objective of the sample project to increase educationally responsible behavior in parents, teachers, and students might be expressed like this:

> To increase educationally responsible behavior in parents, students, and teachers in the XYZ Elementary School *(action verb and statement)* by 25 percent *(performance standard)* at the end of year one *(deadline)* and by 40 percent *(performance standard)* at the end of year two *(deadline)*, as measured by the Responsible Education Scale *(measurement indicator)*.

5. Cost Frame

Include the cost of accomplishing the change in the body of the objective. This will demonstrate that you have *total* command of your proposal. You know *what* you will measure, *how* you will measure it, *when* it will be accomplished, and *how much* it will cost. This provides a stark reminder of how much it costs to accomplish educational change. The one catch is that your grantseekers cannot know the cost until they have completed their project planner.

General Guidelines for Completing a Project Planner

1. *Column A/B — Objectives and Methods*
   - List your project objectives and label each objective. For example, Objective A, Objective B, Objective C, and so on.
   - List the methods you will use to accomplish each of the objectives. Think of the methods as the tasks or activities you will use to meet the need. Label each of the methods under its appropriate objective. For example, A-1, B-1, C-1, and so on.
2. *Column C/D — Month*
   - Record the month you will begin each activity or task and the month you will end each activity or task. For example, 1/4 would mean you intend to begin the first month after you receive funding and carry out the activities over 4 months (16 weeks). If you know the expected start-up month, note it here.
3. *Column E — Time*
   - Record the number of person hours, weeks, or months needed to accomplish each task listed in Column A/B.
4. *Column F — Project Personnel*
   - List the names of the key personnel who will spend a measurable or significant amount of time on each task or activity listed and on each objective. (You have already recorded the time under Column E.)
5. *Columns G/H/I — Personnel Costs*
   - Column G — Salaries and Wages
   - Column H — Fringe Benefits
   - Column I — Total

   For each key personnel listed in Column F you will need to provide an estimate of her or his salary/wage and fringe benefits. You can come up with a rough job description by listing the activities each person will be responsible for and the minimum qualifications you require. You can determine whether personnel will be full- or part-time by looking at the number of hours, weeks, or months they will be needed. Once you have developed a rough job description, you can call a placement agency to get an estimate of the salary needed to fill the position.

Be sure to include services from your organization that will be *donated.* Put an asterisk next to all donated personnel and remember that their fringes as well as their wages will be donated. Identifying donated personnel is crucially important when the grantor requires matching or in-kind contributions. However, it may be advantageous to note donated personnel even when matching contributions are not a requirement. Matching contributions show good faith and make you appear like a better investment. In fact, put an asterisk by *anything* you donate (e.g., supplies, equipment, materials) as you complete the remaining columns.

6. *Columns J/K/L — Consultants/Contract Services*
   - Column J — Time
   - Column K — Cost/Week
   - Column L — Total

   These three columns refer to individuals who are not in your normal employ and to services not normally provided by someone in your organization. (Note: No fringe benefits are paid to those individuals.)
7. *Columns M/N/O/P — Nonpersonnel Resources Needed: Supplies, Equipment, Materials*
   - Column M — Item
   - Column N — Cost/Item
   - Column O — Quantity
   - Column P — Total Cost

   Use these four columns to list the supplies, equipment, and materials needed to complete each activity and to itemize the associated costs. Do not underestimate the resources needed to achieve your objectives. Ask yourself and your key personnel what is needed to complete each activity. Again, designate donated items with an asterisk.
8. *Column Q — Subtotal Cost for Activity*
   - Add Columns I, L, and P — the total for personnel costs, consultant/contract services, and nonpersonnel resources — and note the sum in column Q. You can do this either for each individual activity or for each objective. If you do this for each objective, you will have to add the subtotals for all of the activities that fall under the objective.
9. *Columns R/S — Milestones/Progress Indicators*
   - Column R — List what you will show the funding source to tell them how you are working toward accomplishing your objectives

(e.g., quarterly report). Think of these as milestones or progress indicators.

- Column S — Record the dates the funding source will receive the listed milestones or progress indicators.

Involving Corporate Volunteers in Developing Objectives and The Project Planner

Corporate volunteers can be extremely helpful in preparing the Project Planner. They may have access to computer software that will develop a spreadsheet and a forecast of cash flow forecast for your project. However, as your school's representative to the corporate world, you must be aware of the problems in communication that can occur when you involve corporate people in developing educational programs.

Many corporate staff have been exposed to business seminars on Management by Objectives, or M.B.O. The vocabulary of Management by Objectives, and of the corporate world in general, is much different from that of the field of education. Hence, confusion can result when an edtucator and a corporate individual work together to develop goals and/or objectives. For example, in education, goals are long-range desires. They are normally part of a "guiding statement" and are therefore nonmeasurable and usually nonobtainable. In the corporate world, goals are daily steps taken to accomplish objectives — what an educator would call methods or activities. To make matters even more confusing, objectives in the corporate world are long-range and normally part of a "guiding statement"; in education they are what we want to accomplish and are measurable.

It is easy to imagine how this difference in understanding could extend to a proposal submitted to a corporate funding source. It would therefore be wise to ask one of your corporate volunteers to review the proposal prior to submission to ensure that the vocabulary is appropriate for a corporate funding source.

Project Planner — Sample A

One way to complete a project planner is shown in Sample A (fig. 7.2).

In Sample A the project director's salary is being requested of the funder, as are the salaries of two graduate students who will be assisting the project director. The services of the project director and the graduate students are being contracted from West State University. Therefore, their time commitments and costs fall in columns J, K, and L (Consultants/Contract Services) on the Project Planner.

The project director, Dr. Smith, will ask West State University's Human Subject Institutional Review Board to examine the procedures involved in getting the students, parents, and teachers to agree to write contracts for change. It is

Figure 7.1

PROJECT PLANNER™

Sheet ______ of ______

Proposal Developed for ____________________

PROJECT TITLE: ____________________ PROJECT DIRECTOR: ____________________ Proposed starting date ____________ Proposal Year ____________

A. List Project objectives or outcomes A. B. B. List Methods to accomplish each objective as A-1, A-2, A-3 . . . B-1, B-2 . . .	MONTH		TIME	PROJECT PERSONNEL	PERSONNEL COSTS			CONSULTANTS • CONTRACT SERVICES			NON-PERSONNEL RESOURCES NEEDED SUPPLIES • EQUIPMENT • MATERIALS				SUB-TOTAL COST FOR ACTIVITY	MILESTONES PROGRESS INDICATORS	
	BEGIN	END			SALARIES & WAGES	FRINGE BENEFITS	TOTAL	TIME	COST/WEEK	TOTAL	ITEM	COST/ITEM	QUANTITY	TOT. COST	TOTAL I, L, P	ITEM	DATE
	C / D		E	F	G	H	I	J	K	L	M	N	O	P	Q	R	S

TOTAL DIRECT COSTS OR COSTS REQUESTED FROM FUNDER ▶   T ◀ % OF TOTAL

MATCHING FUNDS, IN-KIND CONTRIBUTIONS, OR DONATED COSTS ▶   ◀

TOTAL COSTS ▶   100% ◀

anticipated that she will work half-time on the project for 12 weeks during months 1 through 6 and full-time for 24 weeks during months 7 through 12.

Sample A shows a considerable amount of matching/in-kind contributions, as indicated by the asterisks. For example, the school district is donating the salary and fringe benefits of the project secretary. In addition, a significant portion of the matching/in-kind contributions are coming from the Jones Corporation, which is donating the use of its corporate video production facility.

While matching and in-kind contributions demonstrate frugality, commitment, and hard work, "overmatching" can become an issue. When a proposal has a huge matching component and requires only a small amount of grant funds, a prospective grantor may conclude that the *entire* proposal should be funded through matching and in-kind contributions. However, *most* matching components are viewed favorably by grantors.

Project Planner — Sample B

Grant writers sometimes create a second, more detailed project planner once they receive word that their proposal has been accepted. For example, Project Planner — Sample B (fig. 7.3) shows how Activity A-4 from Sample A could be outlined in more detail. Naturally, cost estimates could also be developed for each of the activities outlined in Sample B. Keep in mind that some grantors may require such detail.

Using the Project Planner to Prepare a And Defend the Budget

It is best that you, the school administrator, review the Project Planner with the proposal creators to ensure that they have included all the elements necessary for the development of a realistic budget and the success of the plan. With this in mind, there are several key areas that need emphasis.

Budget Negotiation

The budget, in whatever form it is requested, should reflect the Project Planner totals for Personnel Costs (column I), Consultants/Contract Services (column L), and Non-Personnel Resources such as supplies, equipment, and materials (column P). By pointing out the importance of subtotaling the costs for each activity in column Q of the Project Planner, you will be ready to help your grantseekers negotiate a grant award. Initiating discussion of the strategy for negotiating the budget while finishing the plan will enable you to set the stage for an accountable and defensible budget.

Negotiation with a funder for a final grant award should not be based on the budget categories (e.g., personnel, consultants, supplies, and so on). Negotiation should be based on the methods or activities that make up the budget totals.

Figure 7.2

PROJECT PLANNER™

SAMPLE A

Proposal Developed for ______ Sheet ____ of ____

PROJECT TITLE: A Contract for Educational Cooperation - Parents, Teachers & Students Charting a Course for Involvement

PROJECT DIRECTOR: ______ Proposed starting date ______ Proposal Year ______

A. List Project objectives or outcomes A. B. / B. List Methods to accomplish each objective as A-1, A-2, A-3 ... B-1, B-2 ...	MONTH (BEGIN / END) C/D	TIME E	PROJECT PERSONNEL F	PERSONNEL COSTS: SALARIES & WAGES G	PERSONNEL COSTS: FRINGE BENEFITS H	PERSONNEL COSTS: TOTAL I	CONSULTANTS • CONTRACT SERVICES: TIME J	CONSULTANTS • CONTRACT SERVICES: COST/WEEK K	CONSULTANTS • CONTRACT SERVICES: TOTAL L	NON-PERSONNEL RESOURCES NEEDED (SUPPLIES • EQUIPMENT • MATERIALS): ITEM M	COST/ITEM N	QUANTITY O	TOT. COST P	SUB-TOTAL COST FOR ACTIVITY: TOTAL I, L, P Q	MILESTONES PROGRESS INDICATORS: ITEM R	DATE S
Objective A: Increase Educational Cooperation of Teachers, Parents & Students 25% as Measured on The Educational Practices Survey in 12 months at a cost of $																
A-1 Develop the Responsible Educational Practices Survey WIth the Advisory Committee.	1/2	4	Proj. Dir-PD Smith	West	State	U.	2	1000	2000	micro/word perfect			2500			
a. Write questions and develop a scale of responsibility for parents, teachers & students			2 Grad students (GS)	"	"	"	2	500	1000	printer/modem			175			
										phone expense			150			
A-2 Administer the survey to the target population.	2/3	4	2 GS	"	"	"	4	500	2000							
a. develop procedure		4	PD	"	"	"	4	1000	4000							
b. get human subjects approval thru West State University																
c. graduate students to administer survey		4	2 GS	"	"	"	4	500	2000	travel allowance			800			
d. input survey data		*4	Sec'y	800	160	*960				modem/phone expense			150			
e. develop results		1	PD	West	State	U.	1	1000	1000	micro processor			---			
A-3 Develop Curriculum	3/6															
a. review results of pre-test given to parents, students & teachers		1	PD	"	"	"	1	1000	1000							
b. develop a curriculum on		5	PD	"	"	"	5	1000	5000	layot & print			1250			
responsibility concepts in education for each group		*8	Sec'y	1600	320	*1920										
(includes workbook & video on each area of curriculum)		8	Senior High Video Club - Using Jones Corp.	Video	Facility					workbooks	10	200	2000*			
										blank tapes	2	20	40			
o responsible use of time										video studio camera edit character generation	5000	5 hrs	25000*			
o homework responsibility																
o communication skills																
o developing contract for change																
A-4 Promote and Carry-Out Program	6/12	24	PD	West	State	U	24	1000	24000							
		24	Sec'y	4800	960	*5760										
a. use advisory group to announce program																
b. public service spots on radio and television																
c. develop & send home a program																
d. schedule meetings with parents																
e. develop a student video										video camera	1000	6	6000*			
TOTAL DIRECT COSTS OR COSTS REQUESTED FROM FUNDER ▶						0			42000				5065	47065	53% ◀ % OF TOTAL	
MATCHING FUNDS, IN-KIND CONTRIBUTIONS, OR DONATED COSTS ▶						8640			0				33000	41640	47% ◀	
TOTAL COSTS ▶						8640			42000				38065	88705	100% ◀	

Review with your grantseekers the effect of reducing the funds for each activity. What impact will each of these reductions have on attaining the change indicated in the objective? You may be able to reduce the size of your request by eliminating an activity or two without having much effect on your project; however, if you eliminate too many activities you will probably not be able to accomplish your project as outlined. Instead, it may be preferable to modify the objective and reduce the amount of expected change or the number of students or participants the project will impact.

Matching, In-Kind Contributions

As one of the signers of the proposal, the school administrator will be required to document any and all of those costs that have been designated as matching or in-kind contributions.

More and more grantors are requiring that a school/community demonstrate commitment to the project through a *system* of contributions. As funding becomes more limited and competition increases, this practice will become even more common.

How does a school that needs funding demonstrate that it has resources to donate to a grant? While I might agree that this seems contradictory, try to look at the requirement from the funder's point of view. The grantor wants to see commitment!

First, consider the time your advisory group members have volunteered to the project. Can this be considered an in-kind contribution?

Second, review your Project Planner. Are there any personnel costs or non-personnel resources that could be donated instead of requested from the funder?

Finally, are there any hidden costs in your school that could qualify as matching contributions? For example, I once worked on a grant proposal that called for developing an in-service course for teachers as a way of effecting change in the classroom. In seeking to meet the funding source's matching funds requirement, a school administrator revealed that under the teachers' contract the district was required to pay each educator a salary increase after completion of the course. We calculated the average age of the participating teachers and the total number of years that the increase would be paid out to all teachers, multiplied this figure by the salary increase, and were allowed to claim the resulting figure as a match.

While I cannot guarantee what each grantor will accept as a matching or in-kind contribution, be creative. Review your project and look for every possible matching contribution. If you have a grants advisory committee, the members may volunteer some of the match by lending the use of facilities and donating equipment, printing, travel, and so on.

Figure 7.3

PROJECT PLANNER™

SAMPLE B

Sheet ____ of ____

Proposal Developed for ______________________

PROJECT TITLE: A Contract for Educational Cooperation - Parents, Teachers & Students Charting a Course for Involvement

PROJECT DIRECTOR: ______________ Proposed starting date ________ Proposal Year ________

A. List Project objectives or outcomes A. B. B. List Methods to accomplish each objective as A-1, A-2, A-3 . . . B-1, B-2 . . .	MONTH		TIME	PROJECT PERSONNEL	PERSONNEL COSTS			CONSULTANTS • CONTRACT SERVICES			NON-PERSONNEL RESOURCES NEEDED SUPPLIES • EQUIPMENT • MATERIALS				SUB-TOTAL COST FOR ACTIVITY	MILESTONES PROGRESS INDICATORS	
	BEGIN	END			SALARIES & WAGES	FRINGE BENEFITS	TOTAL	TIME	COST/WEEK	TOTAL	ITEM	COST/ITEM	QUANTITY	TOT COST	TOTAL I, L, P	ITEM	DATE
	C / D		E	F	G	H	I	J	K	L	M	N	O	P	Q	R	S
A-4 Promote and Carry-Out the Responsible Education Partners Program																	
a. Set-up a meeting with elementary & junior high teachers to explain the project.																	
1. Get program on teachers' in-service agenda.																	
2. Distribute information package																	
3. Have panel discussion include parents advisory group representative and media representative.																	
4. Break into small groups to discuss program and make recommendation																	
b. Invite local advertising council to take on program and develop public service announcements.																	
c. Invite parents and students to participate in T.V. Busters as a lead activity.																	
1. Set-up prizes by soliciting local industry to provide focus awards for students who complete a contract to not watch any television for 20 days (except news and educ. tv)																	
2. Send home examples of the responsible use of non-t.v. time.																	
3. Invite parents to develop a contact for responsible education that includes homework, school contact, & parental involvement.																	

TOTAL DIRECT COSTS OR COSTS REQUESTED FROM FUNDER ▶ ____ T ____ ◀ % OF TOTAL

MATCHING FUNDS, IN-KIND CONTRIBUTIONS, OR DONATED COSTS ▶ ____ ◀

TOTAL COSTS ▶ ____ 100% ◀

Cash Flow

While the principal may or may not be praised for his or her help in developing the proposal, *you will surely be blamed* if problems with cash flow arise. You can avoid trouble with cash flow by:

- having a project plan that forecasts your cash requirements properly,
- making your school district aware of the cash forecast, and
- having the appropriate administrator sign a proposal that includes the projected cash need of the project.

By reviewing your Project Planner you will have the information necessary to determine your cash flow needs. Column C/D of the Project Planner designates the beginning and end of each activity, and column Q tells how much money will be required to accomplish each activity. Transfer this information to the following Grants Office Time Line and you will have a fairly accurate estimate of your cash flow needs.

Grants Office Time Line

The Grants Office Time Line (fig. 7.4) is a visual representation of your time frame. It also shows an estimate of the cash you will require to stay on your schedule.

First designate your activity number in column 1 of the Grants Office Time Line. (This information will be taken from your Project Planner.) Then draw a line from the activity's projected start date to its completion date. For example, if the activity is to begin in the second month of the project and end in the fourth month, a line would be drawn from 2 to 4.

On the far right of the line, write the total cost of the activity from column Q of the Project Planner.

Federal and many state funders require a quarterly cash forecast. In these cases, place the estimated cash forecast in the appropriate quarterly column at the bottom of the Grants Office Time Line. Estimate the total cash needed for those activities that take place over several quarters or that require advance expenditure, such as equipment purchase.

The subsequent chapters will help you move from the Project Planner spreadsheet to the written proposal.

Figure 7.4

GRANTS OFFICE TIME LINE

ACTIVITY NO.	1	2	3	4	5	6	7	8	9	10	11	12	TOTAL COST FOR ACTIVITY

	1st QUARTER	2nd QUARTER	3rd QUARTER	4th QUARTER	TOTAL

QUARTERLY FORECAST OF EXPENDITURES ▲

CHAPTER 7 CHECKLIST

Planning and Evaluation Worksheet

1. **Do you currently use a spreadsheet or planning document in the preparation of proposals?**

   _____ yes   _____ no

   If yes, does it provide your grantseeker with:

job descriptions for staff & consultants	_____ yes	_____ no
percentage of time allocated to task	_____ yes	_____ no
itemized equipment list	_____ yes	_____ no
cost summary for each objective	_____ yes	_____ no
cash flow or projected cash needs	_____ yes	_____ no
matching or in-kind contributions	_____ yes	_____ no

2. **Can you utilize corporate volunteers to help with:**

proposal editing	_____ yes	_____ no
budget assistance	_____ yes	_____ no
developing computer spreadsheets	_____ yes	_____ no

3. **Do you have a system for helping staff develop behavioral objectives?**

   _____ yes   _____ no

CHAPTER EIGHT

$ Preparing Federal Proposals for Your School

Many principals prepare their school's federal proposals virtually by themselves. While this chapter will provide principals with useful guidelines and techniques for writing grants, its main purpose is to help principals develop a grants system that involves others in writing federal proposals.

Let us assume that one of your grantseekers is looking for federal grant funds to support a project. He or she has completed a proposal sign-on form (see chapter 6) to ensure your support and your district central office's approval, and, with your guidance, has made preproposal contact and procured the information needed to develop a funding strategy and a project planner.

The Federal Grantseekers' Proposal Checklist (fig. 8.1) will ensure that your proposal developers have collected all the information and items necessary to successfully compete for federal funding. Your office should disseminate the checklist and maintain a grants resource file that contains examples of each of the items on the checklist, including sample proposals.

Most schools, even district grants offices, do not have a *system* that enables their grantseekers to examine a proposal (with reviewers' comments) submitted by their district to the federal agency they are approaching or to review a funded proposal submitted by another school district. This is senseless, because studying such a proposal could have a real impact on a prospective proposal writer.

There are several education associations, such as Capitol Publications (see bibliography) and private companies that compile the items on the Federal Grantseekers Proposal Checklist and sell the package. While the information your grantseekers need to help them write a quality federal proposal can be accessed at no cost under the Freedom of Information Act, they would have to travel to Washington, D.C., to gather it. Of course, one advantage in your grantseekers' going to Washington, D.C., is that they would have the opportunity for face-to-face contact with the funding source.

Your school's success rate in the federal grants marketplace will depend upon how well your grantseekers do their homework and follow the stringent rules for completing a federal grant application. For example, applying for funds from CFDA 84.201 (School Dropout Demonstration Assistance

Figure 8.1

FEDERAL GRANTSEEKERS' PROPOSAL CHECKLIST

Put a check mark next to those items that you have a copy of:

- ___ School Grantseekers' Preproposal Endorsement Worksheet
- ___ *Catalogue of Federal Domestic Assistance* — Program Description
- ___ *Federal Register* — Rules and Regulations
- ___ *Federal Register* — Announcement of Proposal Submission Deadline
- ___ Past Grantees for Program
- ___ List of Last Year's Reviewers or Profile of Reviewers
- ___ Sample Funded Proposal
- ___ Sample of Past School District Proposal with Reviewers' Comments
- ___ Grantor Strategy Worksheet
- ___ Federal Research Worksheet
- ___ Federal Funding Staff History
- ___ Scoring System to Be Used in Review

Program) requires a proposal of no more than 30 double-spaced pages, typed in a font allowing at least 12 characters per inch. Thus the body of the proposal *cannot* be 31 pages, or single-spaced! It is important to remind your grantseekers to express their creativity by developing innovative solutions to the problem, not innovative ways of completing the federal grant application.

The basic parts of a federal proposal are usually similar for all applications. Differences between federal agency requirements occur in the preferred ordering of the parts of the proposal, the terminology, and the points allocated to each part. The basic parts of a federal proposal for an education project are listed below.

A. proposal abstract or summary
B. needs statement
C. plan of operation for addressing the need
D. key personnel who will operate the program
E. budget and cost-effectiveness
F. how the effectiveness of the project will be evaluated
G. adequacy of resources
H. assurances

I. attachments

In addition, federal agencies that fund research in education will require a section on the project's hypothesis, specific aims, and research design.

It is most important that the federal proposal be constructed in a manner that the reviewer will understand. The reviewer must be able to read through the proposal rapidly. The salient parts of the proposal must be evident and well documented so that the reviewer can ascribe a point value to each section. The points assigned to each area and the distribution of any additional points will be outlined in each agency's specific proposal guidelines.

A. Proposal Abstract or Summary

Most proposals require an abstract or a summary. The abstract may have to fit into a designated space and/or specific number of lines. Photo-reduction is not allowed. Federal agencies normally state the specific font required so that the grant writer does not use a microtype or laser printer font so small that the proposal cannot be read without magnification.

There is some disagreement over *when* in the proposal development process the abstract or summary should be written. Most experts believe that the abstract should be written *last,* as the grant writer reflects on the completed proposal and summarizes each section; others contend that writing the abstract *first* helps the grantee focus on the ideas the proposal will describe. While one must allow for grantseekers' individual differences, preparing a detailed outline, then writing the proposal, and finally writing an abstract that summarizes the proposal works efficiently for most people.

Whether the abstract/summary is written first or last, make certain that it has the required format and follows all the rules. It should provide a short, concise, and easy-to-read description of the need for the project, the objectives, the solution, and the evaluation. Before writing the abstract, your proposal developers should review the required sections of the proposal and the point system that the reviewers will use to evaluate and rank the proposal. Suggest that they highlight those sections worth the most points and refer to them in the same terms as the federal agency.

In order to convey as much information as possible in a limited amount of space, some grant writers push the abstract to the margins and cram in as many words as possible. This usually results in a summary that is confusing and difficult to read. The federal response to this has been to specify font size as well as number of lines. Especially considering that the reviewer may have already read several proposals, a "crammed" abstract could set a negative tone for the entire proposal and could lead to a low score.

Use the following exercise with your grantseekers to help them prepare to write their abstract/summary.

Review the following abstract and consider whether it:

- shows that the grantseeker has a command of the need,

- indicates that the project has measurable objectives,
- provides a synopsis of the methods, and
- presents the proposal's main points in an interesting manner.

> This project will identify those students at risk for dropping out, will intervene and provide the motivation and tools necessary to complete their high school education, and will encourage post-secondary education and/or training. Over a three-year period, this project will extend services to 450 students including 5 elementary programs that feed into 3 middle schools, which, in turn, feed into 2 high school programs. Activities in this project will increase coping and daily living skills through classroom instruction, utilize community volunteers to tutor students and act as role models, increase awareness and incentive through two field trips, as well as track school attendance and classroom progress acting as a mediator between teachers, parents, and students to resolve problems as they arise.

This abstract indicates that services will be extended to 450 students, 5 elementary programs, and 3 middle schools. It also provides a rough idea of the types of activities prescribed to retain students. In addition, it does this in one sentence of 57 words! However, the abstract does not even *hint* at the need or give any measurement indicators or criteria for success. Also, based on the abstract, the project appears to be geared to high schools, which raises the issue of why 5 elementary and 3 middle schools will be involved. But before we get too critical, we should note that the project summarized in this abstract was funded for approximately $97,000!

B. The Needs Statement

This section may also be referred to as the "Search of Relevant Literature," the "Extent of the Need," or the "Problem." One federal program refers to the needs statement as the "Criterion: Extent to which the project meets specific needs recognized in the statute that authorized the program, including consideration of the needs addressed by the project; how the needs were identified; how the needs will be met; and the benefits to be gained by meeting the needs." One successful grantee responded to this criterion with a description of the extent of the need that included descriptions of the following:

1. Target Area — Where the applicant was located and data that identified a significant needs population in the student body.
2. Needs for Services — What school programs were available, and the void between "what was" and "what should be."
3. How the Needs Will Be Met — A general description of what was to be done.
4. Benefits to Be Gained — The anticipated positive outcomes of the project.

When developing the needs section, your proposal developers should take into consideration the type of reviewer that will be reading the proposal application and try to determine what the reviewer will find motivating and compelling. The needs section must show that your applicant has a command of the current literature in the field. This will demonstrate his or her credibility. Many excellent proposals lose critical points because the grantee fails to command the respect of the reviewer because he or she overlooks the needs section and places the emphasis on the project description and plan of operation.

The following "extent of the need" has been taken from a grant funded by the Department of Education for dropout prevention.[1]

> The target population to be served by the project has experienced low academic achievement, high public assistance rates, high dropout rates, linguistic and cultural differences, geographic isolation, and inaccessibility to existing career and training information. These conditions have combined to create high unemployment, underemployment, poor self-image, and a resultant low standard of living among these people. Astin's study of college attrition clearly identifies family income as a significant factor which negatively impacts student success in postsecondary education and contributes to high dropout rates. Astin does note, however, that this correlation is influenced by such other "mediation" factors as ability, motivation, financial concerns, and parental education.[2]
>
> . . . The target population occupies a rural mountainous and desert region covering over 8,000 square miles which is larger than the combined area of Delaware, Rhode Island, and Connecticut.
>
> . . . It is pertinent to note that 79.3% of the active job applicants are ethnic minority and that 63.5% had less than a high school diploma.

Facts such as those presented in this excerpt convince the reviewer and the federal staff that the writer is knowledgeable about the subject of the proposal. Statistics in the needs section of a proposal show a command of the situation and make a positive impression, unlike "grant-loser statements" such as:

- "Everyone knows the need for . . ."
- "Current statistics show . . ."
- "It is a shame our students do not have . . ."
- "You can't believe the number of times . . ."
- "Several (many, an increasing number of) students . . ."

When reviewers read a needs section containing such weak, banal

[1]Proposal: Four Corners School, College and University Partnership Program, Submitted to U.S. Department of Education, Division of Student Services, CDFA 84-204, by San Juan School District College of Eastern Utah — San Juan Campus, Utah Navajo Development Council, July 9, 1988.
[2]Alexander W. Astin, *Preventing Students from Dropping Out,* San Francisco: Jossey Bass, 1977.

statements they vent their frustration on the scoring sheet, and the grantseeker loses valuable points. A strong needs statement must cite facts, studies, and references and must reflect the commitment and hard work that went in to gathering them.

C. Plan of Operation

The federal application may refer to this section as the "Plan of Operation," "Objectives and Methods," or "Project Methodology." The purpose of this section is to describe an organized solution to the need and problem you have identified; it should thus include your proposal's objectives, methods, and activities. Study a funded proposal to see how successful grantees have organized this section.

Review the section in chapter 7 on constructing behavioral/ measurable objectives and then review the following sample objectives from a proposal for an early intervention dropout program. Keep in mind that the proposal was funded for $750,000!

1. 1,500 kindergarten through sixth-grade at-risk students will benefit from the District's effort to institutionalize instructional improvement and variation by comprehensively upgrading all instructional and support services. This will include: attendance monitoring and immediate follow-up on absences; ombudsmen and advocates for students; junior high at-risk student tutoring of early grade at-risk students; extended school day programs; and off-site activities.
2. Seventy-five kindergarten through sixth-grade teachers and two paraprofessionals will receive training on topics such as: implementation of effective school postulates, individualizing instruction, thematic instruction, ombudsmen and advocates for students, the city as a resource, training parents, managing at- risk student programs, and understanding the needs of ethnic minority (especially Hispanic-American) and low income students.
3. Approximately 500 parents of at-risk students will attend 30 to 60 hours of project-sponsored activities focusing on issues such as: basic literacy, parenting, how to help your child with homework, English as a second language, and social issues information about: drugs and alcohol abuse, AIDS, teenage pregnancy, and suicide.
4. The results of this program will be publicized and disseminated. Strategies will include: a recruitment video, a video that showcases the progress and achievements of students, a program brochure, TV spot announcements, and presentations at community events.

Do these objectives describe *what* will be accomplished or *how* the project will be done? These objectives describe how the project will be done. For three-quarters of a million dollars, we should be told *what area* we can expect to see change in and *how much change* we can expect.

Some of your grantseekers may be misled by objectives that contain numbers. Numbers alone do not mean that an objective is well constructed or even measurable. For example, the above objectives tell us the *number* of parents to be trained but not *what the parents will do differently as a result of the training or what impact the parental training will have on students.*

The following objective is from another proposal funded by the Department of Education under a different program. It demonstrates the measurable component of an objective much more effectively.

> By June 1, 1989, at least 65% of all students enrolled in the academic year program will improve at least 1.5 grade levels in mathematics, language mechanics, language expression, and reading ability as documented by pre-post Comprehensive Tests of Basic Skills scores.

Review chapter 7 on developing a project planner. The Project Planner provides an organized approach for developing the proposed plan. Whether or not you or your grantseekers utilize a project planner, your school's proposal will be evaluated on the thoroughness and clarity of the methods you prescribe to meet the objectives and address the need. Studying a previously funded proposal will provide insight on how successful grantees have organized this section of their proposal.

There are many ways to present the methods or activities. In the following example, the successful grantseeker first presents a main objective, then a subobjective or process objective, and finally the methodologies.

> OBJECTIVE 3: UPGRADE BASIC SKILLS
> PROCESS OBJECTIVE 3.1: Students will be counseled and tutored during the academic year program to meet their individual academic needs and overcome areas of deficiency.
> Methodologies:
> a) Deficiencies of participants will be documented through use of CTBS scores, transcripts, and interviews with teachers, parents, students, and counselors. Through this process, an individual education plan will be prepared based on areas of strengths, but particularly on areas of weakness in which the student needs help. This will be in the form of a contract which the student and counselor will sign to agree to work together to strengthen the academic skills which need improvement.
> b) The counselor will schedule bi-weekly, after-school tutoring, and counseling sessions to provide academic assistance as well as emotional support.
> Personnel Responsible: Project counselors, tutors, and teachers from each high school.
> Resources: Textbooks, testing and teaching materials, media centers of each high school.

D. Key Personnel

This section provides the reviewer with an indication of your project staff's ability to implement the methods aimed at meeting the objectives and closing the gap between "what is" and "what ought to be."

One dilemma that proposal developers face is that key personnel often have not been hired at the time a proposal is submitted. In these cases, the submitted proposal should clearly show that capable staff can be hired or that your school can reallocate individuals who have these skills. Remember, reviewers who are otherwise favorable to a proposal will be put off if they are not convinced that individuals qualified to implement the project are readily available.

Review the following section on key personnel from a funded Department of Education proposal.

> Criterion: The quality of the key personnel the applicant plans to use in the project.
>
> Staff will consist of a full-time project director, a full-time assistant project director, four part-time regular school year counselors, four full-time summer counselors, eight college and peer tutors, 12 part-time instructors, and a full-time secretary. Inasmuch as project staff have not been identified at this time, resumes are not included. The partnership would like to affirm that no problems are anticipated in acquiring qualified, experienced, highly competent personnel. At least one week will be scheduled at the beginning of the project for the orientation of staff to the goals, objectives, plan of operation, etc.

Do you feel confident that this applicant has the expertise necessary to conduct this project? Does the statement that "no problems are anticipated in acquiring qualified . . . personnel" make you feel comfortable? This is like asking someone to bet on a horse she or he has not seen and knows nothing about, simply because you believe that it will be a winner. Every grantor wants to know what horses a prospective grantee has in their stable!

In this example, the applicant could have stated that the project director would be reporting to Dr. Smith, who is currently responsible for managing "X" million dollars or completing "Y" projects. Note, however, that the prospective grantee did at least follow the key personnel criterion with a detailed description of the major positions mentioned in the body of the proposal.

Keep in mind that many government grantors look at the *appropriate* use of personnel as well as their quality. If you are thinking about *minimally involving* one outstanding person in *many* grants, you should be aware that some funders will ask for an outline of the time each staff member will commit to the project and that they may require that the project director or principal investigator commit a significant percentage of her or his time to the project. In other words, you should not have one outstanding and well-known individual spending 2 percent of his or her time on 50 different projects!

E. Budget and Cost-Effectiveness

While federal programs' proposal requirements differ, all applications require a budget. Your proposal's budget and the items that comprise it may be viewed in relationship to how they affect your students, teachers, and/or parents. The amount you request may be divided by the number of beneficiaries so that the federal program officer and reviewer can arrive at the cost per person served by the proposal. One of the primary concerns of a reviewer is that the budget request be reasonable and based on the cost of the activities or methods outlined in the proposal. For example, if a project is supposed to provide a model for other schools, it must be affordable enough to be replicated by schools and districts that may not receive grants.

The following sample is from a federally funded proposal. Note that in the actual proposal, references to the cost per student were removed by federal agency staff. This may have been to prevent readers from *calculating a formula* for what they believed to be the program's/agency's "preferred" cost figure.

> REASONABLENESS OF BUDGET
>
> Criterion: Costs are reasonable in relation to the objective of the project.
>
> Salaries and benefits are based upon institutional schedules and policies. Supplies have been computed on the basis of local vendor prices. Travel and communication costs in such a geographically isolated location may appear to be rather extensive. These have been kept to a minimum with rates on institutional policies.
>
> The overall cost per participant from federal funds amounts to \$________ the first year, decreasing to \$________ the second year and \$________ the third year. The budget is reasonable and cost-effective, particularly considering the geographic isolation of the target area.

The federal funding agency may also require a budget narrative. A budget narrative is an explanation of how the salaries, consultant services, equipment, and materials are related to the completion of each method or activity.

The Department of Education's most common budget information form for nonconstruction projects is Standard Form (SF)-424A. An example of a completed form is shown in figure 8.2. The instructions for completing SF-424A are shown in figure 8.3. If you have completed a project planner (see chapter 7), you already have all the information you need to complete SF-424A.

F. Evaluation

Objectives developed according to the methods suggested in chapter 7 contain the basic steps for evaluation. Most projects demand some sort of preassessment survey so that baseline data can be gathered. Once the intervention steps or model project has been employed, the original baseline data can be compared with posttest evaluation data to demonstrate change in the target population or reduction of the problem.

Using outside consultants to evaluate the project is preferred by many reviewers since this may encourage an unbiased, independent evaluation. By discussing the evaluation section with the prospective grantor before submitting the proposal, your grantseekers should be able to determine the funding source's preferences.

The evaluation section of your school's proposal must clearly delineate:

- what will be evaluated
- when the pre- and postevaluations will occur
- how much change is predicted
- who will perform the evaluation
- how much the evaluation component will cost

In the example provided on the Sample Project Planner (see chapter 7), West State University was named as the evaluator; thus the grantee would not be evaluating the effects of its own program. By including a few West State University professors in the proposal, the grantee built credibility and demonstrated the efficient use of local resources. Using West State University's computer resources and graduate students in the evaluation process also demonstrated the cost-effectiveness of the grantee's proposal.

G. Adequacy of Resources

Every proposal should include this information whether or not the funding source requests it because it lets the funder know why *your* school rather than another should receive a grant. You can play a particularly useful role in gathering this information by having the individuals and groups involved in grantseeking brainstorm a list of reasons why your school deserves a grant. The key is to focus on the resources or unique aspects of your school and its personnel that would appeal to the reviewer.

School Resources Worksheet

Complete the School Resources Worksheet (fig. 8.4) well in advance of your proposal's due date.

Completing the worksheet can be enjoyable and more worthwhile than it might appear at first glance. First, it encourages you to focus on the *positive* aspects of your school, and by brainstorming the positive, you actually combat the negative. Remember, funding sources are not interested in what is wrong with your school and how bad things are. They want to know what forces are at work to ensure success.

Second, the list of your school's positive attributes will empower your grantseekers as they begin to search for external funds. When a potential grantor asks them why their school should be chosen for a grant, they will be able to cite not one but several reasons.

Update your School Resources Worksheet annually and be sure to list all of your school's positive areas, including staff, advisory committees, and so on. The areas that most influence federal grantors and reviewers include equipment, supplies, and facilities.

- Equipment — Demonstrate that you have enough *standard* office equipment (e.g., desks, chairs, and so on) to support the additional staff called for in your proposal. If your proposal calls for nonstandard equipment such as modems and VCRs and you are not requesting funds from the grantor to purchase these items, make it clear in your proposal that they are being donated by you, the grantee, to the project. Your assurance that this equipment is available to support your project demonstrates that you have adequate resources.
- Supplies/Materials — Any supplies and/or materials that you will be making available should also be noted. This will strengthen your case.
- Facilities — Describe the facilities that will be used to support the project, especially unique or different types of facilities such as computer labs, swimming pools, and so on. If another organization will be will be involved in the project, your proposal should show how facilities will be jointly used or shared to ensure the success of the project.

H. Assurances

District officials will be required to provide signed assurances that the project will abide by a myriad of federal rules and regulations. Assurances deal with a wide range of issues such as drug-free workplaces and political lobbying. No doubt your district's central office has signed assurances in the past and will be able to help you in this process. For your general information, *The Catalogue of Federal Domestic Assistance* (CFDA) outlines the federal assurances that are required.

One area of assurances that many school districts overlook is human subjects review. It is not necessary for your school district to organize an Institutional Review Board (IRB) to examine every federal proposal to assure that the human subjects involved are treated humanely; however, as a grantee you should develop a relationship with your local college or university so that you can arrange to have *their* IRB review and approve your federal proposals.

I. Attachments

As we have seen, reactive grantseeking limits the time to write a proposal. Because of this, the applications of reactive grantseekers often have to be submitted without letters of support and agreement from cooperating organizations and community groups. This is a "red flag" to reviewers. It often diminishes potential grantees' credibility and results in the loss of valuable

Figure 8.2

OMB Approval No. 0348-0044

BUDGET INFORMATION — Non-Construction Programs

SECTION A – BUDGET SUMMARY

Grant Program Function or Activity (a)	Catalog of Federal Domestic Assistance Number (b)	Estimated Unobligated Funds		New or Revised Budget		
		Federal (c)	Non-Federal (d)	Federal (e)	Non-Federal (f)	Total (g)
1.		$	$	$	$	$
2.						
3.						
4.						
5. TOTALS		$	$	$	$	$

SECTION B – BUDGET CATEGORIES

6 Object Class Categories	GRANT PROGRAM, FUNCTION OR ACTIVITY				Total (5)
	(1)	(2)	(3)	(4)	
a. Personnel	$	$	$	$	$
b. Fringe Benefits					
c. Travel					
d. Equipment					
e. Supplies					
f. Contractual					
g. Construction					
h. Other					
i. Total Direct Charges (sum of 6a - 6h)					
j. Indirect Charges					
k. TOTALS (sum of 6i and 6j)	$	$	$	$	$
7. Program Income	$	$	$	$	$

Standard Form 424A (4-88)
Prescribed by OMB Circular A-102

Figure 8.2 continued

SECTION C - NON-FEDERAL RESOURCES				
(a) Grant Program	(b) Applicant	(c) State	(d) Other Sources	(e) TOTALS
8.	$	$	$	$
9.				
10.				
11.				
12. TOTALS (sum of lines 8 and 11)	$	$	$	$

SECTION D - FORECASTED CASH NEEDS					
	Total for 1st Year	1st Quarter	2nd Quarter	3rd Quarter	4th Quarter
13. Federal	$	$	$	$	$
14. NonFederal					
15. TOTAL (sum of lines 13 and 14)	$	$	$	$	$

SECTION E - BUDGET ESTIMATES OF FEDERAL FUNDS NEEDED FOR BALANCE OF THE PROJECT				
(a) Grant Program	FUTURE FUNDING PERIODS (Years)			
	(b) First	(c) Second	(d) Third	(e) Fourth
16.	$	$	$	$
17.				
18.				
19.				
20. TOTALS (sum of lines 16-19)	$	$	$	$

SECTION F - OTHER BUDGET INFORMATION (Attach additional Sheets if Necessary)	
21. Direct Charges:	22. Indirect Charges:
23. Remarks	

SF 424A (4-88) Page 2
Prescribed by OMB Circular A-102

Figure 8.3

INSTRUCTIONS FOR THE SF-424A

General Instructions

This form is designed so that application can be made for funds from one or more grant programs. In preparing the budget, adhere to any existing Federal grantor agency guidelines which prescribe how and whether budgeted amounts should be separately shown for different functions or activities within the program. For some programs, grantor agencies may require budgets to be separately shown by function or activity. For other programs, grantor agencies may require a breakdown by function or activity. Sections A, B, C, and D should include budget estimates for the whole project except when applying for assistance which requires Federal authorization in annual or other funding period increments. In the latter case, Sections A, B, C, and D should provide the budget for the first budget period (usually a year) and Section E should present the need for Federal assistance in the subsequent budget periods. All applications should contain a breakdown by the object class categories shown in Lines a — k of Section B.

Section A. Budget Summary

Lines 1 – 4, Columns (a) and (b)

For applications pertaining to a *single* Federal grant program (Federal Domestic Assistance Catalog number) and *not requiring* a functional or activity breakdown, enter on Line 1 under Column (a) the catalog program title and the catalog number in Column (b).

For applications pertaining to a *single* program *requiring* budget amounts by multiple functions or activities, enter the name of each activity or function on each line in Column (a), and enter the catalog number in Column (b). For applications pertaining to multiple programs where none of the programs require a breakdown by function or activity, enter the catalog program title on each line in *column* (a) and the respective catalog number on each line in Column (b).

For applications pertaining to *multiple* programs where one or more programs *require* a breakdown by function or activity, prepare a separate sheet for each program requiring the breakdown. Additional sheets should be used when one form does not provide adequate space for all breakdown of data required. However, when more than one sheet is used, the first page should provide the summary totals by programs.

Lines 1 – 4, Columns (c) through (g.)

For new applications, leave Columns (c) and (d) blank. For each line entry in Columns (a) and (b), enter in Columns (e), (f), and (g) the appropriate amounts of funds needed to support the project for the first funding period (usually a year).

For continuing grant program applications, submit these forms before the end of each funding period as required by the grantor agency. Enter in Columns (c) and (d) the estimated amounts of funds which will remain unobligated at the end of the grant funding period only if the Federal grantor agency instructions provide for this. Otherwise, leave these columns blank. Enter in columns (e) and (f) the amounts of funds needed for the upcoming period. The amount(s) in Column (g) should be the sum of amounts in Columns (e) and (f).

For supplemental grants and changes to existing grants, do not use Columns (c) and (d). Enter in Column (e) the amount of the increase or decrease of Federal funds and enter in Column (f) the amount of the increase or decrease of non-Federal funds. In Column (g) enter the new total budgeted amount (Federal and non-Federal) which includes the total previous authorized budgeted amounts plus or minus, as appropriate, the amounts shown in Columns (e) and (f). The amount(s) in Column (g) should not equal the sum of amounts in Columns (e) and (f).

Line 5 – Show the totals for all columns used.

Section B Budget Categories

In the column headings (1) through (4), enter the titles of the same programs, functions, and activities shown on Lines 1 – 4 , Column (a), Section A. When additional sheets are prepared for Section A, provide similar column headings on each sheet. For each program, function or activity, fill in the total requirements for funds (both Federal and non-Federal) by object class categories.

Lines 6a – i – Show the totals of Lines 6a to 6h in each column.

Line 6j – Show the amount of indirect cost.

Line 6k – Enter the total of amounts on Lines 6i and 6j. For all applications for new grants and continuation grants the total amount in column (5), Line 6k, should be the same as the total amount shown in Section A, Column (g), Line 5. For supplemental grants and changes to grants, the total amount of the increase or decrease as shown in Columns (1) — (4), Line 6k should be the same as the sum of the amounts in Section A, Columns (e) and (f) on Line 5.

Line 7 — Enter the estimated amount of income, if any, expected to be generated from this project. Do not add or subtract this amount from the total project amount. Show under the program narrative statement the nature and source of income. The estimated amount of program income may be considered by the federal grantor agency in determining the total amount of the grant.

Section C. Non-Federal-Resources

Lines 8 – 11 — Enter amounts of non-Federal resources that will be used on the grant. If in-kind contributions are included, provide a brief explanation on a separate sheet.

Column (a) — Enter the program titles identical to Column (a), Section A. A breakdown by function or activity is not necessary.

Column (b) — Enter the contribution to be made by the applicant.

Column (c) — Enter the amount of the State's cash and in-kind contribution if the applicant is not a State or State agency. Applicants which are a State or State agencies should leave this column blank.

Column (d) — Enter the amount of cash and in-kind contributions to be made from all other sources.

Figure 8.3 continued

Column (e) — Enter totals of Columns (b), (c), and (d).

Line 12 — Enter the total for each of Columns (b) — (e). The amount in Column (e) should be equal to the amount on Line 5, column (f), Section A.

Section D. Forecasted Cash Needs

Line 13 — Enter the amount of cash needed by quarter from the grantor agency during the first year.

Line 14 — Enter the amount of cash from all other sources needed by quarter during the first year.

Line 15 — Enter the totals of amounts on Lines 13 and 14.

Section E. Budget Estimates of Federal Funds Needed for Balance of the Project.

Lines 16 - 19 — Enter in Column (a) the same grant program titles shown in Column (a), Section A. A breakdown by function or activity is not necessary. For new applications and continuation grant applications, enter in the proper columns amounts of Federal funds which will be needed to complete the program or project over the succeeding funding periods (usually in years). This section need not be completed for revisions (amendments, changes, or supplements) to funds for the current year of existing grants.

If more than four lines are needed to list the program titles, submit additional schedules as necessary.

Line 20 — Enter the total for each of the Columns (b) - (e). When additional schedules are prepared for this Section, annotate accordingly and show the overall totals on this line.

Section F. Other Budget Information

Line 21 — Use this space to explain amounts for individual direct object-class cost categories that may appear to be out of the ordinary or to explain the details as required by the Federal grantor agency.

Line 22 — Enter the type of indirect rate (provisional, predetermined, final or fixed) that will be in effect during the funding period, the estimated amount of the base to which the rate is applied, and the total indirect expense.

Line 23 — Provide any other explanations or comments deemed necessary.

SF 424A (4-88)

points. Be sure to take the time to gather your letters of support and agreement in advance.

It is a good idea to include your Project Planner as an attachment. Other attachments may include maps, pictures, a layout of your school's building, support data for the statement of need, surveys, and questionnaires.

Reviewers find it helpful when you reference the attachments in the body of your proposal and include a separate table of contents for the attachment section.

CHAPTER 8 CHECKLIST

Evaluation and Planning Worksheet

Which of the following checklists, files, and/or worksheets are already a part of your grants system? Which would you like to add or incorporate into your system?

1. The Federal Grantseekers' Proposal Checklist
   _____ Already Part of Grants System
   _____ Add to Grants System
2. Federal Grants File Containing Samples of the Materials Listed on the Federal Grantseekers' Proposal Checklist
   _____ Already Part of Grants System
   _____ Add to Grants System
3. School Resource Worksheets Compiled into One Comprehensive List of Your School's Positive Attributes
   _____ Already Part of Grants System
   _____ Add to Grants System

Figure 8.4

SCHOOL RESOURCES WORKSHEET

When considering a grant to our school, the funding source will want to be assured that we have the resources to carry out the proposed project. The prospective funding source will want to know what we are good at. Please take a few minutes to help our school put its best foot forward. Prepare a list of possible answers to the grantor's question of why our school should be awarded a grant.

Resources We Can Offer:

- Buildings, Facilities, Space

- Equipment—Computers, etc.

- Supplies/Materials

- Unique Arrangements with Other Organizations

- Our Geographic Location

- Student Composition/Makeup

- Uniqueness of Faculty, Staff

- Awards, Honors, or Other Recognition We Have Received

- Other Unique, Interesting Credibility Builders

CHAPTER NINE

$ Improving Your School's Federal Proposals through a Quality Assurance Program

The main purposes of this chapter are to outline a method for you to improve the proposals your school submits to federal agencies and to review basic information on submission, application transmittal, signature requirements, and the intergovernmental review of federal proposals.

The quality of the proposal your grantseekers submit to the federal funding source will influence how peer reviewers and agency staff *view your school* and *your grantseekers* for many years to come. Just as teachers do not easily forget a bad impression made by a student, reviewers and government staff members do not easily forget the negative impression created by a poorly constructed proposal.

Your school's proposal should be reviewed prior to submittal in order to guarantee that you are sending the federal grantor a proposal you can be proud of and that represents your school's best effort. Even if your proposal is not selected for funding, putting it through a presubmittal review will assure you that it was the high level of competition rather than careless mistakes that accounted for its rejection.

By this time most grantseekers are tired. They want to submit their proposal and get it out of their lives. But you cannot allow them to jeopardize all their hard work by submitting a proposal that has not passed the last test — the mock review. The principal's role in quality control cannot be overemphasized. By instituting and supporting the mock-review process, you give your school's grantseeking effort the attention and credibility that will result in more submissions and greater success.

The more you know about the review system used by the prospective federal grantor, the more closely you can simulate the mock review, and the greater the benefits. Through preproposal contact, your grantseekers should have developed some insights into how the granting agency selects reviewers, the reviewers' backgrounds, and what type of scoring system they follow. This type of information will help you carry out a mock review that closely resembles the official review.

Your grantseekers must be ahead of the submission deadline by at least several days in order to perform a mock review. One way to ensure that there is time for this exercise is to state on your School Grantseekers' Preproposal Endorsement Worksheet that your office *requires* a mock review before it will sign the final proposal and submit it to the district central office. To assure that compliance, instruct your grantseekers to turn the proposal over to you several days before the deadline. This will let your grantseekers know well before they submit the proposal what is expected of them.

The term *quality circle* best describes the mock review process. Invite a few volunteers who are dedicated to improving education and who share a concern for your school's image and reputation to participate in the circle. The participants need not be experts in the grants field or in your proposal's particular subject area. In fact, while you want the quality circle members to resemble the levels of expertise of the reviewers on the federal review committee, you should also invite several individuals with a "clean" perspective to participate. For example, ask a business leader from your grants advisory committee, a college student, a secretary, and/or an accountant. These many different perspectives will help expose your proposal's weaknesses and strengths.

Your help in organizing the mock review will impress on the volunteers the importance of the process. You can either telephone candidates or ask them in writing or in person to participate in the mock-review process. Let them know that your proposal's chance of success will be greatly improved through this presubmission review and that you are asking them to participate because you need their fresh perspective. Brief them on the general approach you would like them to take. It is important to tell them that while you would like the mock review to be as rigorous as possible, this does not mean that they must spend vast amounts of time reading the proposal. You will ask them to spend only as much time reading the proposal as the actual reviewers do, and some of them read proposals pretty quickly! Tell them that you will send them a package that includes a description of the background and types of reviewers, the time allotted to read each proposal, and the scoring system that the reviewers will use. Make sure they know that they do not have to be experts in the subject but that they should make every attempt to read the proposal from the real reviewers' points of view. The sample letter in figure 9.1 can be used to invite individuals to participate in your quality circle.

Each federal agency that makes grants follows a different system for reviewing proposals. For instance, the National Science Foundation's system is very different from the system used by the National Endowment for the Humanities; and the National Endowment for the Humanities' system is much different from that of the Department of Education. These differences in selection criteria and scoring emphasize the need for preproposal contact with the funder and early data gathering about the review process.

Have your grantseekers try to obtain the following information from the granting agency:

Figure 9.1

SAMPLE LETTER INVITING INDIVIDUAL TO PARTICIPATE IN FEDERAL PROPOSAL QUALITY CIRCLE

Date

Name
Address

Dear ________________:

I would like to take this opportunity to follow up on our conversation to secure your input in helping our school district submit the very best grant proposal possible. We are asking that you review the enclosed proposal from the point of view of a federal reviewer. The attached materials will help you role-play the actual manner in which this proposal will be evaluated.

Please read the information on the reviewers' backgrounds and the scoring system and limit the time you spend reading the proposal to the time constraints that the real reviewers will observe. A Quality Circle Scoring Worksheet has been provided to assist you in recording your scores and comments.

A meeting of all the mock reviewers comprising our quality circle has been scheduled for [date __________]. Please bring this worksheet with you to the meeting. The meeting will last less than one hour. Its purpose is to analyze the scores and brainstorm suggestions to improve the proposal.

Sincerely,

Name
Phone Number

- **Where and How the Review Occurs** — Are the reviewers mailed a package of proposals and asked to review them at home? Do the reviewers meet at one place to review the proposals? If so, for how long? Provide this information to your volunteers and replicate the situation.
- **The Average Time Spent Reading Each Proposal** — Most reviewers are very busy people, and the time they spend reading proposals varies greatly.
- **The Number of Proposals Each Reviewer Is Responsible for Evaluating** — A key element in your role playing is to ask your volunteers to think of your proposal as the last one in a pile of proposals. In other words, if the reviewer is responsible for reading 10 proposals, your school's should be thought of as the tenth.

At the very least, you *must* give the members of your quality circle the point system and time constraints they should abide by. Volunteer mock reviewers often want to do such a good job that they spend more time reviewing the proposal than the real reviewers will! Make sure your mock reviewers understand that spending an inordinate amount of time reviewing the proposal will be counterproductive to what you are trying to accomplish through role playing.

In general, the Education Department uses a review system known as EDGAR (Education Department General Administrative Regulation). However, not every agency in the Education Depart-ment follows EDGAR. Some have their own published regulations with a specific set of criteria for evaluating and judging applications for grants. If the agency you are approaching does not have a set of published guidelines, it probably follows EDGAR, but always double check through preproposal contact.

EDGAR's main areas of evaluation include:

1. How the proposed project meets the purposes of the authorizing statute.
2. The extent of the need for the project.
3. How the plan of operation meets the need.
4. The availability of qualified key personnel to implement the plan.
5. Whether the budget is cost-effective and relative to the plan.
6. How the plan's progress in meeting the objectives will be evaluated.
7. Whether the applicant has sufficient resources to house the project and support the plan.

In order to help your volunteers review and evaluate your school's proposal from the proper perspective, provide them with the Selection Criteria Overview (fig. 9.2) and the Scoring Distribution Worksheet (fig. 9.3).

It is important that your grantseekers verify that the point values suggested in parentheses on the Selection Criteria Overview are accurate for each grant program they plan to approach. This verification should be done in preproposal contact with the funding source. In some cases, federal officials may make changes in the point values to reflect a shift in emphasis or to allow grantees with special circumstances to score higher in the review process.

Review with your Quality Circle the Selection Criteria Over-view and the points assigned to each section. Refer them to the Scoring Distribution Worksheet for help in allocating points. The purpose of the Scoring Distribution Worksheet is to promote consistency in scoring within the range of points allowed for each section. Emphasize the need for a candid evaluation and ask the mock reviewers to avoid inflating a positive score or comment in one section to "make up" for a low score or comment in another.

Each mock reviewer should be given a Technical Review Package (fig. 9.4). The worksheets in the Technical Review Package are very similar to those used by the federal reviewers, which makes the mock review resemble the real review as much as possible. In addition, getting acquainted with these worksheets gives the

Figure 9.2

SELECTION CRITERIA OVERVIEW

Meeting the Purposes of the Authorizing Statute (5 pts)

1) What are the purposes of the authorizing statute?
2) What are the objectives of this project?
3) How will these objectives further the purposes of the authorizing statute?

Extent of Need for the Project (25 pts)

1) What needs are outlined by the authorizing statute?
2) What needs does the applicant identify?
3) How did the applicant identify those needs, i.e., what specific documentation or evidence does the application offer to support the applicant's assessment of need?
4) Are the needs identified by the applicant consistent with the purposes of the authorizing statute?
5) Does the applicant identify too many or too few needs for the proposed time frame and resources of the project?
6) Are the outlined needs well defined so that the project can be focused on them, or are the outlined needs very generic?

Plan of Operation (20 pts)

1) Do the project objectives serve the purposes of the authorizing statute?
2) How well is the project designed? Are project objectives consistent with stated needs? Are project activities consistent with project objectives? Are project objectives measurable?
3) How will the applicant use its resources and personnel to achieve each objective?
4) Has the applicant developed an effective management plan that will ensure proper and efficient administration of the project?
5) Do project milestones represent a logical progression of times and tasks?
6) Does the applicant propose a realistic time schedule for accomplishing objectives?
7) Will the proposed activities accomplish the project's objectives successfully?
8) Are the educational approaches planned based on sound research that indicates they will be successful for the population to be served?
9) Does the project have clearly developed provisions for providing equal access to eligible participants who are members of traditionally underrepresented groups (racial or ethnic minorities, women, handicapped persons, elderly persons)?

Quality of Key Personnel (15 pts)

1) Do the job descriptions adequately reflect skills needed to make the project work?
2) Are the duties of personnel clearly defined?
3) What relevant qualifications do the proposed personnel possess, especially the Project Director? (Focus on their experience and training in fields related to the objectives of the project, though other information may be considered.)
4) Will proposed personnel need to be trained for the project?
5) How much time will the proposed personnel actually devote to the project?
6) To what extent does the applicant encourage employment applications from members of traditionally underrepresented groups (ethnic or racial minorities, women, handicapped persons, elderly persons)?

Budget and Cost Effectiveness (10 pts)

1) Is the budget adequate to support the project's proposed activities?
2) Are overall project costs reasonable in relation to project objectives?
3) How much of the project's total cost is devoted to administrative costs?
4) Are budget items sufficiently justified?
5) Is the budget padded?

Evaluation Plan (15 pts)

1) Are the proposed methods of evaluation appropriate to the project?
2) Will the proposed evaluation be objective?
3) Will the proposed evaluation methods measure the effectiveness of project activities in meeting project objectives?
4) Will the evaluation plan produce valid and reliable data concerning the accomplishment of project objectives?
5) Does the evaluation plan measure the project's effect on the project audience?

Adequacy of Resources (10 pts)

1) Are the proposed facilities adequate for project purposes?
2) Is the proposed equipment adequate for project purposes?
3) Does the applicant have access to special sources of experience or expertise?

Figure 9.3

SCORING DISTRIBUTION WORKSHEET

Scoring

The numerical scores you assign to an application's response to the selection criteria must be consistent with the comments you write. Comments and scores should reflect the same overall assessment. You should never attempt to mitigate a negative comment with a positive score, or vice versa.

Comments indicate whether the application's response to the selection criteria is poor, adequate, or good; scores indicate how poor, adequate, or good. If 10 points are possible, 0–2 points is poor, 5–7 points is adequate, and 8–9 points is superior. Four points will indicate a response that is merely weak, whereas 8 points will indicate a response that is above average. Whatever amount of total points is possible, use the midpoint of the scale as adequate and choose your scores accordingly. Do not hesitate to use the full range of points. It is perfectly acceptable to assign a score of 10 or 1, for example. Your guiding rule should be consistency in rating.

Always go back and check your scores to make sure that you have written them correctly and used the appropriate point scale. You should also double-check the scores on the summary page of the Technical Review Form to make sure that they match the scores listed under each selection criterion and that the final total has been computed without error.

You may want to use the following table as a guide when assigning points:

Total	Poor	Weak	Adequate	Superior	Outstanding
25	0–8	9–12	13–19	20–23	24–25
20	0–6	7–9	10–15	16–18	19–20
15	0–4	5–7	8–11	12–13	14–45
10	0–2	3–4	5–7	8–9	10
5	0–1	2	3	4	5

mock reviewers experience that will prove valuable should they ever get the opportunity to "really" review federal grant applications and proposals.

The principal's office (or the grants office) can reproduce the worksheets in the Technical Review Package. Providing them to your mock reviewers in the form of a package will keep the committee focused on each section of the proposal and on the important areas each section contains.

The one major difference in the worksheets your reviewers will be using and those used by the actual reviewers is in the request for suggestions for improvement. As the mock reviewers identify the weaknesses in the proposal, ask them to list any suggestions they have to reduce or eliminate the weaknesses. Stress that the proposal developers still have a few days to

Figure 9.4

TECHNICAL REVIEW PACKAGE

Technical Review Form

School Application No.

CFDA No. ________________

Federal Program: ____

Applicant Organization:

Selection Criteria	Maximum Points	Assigned Points
Meeting Purposes of Statute		
Need for Project		
Plan of Operation		
Quality of Key Personnel		
Budget Cost Effectiveness		
Evaluation Plan		
Adequacy of Resources		
Total Points		

SUMMARY COMMENTS

Strengths:

Weaknesses:

Suggestions for Improvement:

Meeting the Purposes of the Authorizing Statute

Maximum Points _______ Awarded _______

1) What are the purposes of the authorizing statute?

2) What are the objectives of this project?

3) How will these objectives further the purposes of the authorizing statute?

Strengths:

Weaknesses and Suggestions for Improvement:

Figure 9.4 continued

Extent of the Need for the Project

Maximum Points _______ Awarded _______

1) What needs are outlined by the authorizing statute?

2) What needs does the applicant identify?

3) How did the applicant identify those needs; i.e., what specific documentation or evidence does the application offer to support the applicant's assessment of need?

4) Are the needs identified by the applicant consistent with the purposes of the authorizing statute?

5) Does the applicant identify too many or too few needs for the proposed time frame and resources of the project?

6) Are the outlined needs well defined so that the project can be focused on them, or are the outlined needs very generic?

Strengths:

Weaknesses and Suggestions for Improvement:

Plan of Operation

Maximum Points _______ Awarded _______

1) Do the project objectives serve the purposes of the authorizing statute?

2) How well is the project designed?

Are project objectives consistent with stated needs?

Are project activities consistent with project objectives?

Are project objectives measurable?

Figure 9.4 continued

3) **How will the applicant use its resources and personnel to achieve each objective?**

4) **Has the applicant developed an effective management plan that will ensure proper and efficient administration of the project?**

5) **Do project milestones represent a logical progression of times and tasks?**

6) **Does the applicant propose a realistic time schedule for accomplishing objectives?**

7) **Will the proposed activities accomplish the project's objectives successfully?**

8) **Are the educational approaches planned based on sound research that indicates they will be successful for the population to be served?**

9) **Does the project have clearly developed plans for providing equal access to eligible participants who are members of traditionally underrepresented groups (racial or ethnic minorities, women, handicapped persons, elderly persons)?**

Strengths:

Weaknesses and Suggestions for Improvement:

Quality of Key Personnel

Maximum Points _______ Awarded _______

1) **Do the job descriptions adequately reflect skills needed to make the project work?**

2) **Are the duties of personnel clearly defined?**

3) **What relevant qualifications do the proposed personnel possess, especially the Project Director? (Focus on their experience and training in fields related to the objectives of the project, though other information may be considered.)**

Figure 9.4 continued

4) **Will proposed personnel need to be trained for the project?**

5) **How much time will the proposed personnel actually devote to the project?**

6) **To what extent does the applicant encourage employment applications from members of traditionally underrepresented groups (ethnic or racial minorities, women, handicapped persons, elderly persons)?**

Strengths:

Weaknesses and Suggestions for Improvement:

Budget and Cost Effectiveness

Maximum Points _______ Awarded _______

1) **Is the budget adequate to support the project's proposed activities?**

2) **Are overall project costs reasonable in relation to project objectives?**

3) **How much of the project's total cost is devoted to administrative costs?**

4) **Are budget items sufficiently justified?**

5) **Is the budget padded?**

Strengths:

Weaknesses and Suggestions for Improvement:

Figure 9.4 continued

Evaluation Plan

Maximum Points ________ Awarded ________

1) **Are the proposed methods of evaluation appropriate to the project?**

2) **Is the proposed evaluation be objective?**

3) **Will the proposed evaluation methods measure the effectiveness of project activities in meeting project objectives?**

4) **Will the evaluation plan produce valid and reliable data concerning the accomplishment of project objectives?**

5) **Does the evaluation plan measure the project's effect on the project audience?**

Strengths:

Weaknesses and Suggestions for Improvement:

Adequacy of Resources

Maximum Points ________ Awarded ________

1) **Are the proposed facilities adequate for project purposes?**

2) **Will the proposed equipment adequate for project purposes?**

3) **Does the applicant have access to special sources of experience or expertise?**

Strengths:

Weaknesses and Suggestions for Improvement:

incorporate their ideas and suggestions into the proposal.

Your volunteers can review the proposal at home or work, or they may prefer to meet to score the proposal and discuss its positive and negative points. The arrangement you decide on will be based upon how the federal reviewers perform the review. Performing the mock review in a group enables the principal to play a key role as the group facilitator. It is best if the proposal writers are not at this meeting so that the group members will be as candid as possible.

Ask the volunteers to read the proposal and to evaluate and score each section before moving on to the next. Have them put a plus sign (+) beside those areas they think the reviewer will consider positive and a minus sign (-) beside those areas they think will be viewed negatively. Stress that identifying both the positive *and* negative aspects of each section will help the proposal developers understand the mock reviewers scores and enable them to improve the negative areas of their proposal without changing the positive aspects.

Send or give your volunteer reviewers the Quality Circle Information Worksheet (fig. 9.5) and any additional information you and your grantseekers have gathered that might help them. For example, information on last year's grantees may be useful, especially if the mix of grantees is likely to remain the same.

Review with your proposal developers the score each section of the proposal received from the volunteer reviewers. Pay particular attention to the positive points. Then have them focus on how to improve areas that did not score well. Although your proposal writers will be able to explain most of the problem areas to you verbally, remind them that they will not get this opportunity in the real review. By coordinating the mock review process while not participating in the actual critique, you are in a perfect position to summarize the volunteers' scores and comments and to review them in a nonthreatening manner with the grantseekers.

When rewriting and retyping of the proposal are required, it is especially important for you to volunteer any support services your office can offer. Remember, your grant writers are probably beginning to get tired at this point. Think of them as race horses in the home stretch. They may need a little prodding to get to the finish line, but don't push them too hard. This is exactly the time when a true leader will display his or her skills at getting volunteers and staff to put in the extra effort that translates into grants success. For example, making your secretary available for editing will go a long way in ensuring that the mock reviewers' suggestions are incorporated into an improved proposal. Once all the necessary revisions have been made, your school's proposal will finally be ready for submittal.

- **Submittal**

  In most cases, Standard Form (SF) 424 (see fig. 9.6) must be attached as a facesheet to grant applications or proposals

Figure 9.5

QUALITY CIRCLE INFORMATION WORKSHEET

The following information is being provided to assist you in reviewing the attached federal grant application/proposal.

The Setting — The proposals are read at:

_______ the reviewer's location
_______ the federal agency's location
_______ other site selected by the federal agency

The Time Factor

Number of proposals the reviewer evaluates: _________

Amount of time the reviewer spends evaluating each proposal: _________

Background of Reviewers

Age Range: _________

Educational Background: ____

____

Known Viewpoints or Biases: ____________________________________

____

List of Last Year's Reviewers Available? _____ yes ___ no
(If yes, please attach)__

Other Information

Applications/proposals received by the agency last year: # _________

Grants awarded by the agency last year: # _________

$ Range for proposals from schools such as ours: $ _____

being submitted to a federal agency. Instructions for completing this form are shown in figure 9.7.

The proposal should not be bound or stapled together unless the funder gives permission to do so. Usually federal funders prefer that proposals be clipped with pressure tension clips so that they can remove or add forms as needed.

- **Application Transmittal**
  The federal application package will contain specific directions on how to transmit your school's proposal by mail or hand delivery. The following instructions have been taken from the Department of Education's federal guidelines. However, note that the various federal granting agencies have different rules regarding transmittal.

  There are two key elements in submitting federal proposals and transmitting applications: (1) the submittal and transmittal processes outlined by the funding agency should be strictly adhered to; (2)

Figure 9.6

OMB Approval No. 0348-0043

APPLICATION FOR FEDERAL ASSISTANCE

1. TYPE OF SUBMISSION: *Application* ☐ Construction ☐ Non-Construction; *Preapplication* ☐ Construction ☐ Non-Construction	2. DATE SUBMITTED	Applicant Identifier
	3. DATE RECEIVED BY STATE	State Application Identifier
	4. DATE RECEIVED BY FEDERAL AGENCY	Federal Identifier

5. APPLICANT INFORMATION

Legal Name:	Organizational Unit:
Address *(give city, county, state, and zip code)*:	Name and telephone number of the person to be contacted on matters involving this application *(give area code)*

6. EMPLOYER IDENTIFICATION NUMBER (EIN): ☐☐ – ☐☐☐☐☐☐☐

7. TYPE OF APPLICANT: *(enter appropriate letter in box)* ☐

A. State
B. County
C. Municipal
D. Township
E. Interstate
F. Intermunicipal
G. Special District
H. Independent School Dist.
I. State Controlled Institution of Higher Learning
J. Private University
K. Indian Tribe
L. Individual
M. Profit Organization
N. Other (Specify): ____________

8. TYPE OF APPLICATION:

☒ New ☐ Continuation ☐ Revision

If Revision, enter appropriate letter(s) in box(es): ☐ ☐

A. Increase Award B. Decrease Award C. Increase Duration
D. Decrease Duration Other *(specify)*: ____________

9. NAME OF FEDERAL AGENCY:

U. S. Department of Education

10. CATALOG OF FEDERAL DOMESTIC ASSISTANCE NUMBER: 84-201

C.D. 3/26/92

TITLE: School Dropout Demonstration Assistance Program

11. DESCRIPTIVE TITLE OF APPLICANT'S PROJECT:

12. AREAS AFFECTED BY PROJECT *(cities, counties, states, etc.)*:

13. PROPOSED PROJECT:		14. CONGRESSIONAL DISTRICTS OF:	
Start Date	Ending Date	a. Applicant	b. Project

15. ESTIMATED FUNDING:	
a. Federal	$ .00
b. Applicant	$ .00
c. State	$ .00
d. Local	$ .00
e. Other	$ .00
f. Program Income	$ .00
g. TOTAL	$ .00

16. IS APPLICATION SUBJECT TO REVIEW BY STATE EXECUTIVE ORDER 12372 PROCESS?

a. YES. THIS PREAPPLICATION/APPLICATION WAS MADE AVAILABLE TO THE STATE EXECUTIVE ORDER 12372 PROCESS FOR REVIEW ON:

DATE ____________

b. NO. ☐ PROGRAM IS NOT COVERED BY E.O. 12372

☐ OR PROGRAM HAS NOT BEEN SELECTED BY STATE FOR REVIEW

17. IS THE APPLICANT DELINQUENT ON ANY FEDERAL DEBT?

☐ Yes If "Yes," attach an explanation. ☐ No

18. TO THE BEST OF MY KNOWLEDGE AND BELIEF, ALL DATA IN THIS APPLICATION/PREAPPLICATION ARE TRUE AND CORRECT, THE DOCUMENT HAS BEEN DULY AUTHORIZED BY THE GOVERNING BODY OF THE APPLICANT AND THE APPLICANT WILL COMPLY WITH THE ATTACHED ASSURANCES IF THE ASSISTANCE IS AWARDED

a. Typed Name of Authorized Representative	b. Title	c. Telephone number
d. Signature of Authorized Representative		e. Date Signed

Previous Editions Not Usable

Standard Form 424 (REV 4-88)
Prescribed by OMB Circular A-102

Figure 9.7

INSTRUCTIONS FOR THE SF 424

This is a standard form used by applicants as a required facesheet for preapplications and applications submitted for Federal assistance. It will be used by Federal agencies to obtain applicant certification that States which have established a review and comment procedure in response to Executive Order 12372 and have selected the program to be included in their process, have been given an opportunity to review the applicant's submission.

Item:	Entry:
1.	Self-explanatory.
2.	Date application submitted to Federal agency (or State if applicable) & applicant's control number (if applicable).
3.	State use only (if applicable).
4.	If this application is to continue or revise an existing award, enter present Federal identifier number. If for a new project, leave blank.
5.	Legal name of applicant, name of primary organizational unit which will undertake the assistance activity, complete address of the applicant, and name and telephone number of the person to contact on matters related to this application.
6.	Enter Employer Identification Number (EIN) as assigned by the Internal Revenue Service.
7.	Enter the appropriate letter in the space provided.
8.	Check appropriate box and enter appropriate letter(s) in the space(s) provided: —"New"means a new assistance award. —"Continuation" means an extension for an additional funding/budget period for a project with a projected completion date. —"Revision" means any change in the Federal Government's financial obligation or contingent liability from an existing obligation.
9.	Name of Federal agency from which assistance is being requested with this application.
10.	Use the Catalog of Federal Domestic Assistance number and title of the program under which assistance is requested.
11.	Enter a brief descriptive title of the project. If more than one program is involved, you should append an explanation on a separate sheet. If appropriate (e.g., construction or real property projects), attach a map showing project location. For preapplications, use a separate sheet to provide a summary description of this project.
12.	List only the largest political entities affected (e.g., State, counties, cities).
13.	Self-explanatory.
14.	List the applicant's Congressional District and any District(s) affected by the program or project.
15.	Amount requested or to be contributed during the first funding/budget period by each contributor. Value of in-kind contributions should be included on appropriate lines as applicable. If the action will result in a dollar change to an existing award, indicate *only* the amount of the change. For decreases, enclose the amounts in parentheses. If both basic and supplemental amounts are included, show breakdown on an attached sheet. For multiple program funding, use totals and show breakdown using same categories as item 15.
16.	Applicants should contact the State Single Point of Contact (SPOC) for Federal Executive Order 12372 to determine whether the application is subject to the State intergovernmental review process.
17.	This question applies to the applicant organization, not the person who signs as the authorized representative. Categories of debt include delinquent audit disallowances, loans and taxes.
18.	To be signed by the authorized representative of the applicant. A copy of the governing body's authorization for you to sign this application as official representative must be on file in the applicant's office. (Certain Federal agencies may require that this authorization be submitted as part of the application.)

your school's proposal should be submitted *early*, not merely on time. Submitting a week early demonstrates to the granting agency that your school is well organized. In addition, federal bureaucrats may correlate the timely submittal of your proposal with the timely submittal of the reports required after funding, which favorably impresses officials who have to oversee and administer many grants.

Figure 9.8

APPLICATION TRANSMITTAL INSTRUCTIONS

An application for an award must be mailed or hand delivered by the closing date.

Applications Delivered by Mail

An application sent by mail must be addressed to the U.S. Department of Education, Application Control Center, Attention: CFDA Number _____, 400 Maryland Avenue, SW, Washington, D.C. 20202-4725.

An application must show proof of mailing consisting of one of the following:

(1) A legibly dated U.S. Postal Service postmark.
(2) A legible mail receipt with the date of mailing stamped by the U.S. Postal Service.
(3) A dated shipping label, invoice, or receipt from a commercial carrier.
(4) Any other proof of mailing acceptable to the U.S. Secretary of Education.

If an application is sent through the U.S. Postal Service, the Secretary does not accept either of the following as proof of mailing:

(1) A private metered postmark, or
(2) A mail receipt that is not dated by the U.S. Postal Service.

An applicant should note that the U.S. Postal Service does not uniformly provide a dated postmark. Before relying on this method, an applicant should check with the local post office.

An applicant is encouraged to use registered or at least first class mail.

Late applicants will be notified that their applications will not be considered.

Applications Delivered by Hand/Courier Service

An application that is hand delivered must be taken to the U.S. Department of Education, Application Control Center, Room 3633, General Services Administration National Capital Region, 7th and D Streets, SW., Washington, D.C. 20202-4725.

The Application Control Center will accept deliveries between 8:00 a.m. and 4:30 p.m. (Washington, D.C.) daily, except Saturdays, Sundays, and federal holidays.

Individuals delivering applications must use the D Street Entrance. Proper identification is necessary to enter the building.

In order for an application sent through a courier service to be considered timely, the courier service must be in receipt of the application on or before the closing date.

- **Necessary Signatures and Other Requirements**
  Your school's federal grant application cover letter and assurances must be signed by your authorized district representative. Your district grants office may help you procure the necessary signatures and meet all of the requirements. These may include signed and dated school board resolutions that endorse the grant application and any matching or in-kind contributions associated with the grant.

- **Intergovernmental Review**
  The purpose of intergovernmental proposal review is to provide a mechanism for coordinating federally funded projects with state plans. This review process reduces the chances of the federal government supporting a program that a state has decided should not be part of its plan or that does not take the direction that the state wishes. Not all federal programs require an intergovernmental review, and not all

Figure 9.9

STATE SINGLE POINTS OF CONTACT

ALABAMA
Mrs. Moncell Thornell
State Single Point of Contact
Alabama Department of Economic & Community Affairs
3465 Norman Bridge Road
P.O. Box 250347
Montgomery, Alabama 36125-0347
Telephone: (205) 284-8905

ARIZONA
Ms. Janice Dunn
Arizona State Clearinghouse
3800 North Central Avenue
Fourteenth Floor
Phoenix, Arizona 85012
Telephone: (602) 280-1315

ARKANSAS
Mr. Joseph Gillespie
Manager, State Clearinghouse
Office of Intergovernmental Service
Department of Finance & Administration
P.O. Box 3278
Little Rock, Arkansas 72203
Telephone: (501) 371-1074

CALIFORNIA
Chris Kinne
Grants Coordinator
Office of Planning & Research
1400 Tenth Street
Sacramento, California 95814
Telephone: (916) 445-0613

COLORADO
State Single Point of Contact
State Clearinghouse
Division of Local Government
1313 Sherman Street, Room 520
Denver, Colorado 80203
Telephone: (303) 866-2156

CONNECTICUT
Under Secretary
Attn: Intergovernmental Review Coordinator
Comprehensive Planning Division
Office of Policy & Management
80 Washington Street
Hartford, Connecticut 06106-4459
Telephone: (203) 566-3410

DELAWARE
Ms. Francine Booth
State Single Point of Contact
Executive Department
Thomas Collins Building
Dover, Delaware 19903
Telephone: (302) 736-3326

DISTRICT OF COLUMBIA
Ms. Lovetta Davis
State Single Point of Contact
Executive Office of the Mayor
Office of Intergovernmental Relations
Room 416, District Building
1350 Pennsylvania Avenue, N.W.
Washington, D.C. 20004
Telephone: (202) 727-9111

FLORIDA
Ms. Janice L. Alcott
Director, Florida State Clearinghouse
Executive Office of the Governor
Office of Planning & Budgeting
The Capitol
Tallahassee, Florida 32399-0001
Telephone: (904) 488-8114

GEORGIA
Mr. Charles H. Badger
Administrator
Georgia State Clearinghouse
270 Washington Street, S.W.
Atlanta, Georgia 30334
Telephone: (404) 656-3855

HAWAII
Ms. Mary Lou Koayashi
Planning Program Manager
Office of State Planning
Office of the Governor
State Capitol - Room 406
Honolulu, Hawaii 96813
Telephone: (808) 548-5893
FAX (808) 548-8172

ILLINOIS
Jami Owens
State Single Point of Contact
Office of the Governor
State of Illinois
Springfield, Illinois 62706
Telephone: (217) 782-1671

INDIANA
Mr. Frank Sullivan
Budget Director
State Budget Agency
212 State House
Indianapolis, Indiana 46204
Telephone: (317) 232-5610

IOWA
Mr. Steven R. McCann
Division for Community Progress
Iowa Department of Economic Development
200 East Grand Avenue
Des Moines, Iowa 50309
Telephone: (515) 281-3725

KENTUCKY
Mr. Ronald W. Cook
Office of the Governor
Department of Local Government
2nd Floor, Capital Plaza Tower
Frankfort, Kentucky 40601
Telephone: (502) 564-2382

MARYLAND
Ms. Mary Abrams
Chief
Maryland State Clearinghouse
Department of State Planning
301 West Preston Street
Baltimore, Maryland 21201-2365

MASSACHUSETTS
State Single Point of Contact
Attn: Ms. Beverly Boyle
Executive Office of Communities & Development
100 Cambridge Street, Rm. 1803
Boston, Massachusetts 02202
Telephone: (617) 727-7001

MICHIGAN
Mr. Milton O. Waters
Director of Operations
Michigan Neighborhood Builders Alliance
Michigan Department of Commerce
Telephone: (517) 373-7111
Please direct correspondence to:
Manager, Federal Project Review
Michigan Department of Commerce
Michigan Neighborhood Builders Alliance
P.O. Box 30242
Lansing, Michigan 48909
Telephone: (517) 373-6223

MISSISSIPPI
Ms. Cathy Mallette
Clearinghouse Officer
Department of Finance & Administration
Office of Policy Development
421 West Pascagoula Street
Jackson, Mississippi 39203
Telephone: (601) 960-4280

MISSOURI
Ms. Lois Pohl
Federal Assistance Clearinghouse
Office of Administration
Division of General Services
P.O. Box 809
Room 430, Truman Building
Jefferson City, Missouri 65102
Telephone: (314) 751-4834

MONTANA
Ms. Deborah Staton
State Single Point of Contact
Intergovernmental Review Clearinghouse
c/o Office of Budget & Program Planning
Capitol Station
Room 202 - State Capitol
Helena, Montana 59620
Telephone: (406) 444-5522

NEVADA
Department of Administration
State Clearinghouse
Capitol Complex
Carson City, Nevada 89710
Attn: Mr. John B. Walker
Clearinghouse Coordinator

NEW HAMPSHIRE
Mr. Jeffery H. Taylor
Director
Office of State Planning
Attn: Intergovernmental Review Process/James E. Bieber
2 1/2 Beacon Street
Concord, New Hampshire 03301
Telephone: (603) 271-2155

NEW JERSEY
Mr. Andrew J. Jaskolka
State Review Process,
Department of Community Affairs
CN 814, Room 609
Trenton, New Jersey 08625-0814
Telephone: (609) 292-9025

NEW MEXICO
Ms. Aurelia M. Sandoval
State Budget Division, DFA
Rm. 190, Bataan Memorial Bldg.
Sante Fe, New Mexico 87503
Telephone: (505) 827-3640
Fax: (505) 827-3006

NEW YORK
New York State Clearinghouse
Division of the Budget
State Capitol
Albany, New York 12224
Telephone: (518) 474-1605

NORTH CAROLINA
Mrs. Chrys Baggett, Director
Intergovernmental Relations
Department of Administration
116 West Jones Street
Raleigh, North Carolina 27611
Telephone: (919) 733-0499

NORTH DAKOTA
Mr. Jim Boyd
State Single Point of Contact
Office of Intergovernmental Affairs
Office of Management & Budget
14th Floor, State Capitol
600 East Boulevard Avenue
Bismarck, North Dakota 58505
Telephone: (701) 224-2094

OHIO
Mr. Larry Weaver
State Single Point of Contact
State/Federal Funds Coordinator
State Clearinghouse
Office of Budget & Management
30th East Broad Street, 34th Fl.
Columbus, Ohio 43266-0411
Telephone: (614) 466-0698

OKLAHOMA
Mr. Don Strain
State Single Point of Contact
Oklahoma Department of Commerce
Office of Federal Assistance Management
6601 Broadway Extension
Oklahoma City, Oklahoma 73116
Telephone: (405) 843-9770

OREGON
Attn: Ms. Delores Streeter
State Single Point of Contact
Intergovernmental Relations Division
State Clearinghouse
155 Cottage Street, N.E.
Salem, Oregon 97310
Telephone: (503) 373-1998

RHODE ISLAND
Mr. Daniel W. Varin
Single Point of Contact
Department of Administration
Division of Planning
1 Capitol Hill - Fourth Floor
Providence, Rhode Island 02908-5870
Telephone: (401) 277-2656

SOUTH CAROLINA
Mr. Danny L. Cromer
State Single Point of Contact
Grant Services
Office of the Governor
1205 Pendleton Street, Rm. 477
Columbia, South Carolina 29201
Telephone: (803) 734-0493

SOUTH DAKOTA
Ms. Susan Comer
State Clearinghouse Coordinator
Office of the Governor
500 East Capitol
Pierre, South Dakota 57501
Telephone: (605) 773-3212

TENNESSEE
Mr. Charles Brown
State Single Point of Contact
State Planning Office
500 Charlotte Avenue
309 John Sevier Building
Nashville, Tennessee 37219
Telephone: (615) 741-1676

TEXAS
Mr. Tom Adams
Governor's Office of Budget & Planning
P.O. Box 12428
Austin, Texas 78711
Telephone: (512) 463-1778

UTAH
Utah State Clearinghouse
Office of Planning & Budget
Attn: Ms. Carolyn Wright
Room 116, State Capitol
Salt Lake City, Utah 84114
Telephone: (801) 538-1535

VERMONT
Mr. Bernard D. Johnson
Assistant Director
Office of Policy Research & Coordination
Pavilion Office Building
109 State Street
Montpelier, Vermont 05602
Telephone: (802) 828-3326

WASHINGTON
Ms. Marilyn Dawson
Washington Intergovernmental Review Process
Department of Community Development
9th and Columbia Building
Mail Stop GH-51
Olympia, Washington 98504-4151
Telephone: (206) 753-4978

WEST VIRGINIA
Mr. Fred Cutlip
Director
Community Development Division
Governor's Office of Community

Figure 9.9 continued

& Industrial Development
Building #6, Room 553
Charleston, West Virginia 25305
Telephone: (304) 348-4010

WISCONSIN

Mr. William C. Carey
Federal/State Relations Office
IGA Relations
101 South Webster Street
P.O. Box 7864
Milwaukee, Wisconsin 53707
Telephone: (608) 266-1741
Please direct correspondence and questions to:
Mr. William C. Carey, Section Chief
Federal/State Relations Office
Wisconsin Department of Administration
Telephone: (608) 266-0267

WYOMING

Ms. Ann Redman
State Single Point of Contact
Wyoming State Clearinghouse
State Planning Coordinator's Office
Capitol Building
Cheyenne, Wyoming 82002
Telephone: (307) 777-7574

TERRITORIES

GUAM

Mr. Michael J. Reidy
Director
Bureau of Budget & Management Research
Office of the Governor
P.O. Box 2950
Agana, Guam 96910
Telephone: (671) 472-2285

NORTHERN MARIANA ISLANDS

State Single Point of Contact
Planning & Budget Office
Office of the Governor
Saipan, CM
Northern Mariana Islands 96950

PUERTO RICO

Ms. Patria Custodio/
Mr. Israel Soto Marrero
Chairman/Director
Puerto Rico Planning Board
Minillas Government Center
P.O. Box 41119
San Juan, Puerto Rico 00940-9985
Telephone: (809) 727-4444

VIRGIN ISLANDS

Mr. Jose L. George
Director
Office of Management & Budget
Number 32 & 33 Kongens Gade
Charlotte Amalie, V.I. 00802
Telephone: (809) 774-0750

states have the same review requirements. However, if an intergovernmental review is required, and your district has a grants office or a formal grants procedure, the district will most likely handle the review.

If you, the principal, must process the review, find your state's single point of contact on the following list and telephone the contact to ensure that you comply with your state's requirements for coordinating your proposed project with other programs within your state.

CHAPTER 9 CHECKLIST

Evaluation and Planning Worksheet

The following items are essential to a successful grants system. Designate which ones are already part of your system and which ones you would like to add.

1. **Quality Circle Mock Review Committee or Other Proposal Improvement Committee with Same Function**

   _____ Already Part of Grants System
   _____ Add to Grants System

2. **District Submittal and Sign-Off Procedures**

   _____ Already Part of Grants System
   _____ Add to Grants System

3. **School Sign-Off and Prinicipal's Signature System**

   _____ Already Part of Grants System
   _____ Add to Grants System

4. **Federal Grants Submission Checklist Ensuring Funder Compliance in Following Areas:**

   _____ Necessary Signatures
   _____ Inclusion of Board Resolutions
   _____ Inclusion of Consortium Agreements
   _____ Accuracy of Budget Figures
   _____ Number of Copies of Proposal Submitted
   _____ Binding Regulations
   _____ Transmittal Procedures
   _____ Acknowledgement of Proposal Receipt

   _____ Already Part of Grants System
   _____ Add to Grants System

CHAPTER TEN

Developing Foundation And Corporate Grants Support for Your School

While federal grantseeking is characterized by an abundance of rules, regulations, and forms, foundation and corporate grantseeking are typified by a distinct lack of guidelines. Even the terms used by foundation and corporate grantors are not standard. For example, most foundation and corporations prohibit personal contact and request that prospective grantees make their request for a grant in writing. Some will refer to this written request as a letter proposal while others will refer to it as a letter of inquiry, a concept paper, or simply a "letter." About 5 percent will announce that guidelines are available, but most will read the proposal even if the prospective grantee did not request or follow the guidelines.

No matter how private grantors refer to it, grantseekers should develop a distinctly different proposal for each foundation and corporation they approach. There are few private funders with application requirements as stringent as the federal government's, and those are the large foundations, which usually prefer to see a concept paper before even giving an application form to a prospective grantee. Because of this relative lack of requirements, it is imperative that prospective grantees follow any instructions they do receive. For example, restrictions on the number of pages and attachments must be strictly adhered to.

The foundation and corporate grants marketplace is very different from the federal grants arena in other ways as well. As you may recall from chapter 4, private grantors have few office workers, staff, paid reviewers, well-developed proposal review procedures, or predetermined scoring systems for proposal evaluation. Only a very few of the larger foundation and corporate grantors have a specified proposal format and utilize "experts" in the subject area to review proposals. In general, proposals submitted to foundations and corporations are read by board members or trustees who have a limited amount of time to review hundreds of proposals. Most foundation and corporate grants decision makers are not experts in the fields of interest funded by the organization, and none are professional reviewers. These decision makers know what their foundation or corporation is looking for and answer only to their fellow trustees or board members. They prefer short proposals that can be read rapidly. What this means is that your school's proposal must stimulate a prospective funding source's interest right from the beginning and be able to maintain it. The best way for your grantseekers to win the reader's/reviewer's respect is to demonstrate that they have purposefully singled out that particular grantor and have especially tailored their approach to the grantor's needs.

Grantors can sense immediately when the *same* proposal has been "shotgunned" to a list of prospective funders. They know that they were lumped together with a list of prospective funders and that their individual values and needs were ignored for the convenience of the grant writer. Considering the forethought and effort you and your grantseekers have invested in the proactive grants process, you definitely do not want your school to be guilty of taking the shotgun approach. Remember that you are striving for a 50 percent success rate from your grants system. Your school's foundation or corporate proposal is not a direct-mail, fund-raising piece that you expect less than a 1 percent return on. The funding sources your grantors solicit represent one of your school's most prestigious groups of potential supporters. You must be sure that the proposal they are shown reflects your school's best effort rather than the most convenient or easiest solution from the grant writers' point of view.

The Letter Proposal

The most common type of proposal to a foundation or corporation is written in the form of a letter on the prospective grantee's letterhead. Most private funders limit the length of letter proposals to two or three pages and do not allow attachments. The main components of a letter proposal are:

1. an introductory paragraph stating the reason for writing
2. a paragraph explaining why the grantor was selected
3. a needs paragraph
4. a solution paragraph
5. a request for funds paragraph
6. a uniqueness paragraph
7. a closing paragraph
8. signatures
9. attachments (if allowed)

Have your proposal writers draft a letter proposal for your school's project. Encourage them to include all of the components listed above and to use data from their research and Project Planner. Remind them that their letter proposal should be tailored to the grantor's point of view and reflect any information they have on the funding source's preferred format. It is also important to remind your proposal developers that the proposal reviewer/reader probably will not have a degree in education and therefore might not know or understand as much about the proposed project as they do.

The Main Components of a Letter Proposal

1. Introduction

Mention in the introduction any linkages or contacts your school may have with the foundation or corporation. These include any of your school's key volunteers who have name recognition with the foundation or corporation or who are on the board of the funding source. Any contacts who have already talked to the foundation's or corporation's board members or trustees on behalf of your school district should also be mentioned. But keep the focus on the grantor. Under no circumstances should your letter proposal begin with "We are writing to you because we need . . ." What you need is not the primary concern of the grantor; rather, they are concerned about what they value and need. Therefore, place the emphasis on them, as in the following opening: "John Smith suggested I contact the Jones Foundation with an exciting project that deals with ________, an area about which our school and your board share a deep concern."

If your school does not have an established linkage or contact with the foundation or corporation, your letter proposal should start by explaining why your grantseekers selected that particular foundation or corporation to approach or how they knew that foundation or corporation would be interested in the educational need addressed in your proposal.

2. Why the Grantor Was Selected or How Your Proposal Developers Knew the Foundation/ Corporation Would Be Interested in the Educational Need Addressed in Your School's Proposal

Your proposal developers should show that they have done their homework by demonstrating their knowledge of the grantor. For foundations, your proposal developers should invest a few minutes reviewing the organization's IRS 990 PF tax return and analyzing and synthesizing the information. By compiling the statistics on past grants made to the field of education, they might discover an interesting fact or statistic that does not appear in any foundation resource publications. They could also cite a program previously funded by the foundation to demonstrate their familiarity with the foundation's granting pattern and history. For instance, if a foundation's tax return indicates that approximately 25 percent of its grants are related to children, your proposal developers could combine two years of data and say something like:

> My research indicates that in a recent two-year period, the Smith Foundation made _____ grants totaling over _____ dollars for projects focusing on children and their ability to successfully compete in our society. Your granting pattern has prompted us to submit to you this proposal for improving our students' competitive

edge by enhancing our faculty's ability to involve parents in the education of children attending Neighborville Middle School.

Corporate grants are more difficult to research than foundation grants because they are not recorded on publicly available records like the 990 IRS PF tax return. Information on corporate grantors will have to be gathered through linkages, preproposal contact, or company workers who have volunteered to assist your school. As competition for corporate grants increases, companies are focusing their support on those nonprofit organizations to which their workers donate their time and money. Corporate volunteer programs and programs such as "Dollars for Donors" try to increase contact with workers and to get them involved in volunteerism. Your grant developers may therefore want to mention volunteerism in the second paragraph, as the following example shows: "Harry Higgs, chairperson of our volunteer group and a Jones Corporation employee, has stated that the Jones Corporation places a high value on quality education for young people."

Whether you are approaching a foundation or a corporation, this section of your letter proposal should:

- inform the funder that employees of their corporation donate time to your school,
- show that your grantseekers did their homework and are aware of the funding source's giving patterns and priorities,
- state your conviction that the grantor is *special* and has unique needs and interests, and
- inspire the grantor to read on because your school has a special request that fits these needs and interests.

Although the "request for funds" usually appears in a later part of the letter proposal (usually along with the budget information), your proposal developers can mention it in this section if they choose to. Placing the request for funds in this section avoids the problem of getting a grantor interested in your project only to disappoint them later if it turns out that the amount you request is too much for their grants budget. If your proposal developers decide to put your school's grant request in this section they should compare the amount you are asking for with one of the foundation's or corporation's past grants or with their average grant amount for that area of interest. For example: "It is because of your concern for ______ that we encourage you to consider a grant for $25,000."

3. The Need for Your Project

The need referred to here is *not* the proposal developers' need to get the project funded but rather the documented need that your program aims to reduce. However, your proposal developers should not describe your school's project in this section. Unfortunately, overzealous grantseekers have a tendency to jump right into a description of what they want to do. The project and solution should be presented after the funding source understands what the problem is and that it *must* be addressed irrespective of the specific project or grantee. Again, research on the grantor will help your proposal developers tailor the description of the need to them. Your proposal should seek to demonstrate that there is a gap between "what exists" and "what ought to be" for your school, community, students, and so on. The more your grantseekers know about the funder's values and perspectives, the better they will be able to document the need. The needs section must:

- be motivating and compelling so that it captures and maintains the funder's interest,
- demonstrate that your grantseekers have a command of the literature and are aware of the pertinent studies concerning the problem, and
- appeal to the perspective and interests of the grantor.

Have your proposal developers review their research concerning the granting pattern of the foundation/corporation. Being aware of the types of projects the grantor has funded in the past and where the projects were implemented will provide valuable insight and enable your grantseekers to tailor the data presented in the needs section. While federal and state grantors and their paid staff and reviewers expect such material as statistics, literature searches, research references, and quotes, foundation and corporate readers/reviewers may be more motivated by the human element, although they too will expect the proposal to reflect a command of the facts. The best avenue to take with a foundation or corporation may be to present a fact-filled story or case study to help them "see" the problem. The following is an example:

> National studies have demonstrated that children watch television an average of ___ hours per day. A survey of the fourth graders at ABC Elementary School showed that their television viewing surpassed the national average by 20 percent. One possible cause of this disparity could be that the children from ABC Elementary School spend more time alone than many children. One fourth grader surveyed said, "I ride a bus for one hour to get home after school. I'm lonely and tired and my mom doesn't get home until late, so TV is my friend — and a lot better friend than my brother! People who say TV is violent have never lived with my brother."

It is important that your proposal developers determine what type of needs documentation will best motivate the prospective grantor. Does the funding source's distribution of past grants demonstrate any specific geographic preferences? What types of grantees have been supported in the past? Can this information help your proposal developers select the "right" data, studies, or examples to document the need?

When approaching corporate funders, have your proposal developers focus on the corporation's areas of concern and on the locations of company plants or centers of operation. How can the problem addressed in your school's proposal affect the corporation's marketplace and products? You will find that corporations are normally concerned with the education of their future employees, who may well be their employees' children.

4. Solution — What Can Be Done to Solve This Problem

This section of the letter proposal is often difficult to construct because of the limited space available. The previous paragraphs focus on the grantor. If your grantseekers were fortunate enough to make preproposal contact with the funding source to discuss two or three possible solutions to the problem, you can be more confident in choosing *one* specific approach. But even when your proposal developers have limited insight into which solution the grantor might favor, they still must choose one approach and present it in this paragraph.

Naturally, your grant writers have much more information on the proposed solution than they can fit into a few short paragraphs. The challenge is to decide what information to *include* and what to *exclude*. Typically, the proposal writers describe the solution in such great detail that they confuse rather than enlighten the prospective funding source. This is another area where the principal can step in. By playing a supportive role, the principal can help the proposal writers maintain the proper perspective and recognize when they are providing too many details as well as when the proposal's conceptual framework is weak.

The object of this section is to give the prospective grantor a *basic* understanding of the solution your grant writers have chosen to meet the needs they have outlined. In order to do this, your proposal developers should try to think like the grantor. Ask them to keep in mind the qualities they would want to see in the solution if they were on the foundation or corporate board.

The Project Planner (see chapter 7) will help your grant writers keep the project summary short. If possible, include the Project Planner they have developed as an attachment. If attachments are not allowed, include the Project Planner as page two of a three- page letter proposal. The Project Planner will clearly demonstrate to the funder the relationship between your project's activities or methods and its success. The Project Planner is also an excellent basis for the budget section or paragraph, particularly when you consider that it can summarize five or more pages of narrative on one spreadsheet! If your grant writers do not want to develop a project planner, remind them that a spreadsheet will be viewed very positively by the businessperson reading the proposal.

Whether or not a project planner is included with the letter proposal, the plan or solution must appear interesting, plausible, affordable, and well organized. The objectives should be summarized in such a manner that the funder can almost "see" how funding your school's proposal will shrink the gap between "what is" and "what ought to be."

The letter proposal must focus on *one solution* — the one that has the greatest chance of matching the values of the prospective grantor. If your grant writers have done their homework, they know what the grantor values and will have described a need that the grantor will agree is important. By this point in the proposal the prospective grantor should believe that it is *essential* that the gap be closed (indicating commitment) and closed *now* (indicating urgency) and that to put off funding the proposal will only result in a larger gap later. The funding source should feel that they cannot put your school's proposal down until they have read your suggested solution.

While it is likely that the grantor will agree that the need your grant writers have described exists, it is possible that they will disagree with the solution. Even if your grantseekers did their homework, funding sources may have values, feelings, and/or prejudices that remain hidden. Thus the prospective grantor could say:

- that they do not think your solution will work,
- that they have already funded a grant that tried the same solution, or
- that there are other applicants with better or more interesting solutions.

Assuming that at this point the grantor is still interested in the potential benefits of your solution, the next item to be addressed in your letter proposal is cost.

5. Request for Funds — How Much the Solution/Project Will Cost

Grantors have limited funds and can finance only a fraction of the proposals they receive. In fact, estimates are that private funders grant only 10 percent of the requests made to them. Ultimately they must judge *which proposals* produce *what benefits* for *how many* in the target population or field they are concerned with. The choice comes down to which proposal offers the most compelling benefits for the population the funder values.

Your school's letter proposal should clearly state the amount of grant funds being requested. If appropriate, have your proposal writers divide the cost of the project by the number of individuals it will serve. This will provide an estimate of the cost per person served. Remember that your school's project will have a "roll out" or future benefit since each student served will go through life with more skills, better job opportunities, and so on. If your school's proposal deals with parent or teacher training, have your proposal writers "roll out" the project's benefits to the number of individuals these trained people will come in contact with. When they are describing facilities and equipment, have them identify how many students will utilize the resource over its lifetime. For example: "*X* number of families will utilize the Middlesex Recreational Facility for *Y* hours over a 10-year period."

In the situation cited in the example, the cost per person served could be only pennies per hour, depending on the figures!

Multiple Funders

If the proposed project requires funding from more than one source, the letter proposal must state the amount requested from each prospective grantor. This paragraph should inform the grantor that your school will be seeking additional grant funds from other corporations and/or foundations. Your proposal writers should avoid saying, for example, that they *hope* to get funded by the Smith Corporation, the Jones Foundation, and so on. Instead, they should state the exact number of other grantors being approached, the grantors who have agreed to fund the project, the total amount already granted, and the amount outstanding.

For jointly funded projects it is crucial that the grantor know that your school's proposal is being tailored to each prospective funding source and that your grantseekers have done their homework. Some grantors may be justifiably concerned that their part of the project will be overshadowed by the other grantors or that they will not receive appropriate credit. To ensure that the grantors realize how critical their roles are, a colored highlighter can be used to visually separate each grantor's part of the total project on the Project Planner. By referring to this spreadsheet each grantor will see how integral their contribution is to the success of the whole plan.

Matching Costs and In-Kind Contributions

While matching costs and in-kind contributions are usually associated with federal grantors, some foundation and corporate grantors also require that a portion of a project's costs be borne by the grantee. The principal's handling of how matching or in-kind contributions will be secured and documented is particularly important. Even if a matching or in-kind contribution is not required, you, as the principal, may still want to include a documented contribution to demonstrate both your and your school's dedication to the project, because private grantors want to be sure that the organizations they fund are committed to supporting their projects after grant funds are depleted. By demonstrating your school's commitment in advance through a matching or in-kind contribution, you show that you have not applied for the grantor's money without carefully analyzing your own commitment. Matching and in-kind contributions should be designated on your Project Planner with an asterisk (*). The total should be placed at the bottom of the Project Planner in the column headed "Matching Funds, In-Kind Contributions, or Donated Costs."

What to Do if the Grantor Requests a Budget — 32,000 of the 33,000 foundations probably will not require that your school submit a formal budget with the letter proposal. Of the 1,000 who may, only a few hundred will request that a specific budget format be used.

If your proposal writers have developed a project planner, preparing the budget will be a simple task. For a letter proposal budget, they should provide a summary of the major line items on the Project Planner and inform the grantor that more detailed budget information is available upon request.

If no budget format is specified, your proposal developers should present the budget in a paragraph or block form, using a minimum of space and short columns rather than long ones. For example:

> We are requesting a grant of $20,000 from the Smith Foundation. To demonstrate our school's support of this important project we will provide $8,000 in matching support. A detailed budget is available upon request.

	Request	Match	Total
Salaries & Wages	$10,000		$10,000
Stipends/Teachers In-Service		$7,000	7,000
Consultants/Evaluation	3,000		3,000
Equipment/Lab	7,000		
Printing/Materials		1,000	1,000
TOTAL	$20,000	$8,000	$28,000

6. Uniquenesses — Why Your School Rather than Another Should Get the Grant

Since funding sources will be debating this issue anyway, why not address the subject first? Why *should* your school, classroom, or consortium get this grant? Couldn't another school successfully initiate the methods and carry out the proposed project? Your proposal writers need a person with a broader perspective to help them develop the answers to these questions. They need you, the principal, to play the role of "school cheerleader."

First, your school developed the project idea. Second, your proposal writers have documented your school's need. In other words, the *opportunity to act is where you are.* And third, your project idea was developed with the help of experts in curriculum development, evaluation, and so on. You arranged for their input, gathered them together, and worked with them. In short, your school has already invested many, many hours developing a project that will be a successful model.

But in addition to these strong and valid reasons, you still need to examine more closely why your school deserves the funds necessary to implement the proposed solution. Brainstorm with your proposal writers the qualities that can convince the grantor that your school is indeed the best school to fund. For instance, in addition to superior facilities, you may also have unique individuals whose commitment and expertise make your school the funding source's most logical choice. It is extremely helpful when the school's administrator singles out the project director or key personnel in the body of the proposal. For example, "Ms. Jane Doe is slated to direct the project. Ms. Doe has been recognized as an outstanding educator by the State Department of Education and has over twelve years of experience in classroom teaching." Since your signature should appear on the proposal, you are the best person to highlight the exemplary qualifications of the project personnel.

The uniqueness paragraph can also outline the ways that your district's structure will help implement the proposal and, equally important, how the relationship between your school and the district will work to ensure continuation of the project after the grant ends. With the changes in site-based management, more grantors are becoming aware of the emerging role of the building or community-school principal. In addition, grantors are interested in the unique relationship between schools and their districts and in how communities are involved in setting their schools' goals and objectives. The uniqueness paragraph or section provides the opportunity to explain these functions.

7. Closing Paragraph — How to Conclude the Letter Proposal

In the closing paragraph your proposal writers should reaffirm your school's commitment to the project and invite the funder to work with your school to achieve the project's goals. They should also reaffirm your willingness to provide the funding source with any additional materials that may help them make their decision. The grantor should be invited to visit your school to observe both the need and the unique qualities that your staff and volunteers bring to the project. In addition, the name and phone number of your project director should be included in the closing paragraph, especially when the proposal is printed on your stationary or the superintendent's. The final paragraph might include something like: "Please contact myself or Jane Doe, the project director, at 716- 358-4501 with questions about this proposal." If you do not feel comfortable with a grantor asking you detailed questions, it is best to admit up front that neither you nor the superintendent created the proposal. This can be accomplished by offering to arrange a conference call between the grantor and the project director or by suggesting that the grantor speak with the project director and/or your district grants office staff.

8. Signatures - Who Should Sign the Proposal?

Taking the grantor's point of view into consideration, whose signature from your district will have the strongest impact on the funding decision? The general rule is that the letter proposal should be signed by the highest-ranking individual in the school system. In most cases, your school's letter proposal will be signed by your superintendent or you, the building principal. Some schools require the signature of an assistant superintendent for instruction, a business officer, or a curriculum specialist. Some proposals are submitted with two signatures — the president of the school board's and a top-ranking school administrator's. It may be appropriate to have two signatures for proposals that require special cooperation, collaboration, or coordination. For example, a consortium proposal may have the signatures of all the cooperating parties to demonstrate that the collaboration is real.

Unlike foundation and corporate proposals, a federal application may call for a school board resolution that is documented by the inclusion of a signed copy of the board minutes. Even though private grantors do not require this documentation, they may nevertheless respond favorably to a statement confirming that the school/community and district have passed a resolution to apply to their foundation or corporation.

9. Attachments

Most foundations and corporations do not allow or encourage attachments. While attachments may help answer questions that arise during the reading of a proposal, the problems they create for understaffed foundations and corporations often preclude their inclusion.

What about pictures, videotapes, audiotapes, and slides? It seems that in this age of electronics, these components would be not only allowed but encouraged. During *preproposal contact,* electronic tools may be highly effective in helping the grantor "see" the problem. However, it may be inappropriate to include them with the *proposal.* Remember, not all reviewers will have access to electronic playback equipment. The bottom line is to find out what is allowed before submitting the proposal.

What's in Store for the Future?

Foundations in some states are joining together to support a common format for applications for grants. New Jersey has moved ahead on this idea, but it is unlikely to catch on rapidly. If your grantseekers follow the guidelines found in the various resource books, make preproposal contact when allowed, and expand your school's informal linkage with funding sources, you can be fairly certain that your proposal's format will be acceptable to your prospective grantor.

Two sample letter proposals, one to a foundation and one to a corporation, have been included for your review.

Figure 10.1

SAMPLE LETTER PROPOSAL TO A FOUNDATION

January 6, 1993

Ms. Elaine Finsterwald, Trustee
Smith Foundation
123 Money Place
Jonesboro, NC 28699

Dear Ms Finsterwald:

The Smith Foundation is synonymous with the word *children.* Since 1927, your grants have provided creative solutions to the needs of young people in Jonesboro and our state. Your recent annual report highlights your commitment to children's early school years and to family involvement and responsibility in education.. The $1.5 million in grants you have awarded over the past three years to strengthen children and their families clearly demonstrates your dedication and concern.

[You could mention previous support to your school district or the number of children who have been touched by any past support. For example, "Your grant to renovate an elementary classroom into the Smith Computer Lab has directly touched the lives of over 5,000 students in four years. Scores on standardized tests have improved 40%."

If the Smith Foundation has not funded elementary or middle school education directly, show how their support for your school-based project relates to their interest in programs related to the welfare of children, improving family life, parental responsibility and involvement, and so on.]

Previous generations have progressed through our schools with the involvement and encouragement of teachers and parents. Today, classroom leaders lack much of the support they used to get from parents and must compete with television and video games for a child's time and attention.

How much time do children spend watching television versus doing homework? A study of 25,000 middle school children conducted by the Department of Education reported 21.4 hours per week of television versus 5.6 hours of homework (*Wall Street Journal,* March of 1992). When asked if parents placed limits on television, two-thirds of the parents surveyed said yes, while two-thirds of the children said no. These results suggest that some parents may have a problem setting priorities for their children.

Other results of the study point to the deterioration of parental responsibility and involvement in educational activities. For instance, four out of five parents surveyed reported that they regularly discuss school work with their children, while two out of three children said parents rarely or never discuss schoolwork with them. Apparently the breakdown in communication between parents and children is at crisis proportions.

The need exists to develop and implement programs that encourage parents to become involved in their children's education. This means more than just visiting the school. For example, the Department of Education study also showed that 50 percent of parents had visited their child's school for meetings, but only 33 percent had visited their child's classroom.

What happens when parents take responsibility for working with their children and their children's school?

Figure 10.1 continued

- Students whose parents discuss schoolwork with them get higher grades.
- Restrictions on television viewing tend to boost grades.

While some adults may think that the way to improve education is to increase funding for schools, taxpayers in Harrison, Arkansas, do not. While national test scores for students in Harrison rank in the top 10 percent of the country, Harrison ranks 272d out of Arkansas' 327 school districts in education taxes (*USA Today,* November 18, 1991). The key is parental involvement. Almost 100 parents volunteer for one hour a week at each of the town's elementary schools, and parents and teachers meet each year to establish education goals for the next year.

What can we do in Jonesboro to promote the sharing of responsibility for education among schools, parents, and children? Teachers, parents and students at the Jonesboro Elementary School have developed a program entitled Responsibility in Education through Academic *P*artners (REAP). The REAP program is aimed at increasing responsible educational behavior and encouraging parental involvement in the classroom and at home. Teachers will actually work with parents and students to develop tailored, individual contracts to produce increases in all levels of education and the quality of all course work.

The attached Project Planner outlines each objective and the activities that will foster the changes we desire. From increasing test scores to promoting public and volunteer service, the Jonesboro Elementary School will provide the catalyst through the education and involvement of parents in their children's responsible use of "out-of-school" time. The project is not limited to decreasing television viewing, but "TV Busters" are included in the plan.

We are requesting a grant from the Smith Foundation for $20,000 to initiate this project. Based upon our preliminary work with the teachers and Parent Advisory Committee of Jonesboro Elementary School, we anticipate the involvement of 600 students, 360 parents, and 40 teachers. Your grant funds will represent an investment of $20.00 per person served for the first year of the project. Future funding needs will be significantly less once the materials have been developed under your grant award. Our School District will provide $6,000 of in-kind contributions to support the project.

The Jonesboro Elementary School is fortunate to have Renee Weathers as the project director. Ms. Weathers was named the "1992 Outstanding Teacher of the Year" by the North Carolina State Education Department. She will be assisted by the Parents Advisory Committee, chaired by Sam Price. The Committee is supported by a group of 52 parents, who have already volunteered 200 hours to develop the REAP program and this proposal.

We believe that you REAP what you sow in life, and we invite you to "sow with us" by supporting Responsibility in Education through Academic Partners.

Jonesboro Elementary School's tax exempt status is _______, and our tax exempt number is ________. Renee Weathers is available at 200– 861–4000 to answer your questions and to provide additional information that will help you arrive at your funding decision.

Sincerely,

Attachment

Figure 10.2

SAMPLE LETTER PROPOSAL TO A CORPORATION

January 12, 1993

Clyde L. Baker
Contributions Officer
Widget Corporation
4321 Commercial Park
Rocker, NY 14570

Dear Mr. Baker:

John Allen, your marketing manager, advised me to contact you for consideration of a grant from Widget Corporation. John, who has volunteered over 100 hours to our Parents Advisory Committee, has told us of your company's interest in and efforts to promote responsible behavior in your employees and their families. It is with this common interest in mind that the Casper Elementary School requests a grant of $20,000 from the Widget Corporation for the Responsibility in Education through Academic Partners Program (REAP).

John Allen has been instrumental in guiding our school's curriculum group toward understanding the changes technological advances have brought to Widget Corporation and how these changes influence what types of employees and skills your corporation will require in the future.

Technological advances have also brought changes to the family. Everything from health to educational achievement to parent/child communication has been affected by television, videos, and computer games.

We have learned in education that *what* children devote their time to determines the skills they develop. Unfortunately, our children are devoting an inordinate amount of time to television. A study of 25,000 middle school children conducted by the Department of Education revealed that the children surveyed spent an average of 5.6 hours per week on homework and 21.4 hours per week watching television. In addition, when asked if parents placed limits on television, two-thirds of the parents surveyed said yes, while two-thirds of the children said no.

We are not suggesting that television viewing is inherently bad. However, the amount of television children watch is one possible indication of the responsibility parents take for their children's "out-of-school" time and ultimately for their education.

A parent's responsible involvement in his or her child's education can also be evaluated by the time spent discussing schoolwork within the family and the type or quality of parental contact with the child's school. The Department of Education's study revealed some disturbing facts in these areas as well.

- Four out of five parents surveyed reported that they regularly discussed schoolwork with their children, while two out of three children said they rarely or never discussed schoolwork with their parents.
- Fifty percent of the parents surveyed reported visiting their child's school for meetings, while only 33 percent had visited their child's classroom.

When you compare what can result from parental involvement and responsibility in education with what can result from a lack of parental involvement and responsibility in education, the problem is clear and the goal evident. Students whose parents discuss school work with them get higher grades, and restrictions on television viewing tend to boost grades.

Figure 10.2

What can be done? This is the question that brought John Allen and over 100 other parents together to prepare a plan for action. The program they developed is entitled Responsibility in Education through Academic Partners (REAP).

REAP seeks to involve parents, students, and teachers in generating a monthly educational contract for change. Each signed contract is individually tailored and aimed at developing realistic and responsible educational behavior. Each contract outlines a plan to utilize "out-of-school" time more effectively.

The objectives of the project and the activities aimed at bringing about the desired changes are outlined on the enclosed Project Planner spreadsheet. The activities deal with involving parents and students in setting outcomes for education and presenting alternatives such as "TV Busters", a program initiated by a Minnesota teacher, to help kids break the television habit.

Developing the materials and initiating the program generate the project's major costs. Once established, REAP's volunteers and teachers will keep the program going. What is required now is a grant of $20,000 from Widget Corporation.

The Widget Corporation's support will directly affect the lives and education of 600 students, 360 parents, and 40 educators. Over a four-year period, this one-time grant represents an investment of $5.00 per person served. In fact, since the children that participate in the program will learn what can result from a responsible parental role in education, the benefits will accrue over many, many years.

The Widget Corporation's support will be recognized in the REAP program's informational brochure, and space will be set aside on the brochure's inside cover for a statement from Widget Corporation.

Alice Jones has been selected as the project director. She is eminently qualified and has worked with parents in this region for over twenty-five years. As a sign of commitment, the school district has agreed to provide support services valued at $6,000.

The volunteers have done all they can do. The time is right. Please join with us in sowing the seeds for responsible, parental involvement in education.

Money alone does not ensure a great education. Responsible commitment does. In Harrison, Arkansas, national test scores ranked among the top 10 percent in the country, while education taxes rank 272d out of Arkansas' 327 school districts. What's the key? *Parental Involvement.* Approximately 100 parents volunteer one hour per week at each of the town's elementary schools, and parents and teachers work together each year to determine the following year's educational goals.

This project is truly an investment in our community. Alice Jones is ready to provide any additional information you may need to make your funding decision. Please call her at 321–987–0645. Our school's tax exempt status is ______ and our tax exempt number is ___________.

Sincerely,

CHAPTER 10 CHECKLIST

Evaluation and Planning Worksheet

1. Does your school have:

a. a format that helps foundation and corporate grantseekers prepare letter proposals?

_____ yes _____no

2. Are there unwritten rules regarding contact with grantors?

b. a file containing samples of funded foundation and corporate proposals that your grantseekers can examine?

_____ yes _____no

CHAPTER ELEVEN

$ Improving and Submitting Your School's Foundation/ Corporate Proposal

The research your grantseekers have gathered on the prospective funding source will provide them with the deadlines for proposal submission. If possible, validate deadlines through preproposal contact with the grantor. If there are no specific deadlines, your grantseekers should try to determine what time of the year your proposal would receive the most favorable review and have the greatest chance of being funded. Many foundations and corporations will state that proposals are read periodically, or "as needed." Remind your proposal writers that "as needed" does not mean when *they* need the money or want to start the project. Foundations and corporations do not respond to the constraints of their grantees. Instead, they expect their grantees to respond to theirs. One corporate foundation typical of many makes its grants decisions in the summer for the next calendar year. So plan ahead!

If there is a deadline, your school's proposal should be submitted slightly in advance of it. Getting your school's proposal in early eliminates the need for special delivery or express mail service. However, since special delivery is relatively inexpensive, your grant writers may want to send their proposal by this method anyway so that they can obtain a signed assurance that the proposal was safely delivered. Also, your grantseekers should review the exact wording of the funding source's instructions for submitting proposals. Does the grantor want to receive the proposal by a certain date or that it be *mailed* by that date? Many private grantors request the former.

As the principal, you should initiate an early discussion of deadlines to encourage your proposal writers to aim for an early submission. This will allow time for a mock review of the proposal, which will increase its chances of being funded. By emphasizing the importance of the mock review and early submission you will dramatically increase the likelihood that these are carried out. Naturally, it is to everyone's benefit to submit a proposal that reflects your proposal writers' best efforts and is a credit to your school.

Organizing a Foundation/Corporate Proposal Improvement Group

Invite four or five individuals to form a group that will take part in an activity aimed at improving your school's proposals. This proposal-improvement activity or mock review will follow the basic concepts of quality circles and total quality management, where employees volunteer to commit their personal time to improving their company's products and services. Encourage your school's/ community's most talented individuals to get involved in the mock review, including parents, students, educators, foundation/corporate board members, and anyone else you would like to involve in your school's proposal-development process. (Note that a foundation or corporate board member can provide particularly valuable insight into the private grants review and decision-making process.) By inviting a variety of individuals to take part *voluntarily*, you are facilitating a positive grants atmosphere that reinforces the commitment that your grant developers have demonstrated. Once volunteers realize how easy it is to develop a *quality* proposal, they will become valuable resources for your school's grants program and take responsibility for developing their own proposals.

It is much easier (and possibly more enjoyable) to perform a mock review for foundation and corporate proposals than for federal grant applications (see chapter 9). One reason for this is that it is fun to role-play being a wealthy foundation or corporate board member. (Only community foundations actively recruit board members who reflect the economic and racial diversity of the geographic area they fund.) Another reason is that it takes less time to read and make comments on foundation and corporate proposals than federal proposals because the former are usually short one- or two-page concept papers.

Use the sample letter in figure 11.1 as the basis for your invitation to participate in your school's proposal improvement group. Basically, you will be asking individuals to take part in a mock review of a proposal. The volunteers will role-play the actual funders and carry out the real review process as closely as possible. They will be relieved to learn that the purpose of the quality improvement exercise is not to get *their opinions* of the proposal but rather to get their impressions of how the proposal *will look to the proposed funding source.*

In most cases, the group members will spend only five to ten minutes reviewing the proposal. The entire evaluation process will be completed in less than one hour. If the proposal is being submitted to one of the few large foundations that use a longer format and have experts review proposals, you may ask your volunteers to review, comment, and score the proposal before they meet as a group. Even most large foundations utilize a concept paper or outline similar to the one in chapter 10 (the letter proposal). Whether the foundation allows 5

Figure 11.1

INVITATION TO PARTICIPATE IN FOUNDATION/CORPORATE PROPOSAL IMPROVEMENT GROUP

Date

Name
Address

Dear _______________:

I would like to take this opportunity to follow up on our conversation to secure your input in assisting our school district in submitting the very best grant proposal possible. We are asking that you review the enclosed proposal from the point of view of a reviewer. The attached materials have been designed to assist you in role-playing the actual manner in which this proposal will be evaluated.

Please read the information on the reviewers' backgrounds and the scoring system, and limit the time you spend reading the proposal to the time constraints that the real reviewers will observe. The Quality Circle Scoring Worksheet has been provided to help you in recording your scores and comments.

A meeting of all the mock reviewers comprising our quality circle has been scheduled for [date]. Please bring this worksheet with you to the meeting. The meeting will last less than one hour. Its purpose is to analyze the scores and brainstorm suggestions to improve the proposal.

Sincerely,

Name
Phone Number

pages or 10, the best way to get information on the actual review process is to request it during preproposal contact.

The Foundation/Corporate Proposal Improvement Scoring Sheet

Complete the first half of the Foundation/Corporate Proposal Improvement Scoring Worksheet (fig. 11.2) before your group meeting. Give a copy of the worksheet to each member of the group. (The principal or the individual selected to represent your administration should provide the worksheets, set up the meeting, and facilitate the mock review process.)

The first half of the worksheet you distribute to group members should contain information such as the following:

- who at the foundation/corporation reads the proposals,
- how much time is devoted to reviewing each proposal, and
- what scoring system or criteria are used for evaluation.

Unfortunately, in most cases you will not have much information to record. Remember, private grant funds are not public money. *Private grantors are therefore not required* to provide prospective grantees with information on their review process. In addition, most private grantors do not employ an elaborate scoring or evaluation system. They read the proposals quickly and ask their fellow board members what looks good to them.

How can you help your grantseekers obtain background information on private funding officials? Much valuable information can be found in resource books such as *Who's Who* and *Standard and Poor's Register of Directors and Executives.* There are also regional and even local editions of books that describe wealthy and influential individuals. The printed rosters of many membership groups and service clubs may include valuable background information that will give your grantseekers insight into their members. Provide your group with brief biographies on the funding source's board members, or at least basic information such as age and educational background. Since your school's proposal will be based upon educational principles, information on the reviewers' background will help your mock reviewers evaluate the vocabulary in the proposal.

Also give the volunteers a description of the funding source and any information you have on the types of proposals they have funded in the past, the number of projects they have funded, and the amount of each grant. If the grantor is a foundation, a copy of its tax return will also be helpful. At the beginning of the meeting, review the information about the grantor to be sure your group members develop an appropriate impression of the funding source's point of view.

If you are unable to find out the amount of time the grantor is likely to spend reading each proposal, limit the group's time to five minutes.

Instruct your volunteers to read the proposal quickly and to make believe that they have read many such proposals and that they still have a large stack of proposals to review. Ask your volunteers to designate any areas that they *think would appeal to the grantor* with a plus sign (+) and any areas that need improvement with a minus sign (-).

At the conclusion of the time set aside for reading the proposal, you can play a very useful role as the group facilitator and recorder, if you believe your volunteers will speak openly in front of you. If you are in doubt as to your impact on the group, ask a volunteer to act as the recorder/facilitator.

Instruct the recorder to list the positive points on the worksheet (ask her or him to print instead of write). There is no need for consensus on the ideas listed. The participants may then hold a brief discussion about the positive points, after which they should rank order them. Again, this rank order should reflect the grantor's perspective, not the mock reviewers'. The mock reviewers should repeat this procedure for the negative areas. The participants should then suggest improvements for any area they think may be viewed negatively by the grantor.

Figure 11.2

FOUNDATION/CORPORATE PROPOSAL IMPROVEMENT SCORING WORKSHEET

The following information is being provided to help you review the attached foundation/corporate grant application/proposal.

The Proposal Will Be Read by:

______ funding official
______ funding staff
______ review committee
______ board members
______ other ______________________________

Amount of Time Spent Reviewing Each Proposal:

Socio-economic Background of Reviewer(s);

Known Biases or Viewpoints:

Positive Points **Rank Order**

Negative Points **Rank Order**

Other Comments/Suggestions for Improvement:

If an area of the proposal is unclear, it should be listed as a problem area to be improved. Do not allow the proposal developers to take part in the mock review activity. After all, they will not be present to answer questions or offer explanations for the *real* reviewers. In addition, the proposal developers' presence may prevent the reviewers from offering a frank evaluation of the proposal for fear of hurting the writers' feelings.

The group recorder will provide you with the rank orders of the positive and negative areas so that you will know how strongly the mock reviewers felt about specific parts of the proposal. This information, plus the group's list of suggestions for improvement, will help the proposal developers rewrite portions of their proposal and put the finishing touches on the final version.

Review the rewritten proposal to be certain that the proposal developers have not overreacted to the criticisms at the *expense* of the positive areas. Many proposal developers are so sensitive to criticism that in their zeal to "fix" the proposal, they place all their energy in the areas to improve. In general, proposal developers will cut the positive areas in an effort to give themselves more space to improve the negative ones, although this may not be the best thing to do. The principal can be of assistance by keeping the proposal developers focused on the values and perspectives of the funder and by promoting a balance between maintaining the strengths of a proposal while improving the weaknesses.

CHAPTER 11 CHECKLIST

Evaluation and Planning Worksheet

1. **Does you have a system of presubmission review for foundation and corporate proposals to ensure quality?**

   _____ yes _____no

2. **Do you utilize the mock review process to educate and encourage others to become involved in proposal preparation?**

   _____ yes _____no

3. **Who from your school could play a positive, voluntary role in the preproposal review process?**

   ____
   ____
   ____
   ____

4. **List any community members who could provide insight into the preproposal review system and whose involvement in the mock review process would provide a communications link to the community.**

   ____
   ____
   ____
   ____

$ The Principal's Role in Contacting Grantors after Submission and Dealing with the Outcome (Rejection/Award)

As the principal, you will be asked by your anxious proposal developers to check on the status of their submitted proposal. To help you handle this situation and to avoid taking any action that would jeopardize your school's grant at this critical time, consider the following suggestions for contacting funding officials after your school's proposal has been submitted.

Contacting Federal Grantors after You Have Submitted a Proposal

Once your school's proposal has been logged in with the federal granting agency, it is considered in submission. During this time it will be assigned to a review panel and will spend several months in the review process.

The federal agency will consider contact by you or your grantseekers during the period between the deadline and notification of the outcome as an *attempt to unfairly influence the review and outcome.* Therefore, when your school has a proposal in submission, contact with the funder should be made *only* on the rare occasion when you must forward information of major significance that would impact their decision. For example:

- a new breakthrough would allow you to drastically cut the amount requested (new equipment, software, assessment tools, and so on)
- another grantor has *partially funded the project* and the amount of your request can be reduced
- you need to pull your school's proposal from submission and the review process because another funding source has decided to *fund it totally.*

Short of these, or other dramatic reasons, instruct your grantseekers to avoid contact with the grantor while their proposal is being reviewed. This forbidden contact also includes any intervention by elected officials or other advocates.

Contacting Foundation/ Corporate Grantors When You Have a Proposal in Submission

While contact with federal bureaucrats may be a legal issue during this period, contact with corporate and foundation grantors may be an ethical issue. Considering how few grant-related employees the private grantor has, attempts at contact by prospective grantees make their job much more difficult. The situations in which contact is allowed are basically the same as with the federal grantor. Significant changes in the requested amount should be forwarded in writing to the private grantor, with a brief but thorough explanation of what has occurred and how it will modify your school's proposal.

Significant changes in your proposal should be relatively rare. If one occurs, you might consider asking one of your links to the funder to ask them how (and if) you should correspond with them.

The Decision

A key ingredient in an efficient grants program is knowing how to creatively handle your staff's excitement at being notified of a grant award or their disappointment at being turned down. In addition to helping your rejected grantseekers reassess their proposal, you must help successful grantseekers avoid the pitfalls of overexuberance. Grantseekers have put their egos and hard work on the line and deserve special consideration at this critical juncture. There are a few techniques you can apply that will make a big difference in the grantseekers' attitude and involvement in future grantseeking. The techniques vary according to the type of grantor and the grantseeking outcome.

1. Federal Granting Agencies

Strategies for Handling a Rejection

When individuals have expended hard work and energy in applying for a federal grant, the rejection notice hits them very hard. The principal can help prepare the grantseekers *in advance of the notification* by sending them a note or phoning to thank them again for their hard work and to remind them that notification will be made soon and that even a 50 percent success rate means that failure occurs one-half of the time. Remind them that all is not lost if the proposal gets turned down on the first attempt and that the process of preparing a proposal is a learning and growing experience. Talking with your grantseekers prior to notification is particularly useful because most rejected grantseekers go into a denial and withdrawal phase after they receive the dreaded response.

The principal is in a unique position to support the disappointed grantseeker. Many disgruntled grantseekers feel a need to protest the negative decision and appeal the rejection. Remind them that few appeals ever win anything but enemies. Further, since your grantseekers may have to interface with the same program officers again, it is best not to irritate them. Appeals can also hold up the entire award process. For all these reasons they should be avoided in all but the most extreme circumstances. Recognize the grantseekers' disappointment and offer your assistance in writing a thank-you letter (instead of a complaint) to the federal agency.

The purpose of this letter is to thank the official for their time and help, to let them know you understand their limitations and funding constraints, and to request the reviewers' comments. The letter is an opportunity to demonstrate a positive grantseeking attitude and to show your sincere concern for the funder and the difficulty of their job.

In your request for the reviewers' comments, advise the agency that you will use these comments to prepare another proposal. Ask for a list of recipients of this year's grant awards and for any other information they feel would help your grantseekers. Include a self-addressed label for their convenience in returning the information you request.

Explain that your research indicated that this particular grants program presented a great opportunity for funding because of its concern for your school's and grantseekers' area of interest. Inform them that you or your grant writer will be contacting them in the near future concerning their next submission date and grants cycle. You may also ask if they anticipate the availability of any unsolicited funds (funds that are granted at the discretion of the program administrator) or if there is any chance that one of the successful applicants may not expend all of their grant award in the prescribed time frame. (You could utilize any unexpended funds or unsolicited funding to do a *portion of your school's project,* enabling your school to be a more attractive applicant in the future.)

You might receive a letter that gives you a priority score and explains that while you are not yet rejected, the score is not adequate to attract funding. In this case, encourage your grantseekers to react in a constructive, positive way and not to burn any bridges or alienate future funding opportunities.

One pitfall that many temporarily unsuccessful grantseekers fall into is "avoidance of the grantor." Help your grantseekers keep in contact with the funding source. Encourage them to anticipate the next deadline and be sure they realize that their chances for a grant award may actually be greater *after* their rejection since they will have access to the reviewers' comments and a list of recipients.

The principal's encouragement and assistance are key to the resubmittal of a proposal. If resubmitted, the proposal should be judged by a *new* panel of reviewers, which gives it a new chance at being funded. But try to be objective about the likelihood of the project being funded upon resubmittal. If the original proposal got a very low score, ask the federal grantor whether it would be better to develop a whole new approach or solution instead of resubmitting a reworked proposal.

Finally, initiate the process of preproposal contact all over again. Review the list of this year's grantees. Do you know any whom you could contact? What was the average grant size? Where are the grantees located?

Strategies for Handling an Award

Many federal program officers who grant millions of dollars each year *never receive thank-you letters or requests for reviewers' comments* from successful (i.e., funded) grantees. In many cases, applicants do not realize that they will not receive reviewers' comments unless they request this valuable feedback in writing. To make your school stand out as an institution that is dedicated to learning and improving, *be different.* Send a thank-you letter and include a request for reviewers' comments and a self-addressed label. Remember, your grantseekers need to know what they did correctly so they can repeat the techniques that resulted in success. In addition, reviewers' comments can provide the basis for your legitimate praise of your grant writers. Invite the federal granting officials to visit your school. Of course, once you accept federal funds, they have the legal authority to come for a site visit, but it looks better if you invite them.

Negotiating the Final Award

One of the key problems in dealing with federal funds is the art of negotiating the final budget. It is not uncommon for the overexuberant grantseeker to agree to a budget that is significantly different from the grant figure submitted in the proposal. The principal can play a critical role in the negotiation process needed to arrive at a figure that *both* the grantor and the grantee believe will allow the proposal to be successfully carried out. Since the grantseekers have invested hours of work in developing the project, their ability to remain objective in reducing budget items is questionable, and they may jeopardize their future relationship with the funder by being either too flexible or too rigid in arriving at the final figures.

The principal can play the role of negotiator and buffer between the two sides. Your goal is to arrive at a budget that is realistic and *fair to your school,* the granting agency, and your grantseekers. If your grantseekers have developed a project planner you will find that this document is invaluable in helping you set up a realistic basis for negotiating the grant award. If you do not have a project planner to negotiate from, it is never too late. Ask the government granting official to allow you a few days to complete a detailed task analysis and spreadsheet that will document each expenditure proposed in the project. Propose that you send the spreadsheet to them so that together you can analyze how any suggested budget adjustments will impact your program's methods and the accomplishment of its objectives.

Try to remain flexible. Look at the process of negotiating a final award as a team effort aimed at eliminating any waste and inefficiency while ensuring that the program will attain its objectives at the levels specified in the proposal. If the negotiations seriously threaten your program's ability to impact the problem, you should request a reduction in the degree of change (progress) called for in the objectives. Changing the number of students, clients, or individuals served by the project can also bring the costs down. Unfortunately, some grantseekers make up their budget requests out of whole cloth, which often causes the government grantor to view the negotiation process as a search for the "fluff." By referring to your Project Planner, the funding official will be able to relate each expenditure to the successful completion of the project. This will enhance the funder's image of you, your school, and your grants team as *knowledgeable, honest,* and *worthy of their trust.*

The negotiation is further complicated when the federal agency uses a grants or contracts officer to negotiate the budget and a program officer to discuss the project. Fiscal people have difficulty relating the *degree of change* and the *attainment of objectives* to *money.* To deal with this situation, request a conference call between the program and fiscal officers and always defer to the program officer when changing the objectives and scope of the project.

In many ways, the principal has as much of a vested interest in the successful negotiation of the grant as the government officials. All sides want to be certain that the plan proposed by your grantseekers is well designed and that the project will be a credit to the government sponsor and to your school. The Project Planner will provide a way to "see" what happens to the proposed activities and methods when categories of budgets are altered. For example, if the amount proposed for personnel is cut, *whose* time on the project will be reduced and what will be the *effect* on the activities and objectives? When the amount specified for consultants is reduced, what activities will this affect? If the proposal evaluation was to be conducted by consultants, how will the project now be evaluated? Who will collect the data? If the amount for equipment is eliminated or reduced, what will be affected?

In arriving at the final budget, the cash flow, and the reimbursement system, remember that your district's central office, business administrator, or district grants person should be part of the negotiation and final agreement. It is also essential that your central office not agree to budget amounts without agreement from you and your grantseekers.

By involving the staff of your district office staff in the negotiations and utilizing a spreadsheet such as the Project Planner, you will have a sound basis for moving into the implementation stage of the project. Most of the problems associated with administering and carrying out grants can be traced to the improper negotiation of the budget and to the lack of agreement of project staff on the appropriate expenditure of funds called for in the proposal.

2. Foundation/Corporate Grantors

Strategies for Handling a Rejection

The principal can provide a valuable service to the school and the rejected grantseekers by encouraging a thoughtful response to the foundation or corporation's grant denial. Unlike the federal grantor, the private grantor normally does not have the personnel resources or independent review system necessary to provide your grant writers with reviewers' comments and scores. Since private grant funds do not come from tax dollars, there is no Freedom of Information Act to invoke, and you have no legal right to know the basis for the private grantor's decision. What is important here is to maintain your contact with the grantor and to make sure your volunteers' efforts to secure the grant do not go for naught. If you have utilized a personal link to make preproposal contact, you have a responsibility to that person to keep his or her relationship with the foundation or corporation on good terms. Send a letter apprising the person of the rejection and thanking him or her for helping.

Send the foundation or corporation a thank-you letter. Since the principal or the district office may exercise some control over contacts with prospective grantors, you may want to send the letter from your office. In your letter, inform the funding source that your grantseekers will reapply for a grant unless the funder advises you that they should not. Even if the grantor meets only once per year, when they meet next year they will find your thank-you letter from last year along with your school's *new* grant request. In your letter, acknowledge that you understand that they have limited staff so that they can use their resources to make grants instead of payroll. You will not lose anything by sincerely thanking them for the time they invested in reading your proposal and for the opportunity to compete for their grant funds. You might even invite them to attend a school/community meeting or to visit your school before the next round of grants to see your school's unique qualifications firsthand.

To keep your grantseekers' motivation up, you must play the role of both a realist and a cheerleader. You must help your grantseekers understand that some proposals will be rejected and that they must make the best of the situation and get ready to resubmit! For obvious reasons, initiating grantor/grantee correspondence is best not left to the disappointed grantseeker.

Strategies for Handling an Award

You, the principal, must keep your grantseekers from making image-damaging mistakes with funding sources even when their proposals are funded. You might receive a phone call or a letter from your district office or from the grantor informing you of your school's good fortune. Immediately send a thank-you letter to all of your volunteers and/or linkages who helped with preproposal contact and/or proposal preparation. Send the foundation/corporate grantor a thank-you letter. Invite the grantor to visit your school and ask if they would like to view a presentation by your students, teachers, and/or parents. You could also ask if they would like a short video on your project to show at one of their future board meetings. Be sure to request any comments they could provide on your school's proposal, including negative as well as positive feedback. Let them know that as the school's educational leader you are always ready to learn, as are your grantseekers.

Some foundations meet so infrequently and have such limited staff that a check for the entire grant amount is sent with the notification of the award. If a check from the grantor is not included in the acceptance letter, request information on the payment procedure in your thank-you letter.

3. Service Clubs and Organizations

Strategies for Handling a Rejection

When your school's request for a grant is denied by a local service club, civic group, or fraternal organization, the need to send a thank-you letter is even greater than with federal and foundation/corporate grantors because you are likely to see these grantors in your school and community again and again. In your thank-you letter, request suggestions for improvement and directions for resubmittal. Let the club, group, or organization know that the problem your proposal described is not going to go away and that you will be back to seek their support. These funders interpret persistence as commitment. As a committed educational leader and community member, it is your duty to bring to the community's attention the positive aspects of the educational system and to remind these groups of the opportunities they have to help improve it.

Strategies for Handling an Award

Voluntary organizations, service clubs, and fraternal groups like to have their members and donors see and hear about educational changes they have supported. Send them a thank-you letter immediately upon receiving word of your grant award and volunteer to make a presentation at one of their future meetings or conferences. If you can, include your students, teachers, and/or parents in the presentation.

CHAPTER 12 CHECKLIST

Evaluation and Planning Worksheet

Review the following suggested techniques for dealing with grantseeking outcomes and indicate which ones are currently being employed at your school.

1. thank-you letter sent to government officials when proposal is rejected

   _____ yes _____ no

2. thank-you letter sent to foundations/corporations when proposal is rejected

   _____ yes _____ no

3. automatically and routinely request reviewers' comments

   Rejected Proposal: _____ yes _____ no

   Funded Proposal: _____ yes _____ no

4. involved in the final budget negotiation

   School Principal: _____ yes _____ no

   Grantseeker: _____ yes _____ no

   Business Office: _____ yes _____ no

   Grants Office: _____ yes _____ no

5. grantseekers' use of a spreadsheet to justify the budget

   _____ yes _____ no

CHAPTER THIRTEEN

$ The Principal's Changing Role In Administering Grant Funds

The policies and procedures of a school district's grants system have historically been aimed at expending funds and operating programs that are extensions of the central office's federal and state grants programs, particularly federal entitlement programs. Many school districts employ a grants system that mirrors the one used by the majority of public and private institutions of higher education. Colleges and universities have developed extensive centralized grants systems for both securing *and* administering outside grant funds. (They often refer to these as sponsored projects.) However, the challenge of developing resources in the 1990s has demonstrated the weaknesses and limitations of the centralized system. It has become evident that centralized grants offices may not be the best vehicle for encouraging grantseeking or for ensuring high-quality proposals from the *elementary to postsecondary* levels. In fact, *decentralized grants programs generate higher levels of interest and enthusiasm on the local level,* and that translates into grants success! But questions arise regarding the role of decentralized *grantseeking* versus that of decentralized *grants administration.*

As site-based management and school/community empowerment have proliferated across the United States, the role of the principal has expanded to include the seeking of alternative sources of funding and increased responsibility for how those outside funds are administered. This has created quite a dilemma in districts that have encouraged their schools to seek alternative sources of support while trying to retain control of the disbursement and administration of those funds. As one entrepreneurial principal of a junior high remarked, "The easiest part of grantseeking is the actual soliciting of the outside funding. The hardest part is getting the awarded grant funds from the district central office to my school."

Principals now find themselves in the unique position of being given more autonomy and responsibility for marshaling community support and involvement in meeting the challenge of educating our nation's youth. This same movement toward local decision making and responsibility is taking place in colleges and universities. Many institutions of higher education are now adopting the methods that primary and secondary education have initiated to promote change at the local level through grant funding. Many colleges are pursuing a decentralized, departmentally based proposal development system. Some of these revolve around part-time (or released-time) *grant specialists,* whose job is to encourage professors to become more interested, involved, and successful in attracting grant funds from outside the university. Interesting and confusing issues and problems in the development and operation of these emerging systems have arisen throughout all levels of education, primary through graduate school.

Empowering local support through the methods suggested in the preceding chapters will evoke strong motivation, exceptional efforts, and successful grantseeking. Some of the controversial issues in grantseeking begin to appear when multiple approaches are made to the same grantors, and school districts begin to lose their credible image. For example, when six of a district's elementary schools deluge one corporation with requests, the company may feel that the school district should have decided which one project meets its need most closely. They may object to having to assume the responsibility of deciding which of the six school/communities to fund and the accompanying risk of offending the rejected ones.

The complexities of grantseeking and site-based management become increasingly apparent when the administration of grant funds is added to the issues of grantseeking. The grantor gets even more confused over whom to send the grant money to — the district or the school. Our educational resource development systems are in a state of flux, and you must be aware of the potential problems of acting independently, of the benefits of coordinating your actions with those of your district grants office, and of the possibility of developing a new grants system.

The perfect grants system has not yet been developed, and the temptation to copy another district's system should be avoided. The ultimate goal is to capture the energy, creativity, and involvement of your school and community by encouraging them to utilize the potential of grantseeking to reach *their educational goals and objectives.*

The remainder of this chapter presents important issues in the effective administration of your school's grant funds. This information is provided to stimulate your thinking, increase your knowledge base, and help you avoid some of the pitfalls involved in accepting outside funding. This list of considerations is by no means exhaustive; the sources suggested in the bibliography provide a more detailed analysis of each area.

1. Fund-raising vs. Grantseeking

What can you do when your school cannot get a grant to deal with an area of concern? When the grants mechanism is inappropriate or unsuccessful, many schools consider utilizing alternative fund-raising strategies.

Grantseeking is only one strategy for developing financial resources outside your usual tax-based or tuition system. Grantseeking targets government, corporate, and foundation funds. However, grantseeking does not target the over $100 billion donated per year by *individuals*. Individuals give this money away through means other than grants. While slightly over 50 percent of individual donations goes to religious organizations, the sizable amount of $50 billion is distributed to nonprofit groups through other, non-grant-related *fund-raising* strategies. Many school districts and public and private schools are realizing that money can be made through special events (raffles, pancake breakfasts), direct mail (soliciting donations through the mail), bequests (being willed a donation), and a host of other fund- raising techniques.

You will find that the more you empower and involve your community in seeking grants to deal with their school's problems and opportunities, the more they will want to find *other* ways to get the money your school needs. In fact, some schools are so successful at fund raising that they develop a separate foundation to solicit and administer the funds raised. There are a variety of ways that a school district can utilize a separate, local educational foundation that is an Internal Revenue Service designated charitable organization (referred to as a 501–(c)(3) independent from the school district. Of crucial importance is the role a school foundation plays in grantseeking and grant administration.

When submitted through a school foundation, your proposal's chances of being funded by a private grantor may be enhanced. Administering the foundation or corporate grant submitted through a school foundation may also be easier. However, you should always act in agreement with your district central office. While it may seem simpler to go through your school's foundation, your district office's participation is crucial in the case of federal grants since you need their help in following the federal rules regarding compliances and assurances. Your district's personnel and business offices perform the many valuable functions that support a superior grants program.

2. Fiscal Agent

All grantors want to be assured that the school they fund has the fiscal capability to disburse and account for the expended grant funds. Some grantors will request audited budget statements as evidence of fiscal accountability. The district central office is the likely agent to handle and account for a school's grants, although in some school districts the fiscal agent is the business office, the treasurer, or one of the assistant superintendents. The role of the fiscal agent is to monitor the expenditure of grant funds and to request the payment of federal grant funds by submitting an estimate of how the funds will be expended over the period of the grant. The Office of Management and Budget (OMB) has strict guidelines on how these funds are to be transferred and utilized. More sophisticated districts are connected by computers. Once the request is made via computer, the grant funds are deposited automatically in the district's designated bank. In less sophisticated districts, grant funds are expended by the school and then repaid by the federal government.

School principals need to have a basic knowledge of their districts' systems. Many principals complain bitterly about their inability to expend funds. Whether the problem is an outdated system that is slowed by red tape and the need for multiple signatures on request forms or fiscal information that is not timely or usable, your role as facilitator and troubleshooter is critical to grants success. Not providing your fiscal officer with an accurate forecast of expenditures may be the cause of the problem. Federal rules regulate the amount of money to be requested per quarter of the grant cycle and strictly limit the accumulation of unexpended funds. The development of a sound budget, Project Planner, and Grants Office Time Line will help you project an accurate cash forecast (see chapter 7). The school principal can avoid many problems by helping the fiscal agent document the cash needed.

- *Changing Budgets* — You must anticipate changes in your budget because of the impact these changes will have on your cash requests. Government grant rules allow for small changes (i.e., 5 percent of the budget line), but even in these cases the changes must be documented. I always recommend notifying the grantor in writing of the changes. Do not let the rules scare your project director. The implementation of a proactive grants system and adequate planning will provide the basis for documenting your expenditures, making cash requests, and changing the budget. The key to making a budget change is to back up the request with a rationale that is linked strongly to the project's activities/methods and how the change will help accomplish the predetermined objectives. The federal grants or contracts officer will prevent you from getting in trouble and will tell you how to keep your grant transactions legal.
- *Equipment* — Whether your grant is sponsored by the government, a foundation, or a corporation, you are ethically (and in some cases legally) responsible for maintaining an accurate record of all equipment purchased under your grant, including documentation that the equipment was awarded to the lowest bidder. Grantors' rules may vary, and your business

office may have regulations that are more stringent than the grantor's. You should help your grantee(s) forecast the equipment needed to implement each of your school's proposals so that bids can be reviewed and the equipment purchased before the grant is completed. It seems obvious that equipment should be ordered early in the grant cycle, but last-minute ordering does occur. Do not allow your project director to order equipment near the end of the grant award. This is a "red flag" to the funder, since it makes it appear that the equipment was not an integral part of the project. In fact, last-minute orders will probably not be delivered until after the completion of the grant period.

- *Inventory Equipment* — On a recent visit to evaluate a grants process of a major school district, I found several years' worth of equipment-inventory identification stickers filed in a desk drawer. Funders deserve to know where the equipment they purchased for you is located. Do not rely on the district central office or your project director to take care of your equipment inventory. When a piece of equipment is missing or an insurance claim is made, it will be your responsibility to come up with the name of the manufacturer, make, serial number, year purchased, and purchase price. You should also know where each piece of equipment is and make sure that all equipment maintenance is up to date.

  In evaluating one school district's grants system, I discovered that ten lap-top computers were sent out to bid, ordered, inventoried (numbered), and then sent to ten different schools in the district. When I visited the schools, I could locate only five of them. I quickly pointed out to the assistant superintendent how upset a grantor would be if they arrived for a visit and wanted to see children using the computers they had supplied, only to find half of the computers missing. The assistant superintendent immediately telephoned the school principals and began to ask questions. To make a long story short, if your school does not have an inventory system that you are comfortable with, develop one!

- *Personnel Policy and Procedures* — The school principal needs the district office's assistance when hiring individuals to work on a funded project. This important information is often in a manual explaining how to expend grant funds in that district. The manual may describe the procedures for hiring, evaluating, and terminating grant-supported employees. While you may want more control of your grant funds, do not lose sight of the fact that you need your personnel office to provide the valuable functions that keep your grantee(s) in compliance with the labor laws, including those covering the drug-free workplace and many, many other areas.
- *Indirect Costs* — One of the least understood areas in the grants

field is that of the recovery of costs associated with the acceptance of any grant award. The term *indirect costs* is usually identified with federal grants, while the term *administrative costs* or *overhead* is usually identified with foundation and corporate grants. The concept of indirect cost or administrative cost recovery is quite simple and sensible. However, it is hard to explain these costs to grantseekers who see a large piece of their grant going to the district's central office. Point out to your project director that direct costs such as those for project personnel, equipment, and consultants are requested in the budget and covered in the grant and explain that while indirect costs such as those for district personnel and business office staff are not requested in the budget, they too must be covered by the grant. The personnel costs for handling the grant, along with the costs related to supplying the building and office space in which the grant will be carried out , are indirect costs or administrative charges.

Recent newspaper articles on the excessive indirect costs charged by a few of the 3,000-plus universities in the country have generated much negative opinion. Indirect costs are real! It costs your district money to accept and handle outside grant funds, and these costs should be legitimately passed on to the grantor when possible.

Many foundations and corporations have adopted a policy of no payment for indirect costs. However, they do understand that there are costs associated with your taking responsibility for their funds, and some may allow a small administrative cost of 8 percent of the total amount requested of the funder.

You should also be aware that the federal government usually does not repay all of the costs of operation. Different federal agencies and even different grant programs within an agency have different payment policies. For example, government and school districts have a negotiated rate on special government programs involving food and milk. This usually very low (less than 5 percent) rate is referred to as your school's *restricted indirect cost rate.* If your grantseekers are creative they may be able to find funding from a government program that will pay your school's *unrestricted indirect cost rate.*

I once developed a school/community program for prevention education that was funded under a grant from the National Institute for Alcohol Abuse and Alcoholism (NIAAA). The program guidelines requested inclusion of an *unrestricted* indirect cost rate. My fiscal officer had never negotiated an unrestricted rate. Our school had a *restricted* rate of 2.5 percent. When he completed the forms necessary to develop our unrestricted rate (the forms were provided by the federal government's Regional Controller's Office), our rate was calculated at

27 percent of the total grant award, which turned out to be an *additional* $40,000! These funds were used to help the district offset the costs of implementing the project in our school facilities and for handling the personnel, payroll, and equipment transactions.

Many grantseekers are not concerned with recovering indirect costs because they do not see that the funds benefit them. But they may be wrong. By law, the funds recovered under indirect costs go into the district's general funds. Since they are a repayment for genuine costs of operation, they can be reallocated to anything the school district wants, including things that may directly benefit the classroom leader, grantseeker, and so on. In colleges and universities, these funds are used for a variety of purposes such as:

- support for a better grant-prospecting system
- support for a central office grants program
- returning a portion to the schools that have been successful
- funding travel to meet with grantors

3. Evaluating Your School's Grants Effort

The desired result of your grants program is to employ the grant-funding mechanism to meet your school's goals and objectives. This result can be achieved through an efficient system that encourages community and volunteer involvement while maximizing your existing resources.

Review the checklists at the end of each chapter and compile your suggestions for improvement. Note your suggestions on a spreadsheet or a project planner. Be realistic in determining what you can accomplish within the limitations of your setting; and remember, you cannot change your school's grants program overnight.

In order to evaluate the success of your techniques, you need baseline data. Even if your current system allows you to identify the number of proposals submitted from your school and the number funded, there is much more information you need to collect to evaluate your grant system's success. For example, by using a School Grantseekers' Preproposal Endorsement Worksheet (chapter 6) you can analyze the number of proposal ideas generated compared with the number that are submitted, pending, awarded, and rejected. By coding your grant system to the initial proposal idea, you can find out why some proposals were never submitted. Logging or tracking proposals from the principal's office will allow you to give recognition and encouragement to members of your staff who are pursuing grant-funded opportunities.

4. Increasing Your School's Grants Productivity

In an effort to increase grant activity while decentralizing their district grants office, many schools have established the position of school/community grants coordinator. This position varies from school to school. In some it is a volunteer position; in others it is a paid part-time or full-time position. The focus of the job also varies. It can focus entirely on schools and education or it can focus on the community and encompass a variety of concerns, including health, education, job development, and the elderly.

The "best" approach for empowering your school/community through access to grantseeking is up to you to decide. You may choose to discuss the idea of a school/community grant coordinator position with your grants advisory committee and, in doing so, suggest that one way to fund the position would be through a grant from a corporation, foundation, or community group.

A dedicated staff person can focus your school's/community's grants effort and maximize your grants potential.

Your School/Community Grants Office

- *Suggested Goals:*
  - A. increase the number and quality of proposals developed to meet the school's mission
  - B. promote an acceptance rate of 50 percent in submitted proposals and consortium efforts
  - C. promote involvement of community organizations in developing solutions to school/community problems
  - D. provide a focal point for community efforts to find and attract grant funding opportunities.
- *Objectives*
  - A. The school/community grants coordinator will increase the quality of the school's proposals by _____ percent as measured by a pre- and postassessment in one year at a cost of $_____.
  - B. The school/community grants coordinator will increase the quality of school/community consortium proposals by _____ percent in one year at a cost of $_____.
- *School/Community Grants Office Responsibilities:*
  - A. operate a grants resource center for the school/community
  - B. help the school/community develop ideas into fundable proposals
  - C. coordinate and act as a resource to grantseekers who are addressing similar needs or developing similar projects

D. serve as a resource for those with questions on grantseeking

E. organize a system to match community members' skills with proposal development needs

F. provide grantseekers with grants planning tools, videotapes, and other instructional aids

G. maintain files of grant activity, from idea generation to submittal to notices of award/rejection

H. collect examples/samples of funded projects

I. provide grantseekers with grant strategy and consulting

J. help proposal developers with proposal preparation, submittal, and notification of outcome

K. help successful grantees with implementation, grants management, and submittal of reports to grantors

- *Evaluation:* Pre- and postassessment of the objectives specified
- *Budget:* The cost will depend on the percentage of time allocated to the accomplishment of the objectives. You may decide to list in-kind contributions of secretarial or support staff. You may want to include a percentage of the released time for your coordinator.
- *Project Planner:* List on a project planner the duties your committee decides to include in the job description for your school/community grants coordinator position. Break the duties down into the steps that must be taken to support them and develop a cost analysis for each step listed on the planner.

The Sample Project Planner in figure 13.1 will help you develop a plan tailored to meet your school's needs. Remember, you can apply for a grant to develop your school's grant potential. By submitting to a foundation or corporation a cost-effective plan to mobilize your community's involvement in creating and developing funds for change, you may be able to put your plan in place sooner than you think!

Note: The Sample Project Planner suggests some of the steps you may want to take to set up a school grants coordinator. Review with your school grants advisory committee the tasks that will be assigned to this office. Determine whether the office will serve the community and, if so, include those tasks. The committee can then determine the personnel needed to accomplish the tasks. By means of this spreadsheet, a volunteer can immediately see how catalytic they are in the grants process and how their volunteerism impacts the cost of the services.

Designate all donated and volunteer resources with an asterisk (*). List all the supply, telephone, proposal production, and equipment needs. Do not forget that those items that your school will supply should be designated with an asterisk. Remember also that including college or university students in the project may lower the cost of collecting data, developing surveys, and evaluating results.

4. The Use of Consultants in Your Grants Program

Some schools hire consultants to write their proposals because they

Figure 13.1

PROJECT PLANNER™

Sample Project Planner

Sheet 1 of 4

Proposal Developed for ____________________

PROJECT TITLE: School Grants Office/Coordinator

PROJECT DIRECTOR: ____________________ Proposed starting date __________ Proposal Year __________

A. List Project objectives or outcomes A. B. B. List Methods to accomplish each objective as A-1, A-2, A-3 . . . B-1, B-2 . . .	MONTH		TIME	PROJECT PERSONNEL	PERSONNEL COSTS			CONSULTANTS • CONTRACT SERVICES			NON-PERSONNEL RESOURCES NEEDED SUPPLIES • EQUIPMENT • MATERIALS				SUB-TOTAL COST FOR ACTIVITY	MILESTONES PROGRESS INDICATORS	
	BEGIN	END			SALARIES & WAGES	FRINGE BENEFITS	TOTAL	TIME	COST/WEEK	TOTAL	ITEM	COST/ITEM	QUANTITY	TOT. COST	TOTAL I. L. P	ITEM	DATE
	C / D		E	F	G	H	I	J	K	L	M	N	O	P	Q	R	S
OBJECTIVES:																	
A. Increase the number and quality of proposals designed to meet the school's stated mission from % to % as measured by pre and post assessment.																	
A-1. Review school records to determine grants activity (submission and acceptance) prior to grants office.																	
a) check with district office and develop grants history																	
b) input data in computer																	
c) produce report																	
A-2. Develop a School Grants Advisory Committee.																	
a) develop list of members and resources they can contribute																	
b) set up meeting to brainstorm grant area interest-set objectives																	
c) develop webbing and linkages program																	
A-3. Set up grant opportunity searching system.																	
a) review computer based system																	
b) order or locate printed material																	
c) develop audiovisual resources on grants																	
A-4 Develop a school grant seekers support system.																	
a) develop a print a guide for grant seeking for your school																	
b) promote brainstorming and grant ideas to solve problems																	
c) develop a reward and motivation system to provide encouragement to grant seekers																	
TOTAL DIRECT COSTS OR COSTS REQUESTED FROM FUNDER ►															T		◄ % OF TOTAL
MATCHING FUNDS, IN-KIND CONTRIBUTIONS, OR DONATED COSTS ►																	◄
TOTAL COSTS ►																100%	◄

Figure 13.1 continued

PROJECT PLANNER™

Sample Project Planner

Sheet 2 of 4

Proposal Developed for ______

PROJECT TITLE: School Grants Office/Coordinator

PROJECT DIRECTOR: ______ Proposed starting date ______ Proposal Year ______

A. List Project objectives or outcomes A. B. B. List Methods to accomplish each objective as A-1, A-2, A-3 . . . B-1, B-2 . . .	MONTH		TIME	PROJECT PERSONNEL	PERSONNEL COSTS			CONSULTANTS • CONTRACT SERVICES			NON-PERSONNEL RESOURCES NEEDED SUPPLIES • EQUIPMENT • MATERIALS				SUB-TOTAL COST FOR ACTIVITY	MILESTONES PROGRESS INDICATORS	
	BEGIN	END			SALARIES & WAGES	FRINGE BENEFITS	TOTAL	TIME	COST/WEEK	TOTAL	ITEM	COST/ITEM	QUANTITY	TOT. COST	TOTAL I, L, P	ITEM	DATE
	C/D		E	F	G	H	I	J	K	L	M	N	O	P	Q	R	S
B. Achieve an acceptance rate of 50% in submitted proposals.																	
B-1. Set up a pre-proposal contact system.																	
a) procure a long distance phone line from volunteer																	
b) develop budget for travel to D.C. and state capitol																	
B-2. Set up funder files.																	
a) copies of reports, guidelines, and tax returns																	
b) lists of grantees																	
c) lists of reviewers																	
d) records of contact with grantors																	
e) sample proposals and comments																	
B-3. Develop and Implement a Quality Circle or Mock Proposal Review Program																	
a) develop list of volunteers to serve from a variety of school and community backgrounds																	
b) set up procedures booklet to assist mock review by type of grantor:																	
• federal/state																	
• foundation																	
• corporate																	
Evaluation: A & B Compare number of proposals submitted and awarded between pre-assessment and post-assessment.																	
TOTAL DIRECT COSTS OR COSTS REQUESTED FROM FUNDER ▶															T		◀ % OF TOTAL
MATCHING FUNDS, IN-KIND CONTRIBUTIONS, OR DONATED COSTS ▶																	◀
TOTAL COSTS ▶																100%	◀

Figure 13.1 continued

PROJECT PLANNER™

Sample Project Planner

Sheet 3 of 4

Proposal Developed for ____________

PROJECT TITLE: School Grants Office/Coordinator

PROJECT DIRECTOR: ____________ Proposed starting date ____________ Proposal Year ____________

A. List Project objectives or outcomes A. B. B. List Methods to accomplish each objective as A-1, A-2, A-3 . . . B-1, B-2 . . .	MONTH		TIME	PROJECT PERSONNEL	PERSONNEL COSTS			CONSULTANTS • CONTRACT SERVICES			NON-PERSONNEL RESOURCES NEEDED SUPPLIES • EQUIPMENT • MATERIALS				SUB-TOTAL COST FOR ACTIVITY	MILESTONES PROGRESS INDICATORS	
	BEGIN	END			SALARIES & WAGES	FRINGE BENEFITS	TOTAL	TIME	COST/WEEK	TOTAL	ITEM	COST/ITEM	QUANTITY	TOT. COST	TOTAL I, L, P	ITEM	DATE
	C / D		E	F	G	H	I	J	K	L	M	N	O	P	Q	R	S
C. Increase involvement of community organizations in developing and implementing strategies to meet stated school/community objectives by % as measured by consortia grant proposals and sub-contract agreements.																	

TOTAL DIRECT COSTS OR COSTS REQUESTED FROM FUNDER ▶ T ◀ % OF TOTAL

MATCHING FUNDS, IN-KIND CONTRIBUTIONS, OR DONATED COSTS ▶ ◀

TOTAL COSTS ▶ 100% ◀

Figure 13.1 continued

PROJECT PLANNER™

Sample Project Planner

Sheet 4 of 4

Proposal Developed for ____________________

PROJECT TITLE: School Grants Office/Coordinator

PROJECT DIRECTOR: ____________________ Proposed starting date ____________ Proposal Year ____________

A. List Project objectives or outcomes A. B. B. List Methods to accomplish each objective as A-1, A-2, A-3 . . . B-1, B-2 . . .	MONTH		TIME	PROJECT PERSONNEL	PERSONNEL COSTS			CONSULTANTS • CONTRACT SERVICES			NON-PERSONNEL RESOURCES NEEDED SUPPLIES • EQUIPMENT • MATERIALS				SUB-TOTAL COST FOR ACTIVITY	MILESTONES PROGRESS INDICATORS	
	BEGIN	END			SALARIES & WAGES	FRINGE BENEFITS	TOTAL	TIME	COST/WEEK	TOTAL	ITEM	COST/ITEM	QUANTITY	TOT. COST	TOTAL I, L, P	ITEM	DATE
	C / D		E	F	G	H	I	J	K	L	M	N	O	P	Q	R	S
D. Increase grant funded programs to meet community goals and objectives by % as measured by current proposal submissions and funded projects.																	
D-1. Survey community for grant funded activities/programs.																	
a) establish a volunteer group of community advisors to review objectives of a school/community grants office																	
b) develop a survey to document current level of proposal development and grants acceptance and organizational needs																	
c) volunteers meet with groups to complete survey																	
d) data entered into data retrieval system and report generated																	
D-2. Establish a steering committee to develop a list of services that the school/community grants office will provide.																	
D-3. Develop a list of services to be provided.																	
a) budget for services																	
D-4. Construct a proposal to get the office funded on a grant.																	
TOTAL DIRECT COSTS OR COSTS REQUESTED FROM FUNDER ▶															T		◀ % OF TOTAL
MATCHING FUNDS, IN-KIND CONTRIBUTIONS, OR DONATED COSTS ▶																	◀
TOTAL COSTS ▶																100%	◀

lack the funds to hire a permanent, on-staff grants person. Be wary of this. Many funding sources feel that if a grantee cannot *write* their own proposal, they may have trouble *implementing* the proposed solution.

However, the use of a grants consultant may be appropriate if several of the past grantees funded by your prospective grantor utilized one. If you do utilize the services of a consultant, *do not* become involved with one who wants to work for a percentage of the funded proposal. Although this arrangement may seem safe and economical (you pay only when you get an award), it is illegal under federal guidelines because it represents a cost incurred *before* the award date. Federal grantors will pay only for what happens after the funding begins, not for locating and getting the grant.

Consultants should charge you a fee based upon the time they spend developing your proposals, and you should pay them regardless of whether you get funded. Remember, the ability to attract grant funds depends on your school's credibility, quality of ideas, and plan, not on the reputation of the consultant.

CHAPTER 13 CHECKLIST

Evaluation and Planning Worksheet

1. Do you have current, published guidelines on how to administer:

federal grant funds _____ yes _____no
private grant funds _____ yes _____no

2. Does your district have guidelines or policies on grantseeking and fund-raising?

_____ yes _____no

3. Does your district office provide you with the following fiscal support, guidelines, procedures, and so on?

- guidelines for handling personnel paid on grants
  _____ yes _____no
- purchasing assistance, inventory control
  _____ yes _____no
- procedures for easily accessing grant funding information (budget category expenditures, and so on)
  _____ yes _____no
- guidelines for changing budgets
  _____ yes _____no

4. Does your district have federally negotiated indirect cost rates for:

unrestricted federal programs _____ yes _____no
restricted federal programs _____ yes _____no

5. How are the funds recovered from your school's indirect cost reimbursement rate shared with your school and proposal developers?

6. Does your school's proposal development system allow you to evaluate its success?

_____ yes _____no

7. Could your school benefit from a part- or full-time school grants coordinator?

_____ yes _____no

Bibliography

Government Grant Resources

Commerce Business Daily

The government's contracts publication, published five times a week, the *Daily* announces every government Request for Proposal (RFP) that exceeds $25,000 and upcoming sales of government surplus. **Price:** $261 annually or $130 for 6 months. **Order from:** Superintendent of Documents,U.S. Government Printing Office,Washington, DC 20402, 202-783-3238

Catalog of Federal Domestic Assistance (CFDA)

This is the government's most complete listing of federal domestic assistance programs with details on eligibility, application procedures, and deadlines, including the location of state plans. It is published at the beginning of each fiscal year with supplementary updates during the year. Indexes are by agency program, function, popular name, applicant eligibility, and subject. It comes in looseleaf form, punched for a three-ring binder. **Price:** $46 annual subscription. **Order from:** Superintendent of Documents, U.S. Government Printing Office, Washington, DC 20402, 202-783-3238

The Federal Register

Published five times a week (Monday through Friday), the *Register* supplies up-to-date information on federal assistance and supplements the *Catalog of Federal Domestic Assistance (CFDA)*. It includes public regulations and legal notices issued by all federal agencies and presidential proclamations. Of particular importance are the proposed rules, final rules, and program deadlines. An index is published monthly. **Price:** $340 per year. **Order from:** Superintendent of Documents, U.S. Government Printing Office,Washington, DC 20402, 202-783-3238

United States Government Manual

This paperback manual gives the names of key personnel, addresses, and telephone numbers for all agencies, departments, etc., that constitute the federal bureaucracy. **Price:** $23 per year. **Order from:** Superintendent of Documents, U.S. Government Printing Office, Washington, DC 20402, 202-783-3238

Academic Research Information System, Inc. (ARIS)

ARIS provides timely information about grant and contract opportunities, including concise descriptions of guidelines and eligibility requirements, upcoming deadlines, identification of program resource persons, and new program policies for both government and nongovernment funding sources.

Biomedical Sciences Report	$210
Social and Natural Science Report	$210
Arts and Humanities Report	$125
All three ARIS Reports and Supplements	$495

Order from: Academic Research Information System, Inc., The Redstone Building, 2940 16th Street, Suite 314, San Francisco, CA 94103, 415-558-8133

1992 Federal Funding Guide

This guide describes programs that provide grants and/or loans to local, county, and state government, nonprofits, community, and volunteer groups. **Price:** $248 plus $12.50 postage and handling. **Order from:** Government Information Services, 1611 North Kent Street, Suite 508, Arlington, VA 22209, 703-528-1082

Federal Grants and Contracts Weekly

This weekly contains information on the latest Requests for Proposals (RFPs), contracting opportunities, and upcoming grants. Each ten-page issue includes details on RFPs, closing dates for grant programs, procurement-related news, and newly issued regulations. **Price:** $349 for 50 issues. **Order from:** Capitol Publications, Inc., 1101 King Street, PO Box 1453, Alexandria, VA 22313-2053, 800-327-7203

Health Grants and Contracts Weekly

Price: $320 for 50 issues. **Order from:** Capitol Publications, Inc., 1101 King Street, PO Box 1453, Alexandria, VA 22313-2053, 800-327-7203

Education Daily

Price: $537 for 250 issues. **Order from:** Capitol Publications, Inc., 1101 King Street, PO Box 1453, Alexandria, VA 22313-2053, 800-327-7203

Education Grants Alert

Price: $299 for 50 issues. **Order from:** Capitol Publications, Inc., 1101 King Street, PO Box 1453, Alexandria, VA 22313-2053, 800-327-7203

Washington Information Directory, 1992

This directory is divided into three categories: agencies of the executive branch, Congress, and private or "nongovernmental" organizations. Each entry includes the name, address, telephone number, and director of the organization and a short description of its work. **Price:** $72.95. **Order from:** Congressional Quarterly, Inc., 300 Raritan Center Parkway, Edison, NJ 08810, 1-800-638-1710

Foundation Grant Resources

Many of the following research aids can be found through the Foundation Center Cooperating Collections Network. If you wish to purchase any of the following Foundation Center publications, contact: The Foundation Center, 79 Fifth Avenue, Dept. ME, New York, NY 10003-3076, 800-424-9836. In NY State: 212-620-4230

Corporate Foundation Profiles, 7th edition, 1992

This Foundation Center publication contains detailed analyses of 250 of the largest corporate foundations in the United States. An appendix lists financial data on hundreds of additional corporations with assets of $1 million or that give at least $100,000 in grants every year. **Price:** $135. **Order from:** The Foundation Center

The Foundation 1,000

This research aid profiles the 1,000 largest U.S. foundations by foundation name, subject field, type of support, and geographic location. There is also an index that allows you to target grantmakers by the names of officers, staff, and trustees. **Price:** $195. **Order from:** The Foundation Center

The Foundation Directory, 1993 Edition

This is the most important single reference work available on grantmaking foundations in the United States. It includes information on foundations having assets of at least $2 million or annual grants exceeding $200,000. Each entry includes a description of giving interests, along with address, telephone numbers, current financial data, names of donors, and contact person, and IRS identification number. Includes six indexes: state and city, subject, foundation donors, trustees and administrators, and alphabetical foundation names. The trustees index is very valuable in developing linkages to decision makers. **Price:** $185 hardcover. $160 softcover. **Order from:** The Foundation Center

The Foundation Directory Supplement, 1993

The *Supplement* updates the 1993 edition of the *Directory* so that users will have the latest addresses, contacts, policy statements, application guidelines, and financial data. **Price:** $110. $275 hardcover: *Directory* and *Supplement.* $250 softcover: *Directory* and *Supplement.* **Order from:** The Foundation Center

The Foundation Directory Part 2, 1993 Edition

This *Directory* provides information on over 4,500 midsize foundations with grant programs between $50,000 and $200,000. Published biennially. **Price:** $160. $415 hardcover: *Directory, Supplement, Part 2.* $390 softcover: *Directory, Supplement, Part 2.* **Order from:** The Foundation Center

The Foundation Grants Index, 21st edition, 1993

This cumulative listing of over 55,000 grants of $5,000 or more made by over 800 major foundations is indexed by subject and geographic locations, by the names of recipient organizations, and by key words. **Price:** $125. **Order from:** The Foundation Center

Foundation Grants to Individuals, 8th Edition, 1993

Comprehensive listing of over 2,300 independent and corporate foundations that provide financial assistance to individuals. **Price:** $55. **Order from:** The Foundation Center

The National Guide to Funding for Elementary and Secondary Education, April 1993

Includes over 1,600 sources of funding for elementary and secondary education and over 4,500 grant descriptions listing the organizations that have successfully approached these funding sources. **Price:** $135. **Order from:** The Foundation Center

Education Grant Guides, 1992/1993 Editions

There are 7 Grant Guides in the field of education including: Elementary and Secondary Education, Higher Education, Libraries and Information Services, Literacy, Reading and Adult/Continuing Education, Scholarships, Student Aid and Loans, Science and Technology Programs, and Social and Political Science Programs. There are 23 other guides in areas other than education, such as children and youth, alcohol and drug abuse, minorities, etc. Each guide has a customized list of hundreds of recently awarded grants of $10,000 or more. Sources of funding are indexed by type of organization, subject focus, and geographic funding area. Price: $60 each. Order from: The Foundation Center

Foundation News

Each bimonthly issue of the *News* covers the activities of private, company-sponsored, and community foundations, direct corporate giving, and government agencies and their programs, and includes the kinds of grants being awarded, overall trends, legal matters, regulatory actions, and other areas of common concern. **Price:** $29.50 annually or $53 for 2 years **Order from:** Foundation News, PO Box 96043, Washington, DC 20077-7188, 301-853-6590

LRCW Newsbriefs (Lutheran Resources Commission Newsbriefs)

This monthly is geared to providers of human services and to anyone wanting to keep up-to-date on government grant deadlines. It is a 30-page bulletin of resource material for program development in over 28 subject areas as well as for resource development in general. **Price:** $70 per year. **Order from:** Lutheran Resource Commission, Woodward Bldg., Suite 900, 733 15th St., NW, Washington, DC 20005, 202-667-9844

The Taft Foundation Information System

Foundation Reporter: This annual directory of the largest private charitable foundations in the United States supplies descriptions and statistical analyses.

Foundation Giving Watch: This monthly publishes news and the "how-to's" of foundation giving, with a listing of recent grants.

Foundation Updates: This publication supplies new information on 100 foundations per year. **Price:** $443 (all three publications); $327 (*Foundation Reporter* only); $139 (Newsletter only, one year/12 issues). **Order from:** Taft Group, 835 Penobscot Building, Detroit, MI 48226, 800-877-8238

Education Funding News

This weekly report also provides funding information. **Price:** $239 for 50 issues. **Order from:** Government Information Service, 1611 N. Kent Street, Suite 508, Arlington,VA 22209, 703-528-1082

Foundation and Corporate Grants Alert

Price: $227 for 50 issues. **Order from:** Capitol Publications, Inc., 1101 King Street, PO Box 1453, Alexandria, VA 22313-2053, 800-327-7203

Private Foundation IRS Tax Returns

(Available from the IRS or free to use at Foundation Center)

The Internal Revenue Service requires private foundations to file income tax returns each year. Form 990-PF provides fiscal details on receipts and expenditures, compensation of officers, capital gains or losses, and other financial matters. Form 990-AR provides information on foundation managers, assets, and grants paid and/or committed for future payment. The IRS makes this information available on aperture cards that may be viewed at libraries operated by the Foundation Center or at its regional cooperating collections. You may also obtain this information by writing to the appropriate IRS office (see accompanying list). Enclose as much information about the foundation as possible, including its full name, street address with zip code, its employer identification number if available, and the year or years requested. It generally takes four to six weeks for the IRS to respond, and it will bill you for all charges, which vary depending on the office and number of pages involved.

INTERNAL REVENUE SERVICE CENTER REGIONAL OFFICES

Central Region (Indiana, Kentucky, Michigan, Ohio, West Virginia)

Public Affairs Officer, Internal Revenue Service Center, PO Box 1699, Cincinnati, OH 45201

Mid-Atlantic Region (District of Columbia, Maryland, Virginia, Pennsylvania — Zip Codes 150-168 and 172)

Public Affairs Officer, Internal Revenue Service Center, 11601 Roosevelt Blvd., Philadelphia, PA 19154

Midwest Region (Illinois, Iowa, Minnesota, Missouri, Montana, Nebraska, North Dakota, Oregon, South Dakota, Wisconsin)

Public Affairs Officer, Internal Revenue Service Center, PO Box 24551, Kansas City, MO 64131

North Atlantic Region (Connecticut, Delaware, Maine, Massachusetts, New Hampshire, New

York, New Jersey, Rhode Island, Vermont, Pennsylvania — Zip Codes 169-171 and 173-196)
Public Affairs Officer, Internal Revenue Service Center, PO Box 400, Brookhaven, NY 11742

Southeast Region (Alabama, Arkansas, Georgia, Florida, Louisiana, Mississippi, North Carolina, South Carolina, Tennessee)
Public Affairs Officer, Internal Revenue Service Center, PO Box 47-421, Doraville, GA 30362

Southwest Region (Arizona, Colorado, Kansas, New Mexico, Oklahoma, Texas, Utah, Wyoming)
Public Affairs Officer, Internal Revenue Service Center, PO Box 934, Austin, TX 78767

Western Region (Alaska, California, Hawaii, Idaho, Nevada, Washington)
Public Affairs Officer, Internal Revenue Service Center, PO Box 12866, Fresno, CA 93779

Corporate Grant Resources

Annual Survey of Corporate Contributions
This annual survey of corporate giving is sponsored by the Conference Board and the Council for Financial Aid to Education. It includes a detailed analysis of beneficiaries of corporate support but does not list individual firms and specific recipients. **Price:** $20 for Associates. $80 for Nonassociates. **Order from:** The Conference Board, 845 Third Avenue, New York, NY 10022, 212-759-0900

The National Directory of Corporate Giving, 2d Edition
This directory provides information on over 1,500 corporate foundations plus an additional 600 direct, corporate giving programs. It also has an extensive bibliography and six indexes to help you target funding prospects. **Price:** $195. **Order from:** The Foundation Center, 79 Fifth Avenue, Dept. ME, New York, NY 10003-3076, 800-424-9836. In NY State 212-620-4230

Directory of Corporate Affiliations
This directory lists divisions, subsidiaries, and affiliates of thousands of companies with addresses, telephone numbers, key persons, employees, etc. **Price:** $687 plus handling and delivery. **Order from:** Reed Reference Publishing, PO Box 31, New Providence, NJ 07974, 800-323-6772

Dun and Bradstreet's Million Dollar Directory, 5 volumes
The five volumes list names, addresses, employees, sales volume, and other pertinent data for 160,000 of America's largest businesses. **Price:** $1,310 for 5 volumes. **Order from:** Dun and Bradstreet Information Services, 3 Sylvan Way, Parsippany, NJ 07054, 800-526-0651

Standard and Poor's Register of Corporations, Directors and Executives
This annual register provides up-to-date rosters of over 400,000 executives of the 46,000 nationally known corporations they represent, with their names, titles, and business affiliations. **Price:** $550 for one year, includes quarterly supplements. **Order from:** Standard and Poor's Corporation, 25 Broadway, 17th Floor, Attn: Sales, New York, NY 10004, 212-208-8786

Taft Corporate Giving Directory, 13th Edition, 1992
This directory provides detailed entries on 589 company-sponsored foundations. Included are nine indexes. **Price:** $327 plus postage and handling. **Order from:** Taft Group, 838 Penobscot Building, Detroit, MI 48226, 800-877-8238

Corporate Giving Watch.

This monthly reports on corporate giving developments. **Price:** $139 a year. $442 plus postage and handling for *Taft Corporate Giving Directory* and *Corporate Giving Watch.* **Order from:** Taft Group, 838 Penobscot Building, Detroit, MI 48226, 800-877-8238

Computer Research Services

Congressional Information Service Index (CIS Index)

CIS covers congressional publications and legislation from 1970 to date. It covers hearing, committee prints, House and Senate reports and documents, special publications, Senate executive reports and documents, and public laws. It includes monthly abstracts and index volumes. Noncomputer grant-related materials are also available from CIS. Including a CIS Federal Register Index, which covers announcements from the Federal Register on a weekly basis. **Price:** $1,040 hardbound annual edition. Monthly service (including hardbound annual edition) is on a sliding scale ranging from $1,045 - $4,310, depending on your library's annual book, periodical, and microform budget. **Order from:** Congressional Information Services, Inc., 4520 East West Highway, Suite 800, Bethesda, MD 20814, 800-638-8380

DIALOG Information Services

3460 Hillview Avenue, Palo Alto, CA 94304, 800-3-DIALOG. A commercial organization that provides access to hundreds of databases in a range of subject areas. DIALOG has no start-up fees or monthly minimum charges, but there is an annual fee of $35. Foundation Center files cost $1.10 per minute to search on line. Each full record printed off line or by DIALOG costs an additional $.40.

Federal Assistance Program Retrieval System (FAPRS)

The *FAPRS* list more than 1,250 federal grant programs, including planning and technical assistance. All states have *FAPRS* services available through state, county, and local agencies as well as through federal extension services. For further information, call 202-708-5126 or write to:

1. Your congressperson's office; they can request a search for you, in some cases at no charge.
2. Federal Domestic Assistance Catalog Staff, GSA/IRMS/WKU, 300 7th Street, SW, Reporters Building, Room 101, Washington, DC 20407

Foundation Center Databases

The Foundation Center offers the public two online computer databases — *The Foundation Directory* file and *The Foundation Grants Index* file. Both databases are available online through DIALOG. The cost for this service is $95 for up to 75 records and $.50 for each additional record. **Contact:** The Foundation Center, 79 Fifth Avenue, New York, NY 10003-3076, 800-424-9836. In NY State 212-620-4230

The Sponsored Programs Information Network (SPIN)

This is a database of federal and private funding sources. A microversion is available as well as online. **Price:** Online - $500 annually plus $10 per search or $3,500 annually with unlimited searches. Microversion — $2,995 for biweekly — updates; $1,995 for monthly updates; $1,195 for quarterly updates; $695 for annual updates. **Order from:** InfoEd, 453 New Karner Rd., Albany, NY 12205, 518-464-0691